Paul Kimmage was a professional cyclist before he turned to journalism, competing in the Tour de France on three occasions. His book *Rough Ride* is widely acknowledged to be the most honest account of life in the professional ranks and won the William Hill Sports Book of the Year award. He has been named Sports Interviewer of the Year at five Sports Journalists' Association awards. He is the co-author of the critically acclaimed *Full Time*, the autobiography of Tony Cascarino.

ENGAGE

On a cold Tuesday morning in March 2005, the cream of young English rugby gathered in Northampton. Matt Hampson was one of them. He had dreamt of playing rugby for England ever since he had picked up a rugby ball. He was playing in an England Under 21 team that included James Haskell and Toby Flood. But during the training session that morning, as the forwards engaged, the scrum collapsed and Matt took the full force of the blow. He woke up in an intensive care unit, paralysed from the neck down and dependent on a ventilator to breathe. In *Engage*, award-winning journalist Paul Kimmage combines with Matt to tell this uplifting true story about one man's strength and determination to overcome the odds.

PAUL KIMMAGE

ENGAGE

The Fall and Rise of
MATT HAMPSON

Complete and Unabridged

CHARNWOOD
Leicester

First published in Great Britain in 2011 by
Simon & Schuster UK Ltd.
London

First Charnwood Edition
published 2012
by arrangement with
Simon & Schuster UK Ltd.
London

British Library CIP Data

Kimmage, Paul, *1962* –
Engage: the fall and rise of Matt Hampson.
1. Hampson, Matt. 2. Rugby Union football
players- -Great Britain- -Biography.
3. Paraplegics- -Great Britain- -Biography.
4. Rugby football injuries. 5. Large type books.
I. Title
796.3′33′092–dc23

ISBN 978–1–4448–1229–9

Published by
F. A. Thorpe (Publishing)
Anstey, Leicestershire

Set by Words & Graphics Ltd.
Anstey, Leicestershire
Printed and bound in Great Britain by
T. J. International Ltd., Padstow, Cornwall

This book is printed on acid-free paper

In memory of Stuart Mangan (1983–2009)
. . . some birds aren't meant to be caged.

Contents

Why is life worth living? That's a very good question. Ummm . . . Well there are certain things, I guess, that make it worthwhile. Uh, like what? Okay. Um, for me . . . oh, I would say . . . what, Groucho Marx, to name one thing, and . . . Willie Mays, and . . . the second movement of the Jupiter Symphony, and . . . Louis Armstrong's recording of 'Potatohead Blues' . . . Swedish movies, naturally . . . *Sentimental Education* by Flaubert and Marlon Brando, Frank Sinatra . . . those incredible apples and pears by Cézanne.

— Woody Allen, *Manhattan*

PART 1

INSOMNIA

1

There's a portrait at home that often makes me smile. It was taken six years before the accident, in the summer of 1999. What does it say about the Hampson family? Well, let's see now: Dad has just kicked off his boots and looks slightly hot and bothered after a long day on the building site. He is hungry, and can 'do without the photoshoot with David bloody Bailey', but that's his father-in-law holding the camera, and they've had 'issues' in the past, so he's doing his best to grin and bear it. Mum detests having her portrait taken at the best of times and also looks under pressure; reserved and slightly matronly in bearing, if she had 'Head Teacher' stamped across her forehead it could not be more obvious, but her true nature, her warmth and goodness, is also revealed — you can see it in the softness around her eyes. Amy? Well, what can I say about my beautiful sister that won't earn me a slap? Is she saying 'cheese'? Only like her life depends on it! She's running late for a date in Stamford with a new boyfriend and wants out of there as quickly as possible. My brother, Tom, is really smiling. Grandad isn't pleased; every time he raises his camera, the kid is grinning back at him like Wallace from *Wallace and Gromit*. 'Stop pulling that stupid face, Tom! You're wrecking the photo,' Grandad pleads. But try selling reason to an eleven-year-old. Me? Well, you

would never say I was faking it. No, I look
happier and more content at the age of fifteen
than any member of the family. But then, why
wouldn't I? I am wearing an England shirt.

2

Follow your dreams, they say. This is where they lead me, to a kingsize bed with lush cotton sheets on a Saturday morning at the Chiswick Moran Hotel in London. I lie motionless for a while, staring at the ceiling. A shaft of morning sunlight splits the room. The purr of my girlfriend, Jennie's, breath laps gently against the silence. I gaze at her beautiful face and envy her peace. The game is almost eight hours away but I'm already starting to twitch . . .

Do you have the bottle for this?

★　★　★

The day, like most others, begins with a pee. I note the colour (pale yellow) and flow-rate (a strong throaty splash) of my urine, and study my face in the mirror and decide not to shave. The room is like a bombsite. I pluck a T-shirt and tracksuit from the heap of discarded kit and slip quietly out the door.

Jonny Wilkinson and Toby Flood are weighing themselves in the corridor.

'Morning, guys.'

'Morning, Hambo.'

I follow them on to the scales, make a note of my weight — 118 kg — and take the lift to the team room for breakfast. Some of the guys have already finished; most are still in bed. I choose a

5

setting at the table between James Haskell and Tom Rees.

'Morning, Hambo,' Reesy says, dipping his spoon into a large bowl of fruit and yoghurt.

'Morning, Reesy . . . James.'

'Is your arsehole twitching yet?' Haskell grins.

'No, slept like a baby, mate,' I lie.

'Slept like a fog-horn you mean,' he snorts. 'How does Jennie abide your snoring?'

'It's called love, mate,' I grin. 'And anyway, I'm not that bad.'

'You fucking are!' he insists. 'I've roomed with you before, remember? The Under-18s? That crummy hotel in Castlecroft?'

'I remember that. It was like *Fawlty Towers*,' Reesy says.

'Yeah,' Haskell concurs. 'I nearly freaked when I saw the room list: Oh Christ! They've put me with a prop! It was the first time I roomed with Hambo.'

'I thought you were going to be a right posh twat,' I counter.

'I thought you'd smell,' he says.

'And we were both right.' I smile.

'Yeah, but don't tell me you don't snore.' He laughs.

A waiter arrives with porridge and a green tea for Haskell. I order beans on toast and a pot of proper, breakfast, tea. The head coach, Brian Ashton, saunters in from the lobby with a copy of the *Guardian* under his arm. 'Looking forward to reading your new column, James.' He smiles. 'But I hope you're not as hard on me as Dallaglio!'

'You have nothing to worry about, Brian,'

6

Haskell replies, slightly unnerved.

'Yeah, as long as you keep picking him,' I add.

★ ★ ★

The first business of the day — a team meeting with the coaching staff — is scheduled for 10.30. Ashton clears his throat and begins his address in soft, measured tones. 'Okay, it's the start of another Six Nations campaign . . . a massive opportunity for everyone, and it's important we begin with a performance against Wales. I will talk to you again in more detail before the game, but for now I just want to check that there were no problems during the night and that you are all fit and well.'

He pauses and scans the room. A huge, ripping fart (dispatched, I suspect, from the fertile loins of Mark 'Ronnie' Regan) almost shakes the walls.

'You smelly bastard, Ronnie,' someone roars.

'I'll be fucked if I'm packing down behind you,' Steve Borthwick chimes.

Five minutes pass before Ashton resumes. 'Okay, we have two new caps today,' he announces, 'and I would ask them both to step forward now for a small presentation. Luke Narraway . . . '

There is a round of applause as Luke is presented with his first England jersey.

' . . . and Matt Hampson.'

I follow Luke to the top of the room with a lump in my throat.

★ ★ ★

A line-out session has been called in the physio room. John Wells, the forwards' coach, oversees the walk-through; Steve Borthwick makes the calls; we spend an hour pretending to throw, lift and jump and honing our driving play. Then Haskell suggests I join him for a run: 'Come on, you fat bastard, it will do you good.'

We leave the hotel and turn left along Chiswick High Road, but haven't gone 500 yards before we're gasping on exhaust fumes. 'James, you do realize this is one of the busiest roads in London?' I scoff.

'What would a Leicester mute like you know about London?' he retorts.

We double back on to Thorney Hedge Road and find a patch of derelict ground to jog and stretch.

★ ★ ★

Jennie has showered and changed and is packing when I get back to the room. She has been invited to Richmond for lunch with the other wives and girlfriends and looks a million dollars. I remind her of our first date when she professed to dislike rugby. 'It's growing on me.' She laughs.

'So who have you been hanging out with?' I ask.

'Haskell's girlfriend is lovely and David Strettle's . . . and I really like Lewis Moody's wife. Did you know he was married?'

'Doh! We're team-mates at Leicester, remember?'

'That's mean.' She pouts.

'Sorry.' I smile, wrapping my arms around her. She plants a gentle kiss on my lips and prepares to leave. 'I know how much this means to you, Matt. I really hope it goes well.'

'Thanks, Jennie. Have you got your ticket?'

'Yes.'

'Okay, see you later. Go easy on the bubbly.'

★　★　★

I take a long refreshing shower and lie on my bed for half an hour before the pre-match meal. Matt Stevens and Michael Lipman are sitting at an adjoining table. I chinned Matt recently during a brawl at Welford Road, but we've been getting on great this week. He's still carrying the bruise on his eye, but I joke that he has rarely looked as well. 'Thanks, buddy.' He smiles. 'I really appreciate that.'

The pre-match lunch is the usual fare: pasta, potatoes and chicken breast, washed down with chilled litres of Powerade. The banter is negligible — we have started to retreat into game-mode. I clear my plate and collect my presentation jacket from a rail by the door and return to my room.

There's a 'Good Luck' card from a boyhood coach on my bedside locker. I pick it up and gaze at the inscription:

The first of many! Best of luck, Hambo. I always knew it would come to this — John Cornwell

. . . and my pulse starts to race. The game will be brutal. The Welsh front row isn't the meanest or most powerful in international rugby but they will relish the prospect of turning the screw on a debutant England prop. My deepest fears return.

Are you good enough, Hambo?

★ ★ ★

Lewis Moody pokes his head around the door. 'You have a visitor.' He grins.

'Not now, Moodos,' I reply, suspecting a joke.

But there, standing in the doorway, is the towering frame of Martin Johnson.

'Johno! What are you doing here?'

'I had to pick up a couple of tickets from Wig [Graham Rowntree] and just thought I'd pop up to see how you are,' he says.

'Yeah, not bad, a bit nervous.'

'That's good. The adrenaline will help you perform. Just remember, there will be fifteen guys sitting across the corridor in the Welsh dressing room feeling just as nervous as you are.'

I flick on the kettle and suggest a cup of tea. He shifts a pile of kit from the chair and sits down.

'What age are you now, Hambo?' he enquires.

'Twenty-three,' I reply.

'Same age I was when I made my debut.'

'Were you nervous?' I ask.

'Absolutely shitting myself.' He smiles.

'What was it like?'

'Crazy. Did I ever tell you that story?'

'No.'

10

'A day before the game, I'm walking around Leicester thinking of having my hair cut when this call comes through to get my arse down to London.'

'What?'

'I hadn't been selected for the squad but Wade Dooley had picked up an injury and they wanted me for cover.'

'You're joking!'

'It gets better. I jump into the car, drive to Richmond, and the first person I meet at the England hotel is Kevin Murphy, the team physio. 'Congratulations,' he says, sticking out his hand. 'You didn't hear it from me but you're playing . . . Wade is out.' And before I can blink, I'm standing in front of 70,000 people at Twickenham, listening to the national anthem.'

'Fuck!'

'Yeah . . . Blessing in disguise, really,' he says. 'I didn't have time to think about it. The big worry was the line-out calls but there was no lifting back then and only two or three combinations to remember, so it wasn't too bad.'

'How did you sleep that night?' I ask.

'Thought I might have trouble, but I went out like a light. And Wade was great. It was his last season. He called to my room next morning to calm me down and pass on a few tips about the French. That's when the nerves kicked in. There was a team meeting for the forwards in Brian Moore's room. He warned me to expect a bumpy ride. 'You're going to be terrified out there for the first five or ten minutes,' he said. 'But then you'll realize it's just another game of

11

rugby; you'll find you are doing okay and realize you can handle it.' That really helped my confidence and I will say the same to you, Hambo: the first five or ten minutes will be brutal, but I have no doubts whatsoever that you will handle it.'

'Thanks, Johno.'

I pour the tea and remind him of the day we almost played together.

'It was a year after you won the World Cup . . . your testimonial year, remember? You had just come back from a trip to Singapore and we were playing Wasps at Adams Park.'

'Was that the drawn game?'

'Yeah, the first time I'd been picked for Tigers. Wellsy had put me on the bench, but I didn't get on. That's always been a regret, Johno, I'd have loved to have played with you.'

'Forget all that,' he says, visibly perturbed. 'I'm not here to give you a kiss. Don't get me wrong, I'm flattered, mate, but this is not the time or place. I want you to finish your tea and pack your bag and start thinking about that Welsh front row. They're fucking licking their lips now, thinking about what they are going to do to you. They are going to hit you harder than you've ever been hit before and the question you must ask is: how am I going to respond? Well, let me give you the fucking answer: put your body on the line, put your mind on the line; nothing else matters. There will be plenty of time later to reminisce.'

'Okay, Johno.'

He points his finger and fixes me with a glare.

'Do not let me down.'

'I won't, Johno.'

'Okay, see you after the game.'

'Thanks, Johno.'

I pull on my tracksuit and presentation top and drop my bags to the bus. A group of fans are lingering by the door. I sign some autographs and hurry back to the team room, where Reesy is stretching and Haskell is wired to something weird on his iPod.

'What's that?' I ask.

'Drum 'n' bass,' he says. 'It's called 'Granite' by a group called Pendulum.'

'A bit highbrow for me.' I laugh. 'Got any Spice Girls?'

The final meeting is called. Ashton reminds us of our work on the training ground and we troop downstairs to the bus. Traffic is manic as we edge towards Twickenham. I gaze out the window and there are hundreds of people marching towards the ground. They nudge each other and point cheerfully at the coach, oblivious of the tension beyond the tinted glass.

★ ★ ★

We arrive at Lion Gate. I sit for a moment to compose myself and follow Simon Shaw towards the door. The noise is exhilarating. There are thousands banked on the steps of the West Stand, cheering us off the coach. I grab my bag and my suit carrier and follow Shawsy into the tunnel. The hairs are standing on the back of my neck. The walls of the changing room are

13

plastered with motivational signs:

'Maintain the momentum.'

'Play with aggression.'

I search for the locker engraved with my name but they all seem to be occupied. 'Wellsy! What the fuck! Where's my peg?' I exclaim.

He shakes his head and points to the door where my brother, Tom, is standing with two security men. His eyes are bloodshot. His face is deathly pale.

'Tom! What are you doing here?' I gasp.

'There's been an accident,' he says. 'We need you to come upstairs.'

'What! You must be joking. What kind of accident?'

But he turns and leaves without reply.

'WHAT KIND OF ACCIDENT, TOM?'

Haskell places a comforting arm on my shoulder. 'Go with them, Hambo,' he says. 'Leave your stuff with me.'

'Okay, sort me a peg, mate,' I reply. 'I won't be long.'

I follow the security men back down the tunnel and out the players' entrance. The ground feels different. Something has changed. A young boy is staring at me like he has just seen an alien. Nobody is stopping to cheer or call my name. We reach the lift at the bottom of the Spirit of Rugby suite and an official hurries inside to hold the doors for me. I stare at him, bewildered. My pulse has started to race. The only thing that makes sense is the screaming voice in my head: *You have got to get back to the changing room, Hambo!* I bolt

14

from the lift and start sprinting down the corridor towards the players' entrance.

★ ★ ★

I'm almost there now. The guys are stripped and ready to go. Haskell is standing at the door with my jersey in his hand. He is waving and urging me to quicken but it's as if I'm running on a conveyor belt. I can't close the gap. I can't get back to the changing room. And that's where it ends. That's where it always ends; with me, stranded in the tunnel as my friends run out at Twickenham; with me, cursing my brother, night after night in my dreams: *Fucking Tom! Always wrecking things!*

3

There's a girl sizing me up from the other side of the dance floor. She has a lovely face, tangled blonde curls and a rack like Jordan. Perhaps it *is* Jordan — they say she's a regular here. Perhaps I'm hallucinating and she's not looking at me at all. Here is Chinawhite in Piccadilly, the playground of the chic. It's a Saturday night in London and I've been invited to the VIP room with Haskell and a few of the England boys. It's been a while since I've been clubbing, and even longer since I've danced, but this place is beginning to grow on me. And the night has definitely improved since Jordan started giving me the eye. I smile warily as she comes sashaying across the floor, squeezed into a delightfully skimpy dress from Prada or Dolce. She has deep brown eyes, skin like burnt butter and a brain the size of a pea.

'What's that pipe sticking out of your neck?' she enquires, by way of introduction. 'Is it a snorkel?'

They don't do chat-up lines like that in Leicester and I have to fight the urge to strangle her. Or have Haskell strangle her. But she's gorgeous, and I'm curious, and like I say, it's been a while . . .

'It's a tracheostomy,' I reply. 'There's a machine at the back of my wheelchair that pumps air through the snorkel and into my lungs.'

16

'So you're like . . . paralysed,' she says.

'The penny drops.' I smile.

'How did it happen?'

'Have you seen *Casino Royale*?'

'Yes.'

'That scene with Daniel Craig on the building site? That was me. I'm a stuntman . . . Or at least I was before my accident.'

'Were you really?'

'Naah. I did it playing rugby.'

'How awful!'

'Well, it's certainly not ideal,' I concur, 'but it has its perks. There's always a seat in the bar when it's crowded, and girls love a man with his own set of wheels.'

'You're funny,' she says, laughing.

'You're hilarious,' I reply.

'I'm Kate,' she says, extending her hand.

'Matt.' I smile, glancing pointedly at her fingers.

'I'm so sorry,' she shrieks, whipping her hand away.

'That's okay, I'm used to it.'

'I had leukaemia once as a kid,' she professes. 'They thought I was going to die.'

'But you didn't.'

'No, I didn't.' She chuckles.

'Can I buy you a drink, Kate?'

'I'll have a vodka and orange, thanks.'

Kate lives in Kensington and works in fashion. Or is it photography? I'm not sure. I can't remember. What I do recall is that she was full of surprises.

'Who's that bloke standing behind you?' she enquires.

17

'That's Dean. He's one of my carers.'

'Tell him to fuck off.'

'Why?'

'I'd like to speak to you alone.'

'I can't do that, I'm afraid. He's not allowed to leave my side.'

'Why not?'

'Because if something happens to my snorkel, I'll have a very serious problem.'

'Do you mind if I sit on your knee?'

'You better not, I might spasm.'

'Spasm?'

'A sudden, involuntary contraction of a muscle.'

'Sounds lovely,' she coos. 'We could spasm together.'

'Believe me, I'd consider myself to be the luckiest guy in the world if that happened but . . . '

'What can you move?' she asks.

'Not a lot from the neck down.'

'Really?'

'No.'

'How's your cock?'

'Hasn't seen much action for a while now, I'm afraid.'

'I'll just have to sit on your face then.'

'Yeah, that might work,' I reply, laughing. 'Dean? Would you mind lowering my backrest please?'

'What about a date?' she enquires.

'Hmmm, dunno. What do you have inside that would make me want to know you more?'

'What?'

'Beauty is common, but what's rare is a great energy and outlook on life. Do you possess that energy and outlook, Kate?'

'You're taking the piss again, aren't you?'

'Yeah, sorry, read that somewhere in a book.'

'What about a date?'

'Sounds good.'

'Just me and you,' she insists.

'That might cause problems, Dean gets very jealous.'

'Be serious,' she says, slapping my hand.

'Okay, that would be great.' I smile.

She scribbles her number on a slip of paper and slips it into my jacket. We continue flirting way past midnight, and it's five-thirty in the morning when I get to my hotel. Sleep does not come easily. I'm thinking about the girl; she has rekindled a fire I was sure had extinguished.

What if it's not over? What if there is still someone out there for me?

I close my eyes and my thoughts turn to Jennie.

4

If disability teaches you one thing, it's that there are a lot of dumb people in this world. I went shopping for some new shoes recently during a trip to Sheffield and tried on a pair of Timberland boots. So I'm sitting, in my wheelchair having them fitted, with my pipe out and the ventilator on: 'You'll get great wear out of these,' the shop assistant assures me. 'They've got a good thick sole.'

And what is it about photographers? I attended an open day at Billesdon Fire Station last month and was invited to pose for a couple of shots out the back. There was a thick power cable running across the exit and I wasn't sure I was going to be able to cross it in my chair without a ramp. 'This way, Matt,' the snapper chirps. 'Take a run and jump.'

Which was almost as good as his colleague a week before during a photoshoot with Martin Johnson and a couple of the Leicester boys. 'Okay, everybody thumbs up,' he says. 'And you, Matt, come on!' I thought Johno was going to flatten him.

Of course, the one place you don't expect it is at the National Spinal Injuries Centre at Stoke Mandeville. I was back recently for a check-up and had a long chat with one of the nurses about my plans to write a book. This nurse knows me intimately. She has winched me from my bed and showered me; she has shaved me, dressed me, clipped my toenails, brushed my teeth and wiped my bum. But when I told her I was working with a ghostwriter she was almost shocked.

'Oh!' she exclaimed. 'Are you not writing it yourself?'

5

and showed me, she has shaved me, dressed me, clipped my toenails, brushed my teeth and wiped my bum. But when I told her I was working with a ghost-writer, she was almost shocked.

The first time I met Paul Kimmage was a year after my accident, when he came to interview me for the *Sunday Times*. He was wearing a black pin-stripe suit and arrived at my bedside with an umbrella tucked under his arm and a matching briefcase. He looked more like a barrister than a journalist . . . and the questions, Christ! Talk about the Spanish Inquisition! And as odd as two left feet. I still can't figure him out. A couple of months ago, when we first started working on the book, I was telling him a story about some coaching I've been doing at Oakham when I noticed him scanning the titles on my bookshelf.

'I KNEW IT!' he explodes.

'Knew what?'

He is waving a copy of Lance Armstrong's *It's Not About the Bike*.

'Let me guess,' he says. 'He's your hero, your inspiration.'

'Well, to be honest . . . '

'I know, I know,' he spits. 'It's the best book you've ever read.'

'Well, actually . . . '

'IT'S SHITE! I'm sorry, Matt, I know you really admire this guy and that you've been inspired by his cancer, blah, blah, blah but if we're going to do this book together . . . '

'I haven't read it,' I protest. 'Someone left it as

22

a gift. I don't know anything about Lance Armstrong.'

'You don't?'

'Well, I know he's an American who had cancer and won the Tour de France, but that's it.'

'So we don't have to mention him?'

'No, not at all.'

'Okay, that's fine.'

Then he says, 'What about your carers?'

'What about them?'

'Do any of them wear those yellow wristbands?'

I start laughing. 'Why? Is that a problem?'

'They'll have to come off when I'm around.'

'Okay,' I say. 'I'm sure we can arrange that.'

'Good. Now . . . where were we?'

Thankfully, it's been plain sailing ever since . . . well, mostly. He likes a moan — grumpy is his default mode — and gets on like a house on fire with my father, but sometimes I have to remind him that I'm the guy in the wheelchair. So you can imagine my surprise this morning when he arrived for another session looking cheerier than Peter Kay.

'What's wrong, Paul?' I tease. 'Has Lance Armstrong broken his leg?'

'No, better than that.' He smiles.

'Really?'

'Well, no, but almost as good.'

He pulls a small typed manuscript from his bag: 'Ta da! The first chapter. I finished it last night.'

The cover isn't quite what I expected . . .

23

based on an original screenplay
by Frank Darabont

FIRST DRAFT: 1/2/08

'I know I'm dyslexic,' I say, 'but this looks like a screenplay.'

'It *is* a screenplay.'

'I thought we were doing a book.'

'We are, but it's a book that reads like a screenplay . . . or at least it starts like a screenplay. It will have a kind of split narrative running through it.'

'Sounds complicated.'

'It's different,' he insists.

'Who's Frank Darabont?'

'The genius behind your favourite film.'

'What? *The Shawshank Redemption?*'

'Yeah. See . . . I think there are a lot of parallels between what happened to you and what happened to Andy Dufresne: the poster you hung by your bed in Stoke Mandeville . . . the emphasis you place on hope . . . the fact that you were both unjustly incarcerated.'

'There's one obvious difference,' I observe. 'Andy escapes.'

'Yeah, well, that's true.'

'How are you planning mine?'

'I haven't quite figured that yet,' he concedes. 'But hey, it's a work in progress. Want to hear how it starts?'

'Sure.'

He starts to read:

Scene 1: EXTERIOR — SWIMMING POOL — DAY

The body of a young boy is floating face-down in a swimming pool. From an underwater camera we are looking up at the seemingly lifeless corpse of twelve-year-old Indeep 'Indy' Sidhu as it bobs up and down. He appears to be smiling.

INDY (voiceover)
They say your life flashes before you the moment before you die. I didn't see it. There was no distress or pain. One moment I was this happy-go-lucky kid diving into a pool on a beautiful Sunday morning, and the next I was floating merrily on some distant cloud with a dislocated neck.

A woman screams. Two men retrieve the boy from the water and begin frantic efforts to revive him. The boy is not responding. They pound his chest and blow into his mouth. Finally, he coughs.

FADE TO

Scene 2: INTERIOR — STOKE MANDEVILLE — NIGHT

A wheelchair is gliding slowly through the shadows of a corridor towards the sound of distant sobbing. Twenty years have passed since Indy Sidhu ruptured his spinal cord in the pool and he spends his spare days and nights at Stoke Mandeville, counselling the newly afflicted.

25

INDY (voiceover)
There's a guy like me in every spinal ward in
England. We're called 'old legions' and specialize
in misery, I guess. How it feels . . . what it tastes
like . . . how to swallow it and move on. The
acceptance is hardest, no doubt about that. You
wake up hoping life will resume as before but
find that God has changed the game plan: 'No
more diving for you, son.'

The camera tracks Indy's wheelchair as it moves
through the darkness towards the source of the
crying — a young equestrian who has fallen at a
horse trials. He arrives at her bedside and tries to
console her . . .

INDY (voiceover)
Those first nights are the toughest, no doubt
about it. They wheel you in, helpless as the
moment you were born and leave you locked
inside the shell of your shattered corpse, unable
to twist or turn or scratch or wipe, distraught
with grief for all you have lost, and tormented
by the fear of what happens next. Old life
blown away in the blink of an eye . . . a
long cold season in hell stretching out
ahead . . .

FADE TO

Scene 3: EXTERIOR — STADIUM — NIGHT

The 66th minute of an Under-21 rugby international between Ireland and England in Dublin. A

26

scrum has collapsed on the Irish 22 and as the players begin to extricate themselves from the wreckage, the camera zooms to the muddied white shirt at the bottom of the pile — a young English prop with blue eyes and mousy blond hair. He rises and wipes a trickle of blood from his lip.

INDY (voiceover)
This is Matthew Hampson. He plays rugby for England and Leicester Tigers. The game is his life, but in a few more days they're going to take that life away from him and lock him in the toughest place imaginable. Of course, he doesn't know that yet, which is probably just as well . . . I mean, can you imagine how terrifying life would be if we could see what was coming down the track?

The two packs bind and prepare to reset. From a ground-level camera, we're shooting upwards from beneath the scrum as the six front-row forwards crouch and hold. Their faces are portraits of controlled fury. A smile dances briefly across Hampson's lips and we hear the call to engage. The packs collide with a deafening thud and we

FADE TO

Scene 4: INTERIOR — CAR — NIGHT

A taxi travelling into the city of Dublin. The driver — a middle-aged man with flecked grey hair — has picked up a fare from an airport hotel and is listening to commentary from a game.

COMMENTATOR (voiceover)
Hampson picks and drives and brushes Andrew
Trimble off with contemptuous ease . . . great
work from the young English prop.

His eyes flicker between the road and the exquisitely
scented passengers he can see in his rearview mirror.
Blonde, busty and beautiful, they are dressed to thrill.

DRIVER
You sound English, girls.

BLONDE 1
Yeah, Bolton.

DRIVER
Over for the game?

BLONDE 1
What game is that?

DRIVER
The rugby. The Six Nations.

BLONDE 1
No, we're here for Brad Pitt.

DRIVER
(Confused) Brad Pitt?

BLONDE 1
Yeah. (Giggles) Do you not recognize us from the
film?

DRIVER
No.

BLONDE I
She's Thelma, I'm Louise; we've left the two use-
less bastards we married in Bolton and we're
looking for Brad Pitt.

DRIVER
(Laughs) Nice one . . . You're not going to tie me
up and rob me, now, are you?

BLONDE I
No, you're safe enough.

DRIVER
Please . . . I promise not to call the cops.

BLONDE I
(Laughs) Maybe on the way back. So what's this
Temple Bar like? We're told it's the place to go in
Dublin.

DRIVER
Yeah, there's plenty of clubs and restaurants and
bars and any number of wannabe Brad Pitts
. . . The wife's more of a George Clooney fan.
Did you notice the resemblance?

BLONDE I
(Laughs) Yeah, now that you mention it.

FADE TO

Scene 5: INTERIOR — HOTEL — NIGHT

A dark, empty room. We hear the click of a plastic card in a slot and the door opens. Thelma enters with a man on her arm. They're tipsy and giddy and horny as hell. She closes the door and kisses him passionately against the wall. A small gash on his lip starts to bleed; she licks it and slips her tongue into his mouth. The taste excites him.

They're all over each other now, ripping at clothes and pawing at flesh. He fondles her breasts and snatches at the zipper of her dress. She pulls at the buckle of his belt and unzips his fly. He enters her right then and there, impaling her against the wall. She grinds against him, her body shuddering with pleasure. She clasps his muscular shoulders and implores him not to stop. He carries her across the room and they fall into bed.

She wrestles him on to his back and straddles him. The lovemaking becomes louder and more frenzied until she cries out in orgasm and rolls on to her side. Within minutes, she is sleeping. The camera moves across the pillow. A shaft of moonlight dissects the room and for the first time we discern the handsome face of her lover — the young English prop, Matt Hampson. His eyes are half-closed in a post-coitus glaze, a smile flickers on his lips.

INDY (voiceover)
Dublin was one of the great nights. The England boys still laugh about it now: the drinking contest; the rickshaw race; and how the props, Hampson

30

and Cusack, had shifted the drop-dead-gorgeous Thelma and Louise. They had no idea, of course, what was lurking around the corner, the nightmare awaiting Cusack, Matt's last game.

Paul closes the manuscript and fixes me with a gaze. 'Well, what do you think?'

'Yeah, it's certainly different,' I demur.

'You sound unsure. Let me guess, you're worried about what your grandmother will think.'

'No, it's not that.'

'Your mother?'

'No.'

'Jennie?'

'Well, she did cross my mind, but it's more . . . '

What?'

'You said the book was going to hurt and that it had to be honest.'

'Yeah.'

'Well, I'm not sure how honest the bedroom scene is.'

'What? You didn't spend the night with Thelma in Dublin?'

'No, I mean the sex. It was never that good.'

6

Tonight is the night. France are playing Argentina in the opening game of the 2007 Rugby World Cup at Stade de France. I thought about making the trip to Paris — there was a chance of tickets from the RFU — but decided to stay at home and watch on my giant (65″) plasma screen. It's standing room only *chez* Hambo tonight. Three of my closest friends — Matt Cornwell, Alex Dodge and Dave Young (batting well above his average with a new girlfriend, Emily) — have come for dinner; Mum and Dad have wandered over with a bottle of (French) wine, and *les chiens*, Bruno and Ellie, sprawled out, have claimed most of the floor.

The teams line up for the singing of the national anthems. I watch as the Argentinians link arms and my eyes well with tears. It's funny, but I get really emotional now watching the anthems; for the first eighteen years of my life I never gave them a second thought and then I made my England debut and was almost overcome by ... Is patriotism the word? I don't know, but I can see it and feel it again now in the faces of the Argentinians: the unbreakable sense of fellowship, the almost unbearable sense of pride ...

God save our gracious Queen
Long live our noble Queen
God save the Queen
Send her victorious
Happy and glorious
Long to reign over us
God save the Queen.

The protocols end. The Stade erupts with a stupendous roar and the moment we've waited for arrives. I am so looking forward to this game and the tournament.

'Dad! Have you noticed the referee?' I ask.

'Yeah, I was just going to say,' he replies. 'Spreaders!'

7

This is the sound.

whooooooosh

The first sound I hear when I open my eyes each morning.

whooooooosh

The sound of the ventilator.

whooooooosh

The sound of the air being pumped through the tube into my lungs.

whooooooosh

The rhythm of my life.

whooooooosh

I hear it every four seconds.

whooooooosh

Or fifteen times a minute.

whooooooosh

Or 900 times every hour.

whooooooosh

Or 21,600 times a day.

whooooooosh

After a while you stop counting,

whooooooosh

But you never stop listening to the sound.

8

There are other sounds, distant sounds, things I never imagined I'd hear: the sounds of that second summer at Stoke Mandeville. The hiss of the water in the shower cascading on to my skin; Alfred, the attending nurse, going about his business: the gathering and the wiping; the strapping and the winching; the soaping and the rinsing. For me, the humiliating rituals of my new condition; for him, the simple automations of a working day. 'Just washing your foreskin, Matt,' he announces with a chuckle. And then we laugh, because you've got to laugh.

★　★　★

Another sound. The sound of one of our weekly rehabilitation lectures at Stoke Mandeville. The theme today is 'Sex and Disability'. A fairly dated instructional video is shown on a large projector screen. Then a nurse, who doesn't look like she has had much practical experience, gives a talk on the nuts and bolts of having sex in wheelchairs. The floor is opened to questions. A traumatized 35-year-old complains of being able to ejaculate only when 'this thing is shoved up my arse'. A fat, fifty-year-old wails in frustration about her unsatisfied clitoris and gives a much too detailed account of a disastrous recent coupling. The lecture ends. We stagger from the room, gasping and nauseous. And then we laugh, because you've got to laugh.

★   ★   ★

Another sound. The sound of rain pounding the skylight above my bed. It's morning. Dean and Michelle are doing my bowels. How does that feel? Well, it's a bit like sitting in your car with the bonnet up as the mechanic changes a filter — you are vaguely aware of the prodding and probing but don't feel a thing except for the sweating. I always sweat. Why? Well, if you've ever had a latex finger inserted in your rectum you will probably understand. They have almost finished now. Dean wraps the waste for disposal, and as Michelle removes her glove with a snap I feel the sudden hint of moisture on my lip. What is it? A drop of condensation from the skylight? A dash of sweat from my brow? I swat it with my tongue. It doesn't taste like sweat! Michelle looks horrified. Dean is stunned.

'That wasn't a flick of poo from the glove, was it?' I enquire.

'Oh God, I'm so sorry, Matt,' Michelle cries.

'I'll get the mouthwash,' Dean says.

I swallow and spit and cough and try to quell the urge to gag.

'Fucking great! Just when I thought things couldn't get much worse, I am eating my own poo!'

And then we laugh, because you've got to laugh. If you didn't you'd just cry.

9

Why me?

These are the words.

Why me?

The words that haunt you at night.

Why me?

The words that make you cry.

Why me?

The words that fucking destroy you.

Why me?

There are 20,000 front-row forwards playing the game regularly in England.

Why me?

They play (on average) twenty games each season.

Why me?

There are (on average) fifteen scrums per game.

Why me?

The risk of sustaining a serious injury has been calculated at 0.84 per 100,000 players.

Why me?

That's the question.

Why me?

The fight I'll pick with God.

10

They say he works in mysterious ways. God, that is. This is what I would like him to explain to me.

The month is May 1986. I am eighteen months old. My mother, Anne, has strapped me into the back seat of the car with Amy, my four-year-old sister. We are driving to the shops in Oakham. I don't like cars, hate the bloody restriction, but my sister has become quite adept at unpicking buckles and I go tumbling out the door as we round a corner. Imagine my mother's horror as she glances in the rearview mirror and sees her son bouncing down the road. Does the child-seat disintegrate? Is it hit by an oncoming car? Do I suffer an appalling injury? No, there isn't a mark on me.

The month is November 1989. I am five years old. Mum is in the kitchen preparing lunch; Amy is in the sitting room playing with her dolls; I'm flying up and down the hallway of our home in a plastic McLaren, pretending to be Ayrton Senna. There's a plate-glass door at the end of the finishing straight. I don't like doors, doors are restrictive. I accelerate down the hallway and decide not to stop. The glass shatters into a thousand pieces. Is the floor covered in blood? Have I lost a limb or been guillotined? No, there isn't a mark on me.

The month is December 2002. I am eighteen years old. It's Christmas. The boys at the Leicester Tigers Academy are high on festive spirit. A pub golf night has been organized — the annual Open Championship — and we report for this Royal and Ancient contest to Time, a bar near Leicester station, wearing lairy Pringle tops and chequered pants. The opening hole — an inviting par 3 — requires a pint of Stella with a depth-charge of vodka to be drained in three gulps. Take four and you make bogey; two and you make birdie. Each score is recorded on a card and the round consists of a different drink at eighteen of the city's finest pubs. I start brilliantly, blitzing the front nine with an albatross and three birdies but triple-bogey the last to end up one over for the round.

The game finishes at three in the morning. The championship has taken its toll. Two of the boys have been arrested for climbing the Christmas tree on Granby Street; three more have collapsed unconscious on Charles Street. I'm struggling to walk and starting to hallucinate. My friend Alex Dodge invites me to crash at his place.

We hail a cab to Leicester Forest and are staggering up the driveway to his home, when I spot the antichrist, Lawrence Dallaglio, sneering at me from the garden next door. 'So, Hambo, think you can play with the big boys?' Enraged, I charge and smash him in the ribcage and drive him across the lawn. 'Take that you c ★ ★ t.' It's the last thing I remember before drifting off to sleep.

The fallout next morning is ugly. Alex's parents' home has been vandalized. Some lout has spewed all over their couch, attempted to clean the mess with Windolene and blocked the downstairs toilet. He has also charged into the neighbours' garden and uprooted an ornamental lamppost with his head. Did the culprit fracture his skull? Did he choke on his vomit and die? No, there isn't a mark on me.

The month is September 2004. I am nineteen years old. Training at Leicester has finished for the day and I'm racing Dave Young down the A563 to Starbucks in Fosse Park. He's driving 'the bogey', a spectacularly ugly green Hyundai; I'm driving 'the silver bullet', a flash VW Polo. We've been wheel to wheel since the flag dropped in Oadby and have reached the big roundabout at the entrance to the mall. The lights turn amber; we brake and prepare to stop. The lights are red; I floor the accelerator. There's a car coming from the right; I squeeze through the gap, forcing him to brake violently; the air erupts with the squeal of burning rubber. Is my act of folly punished? Am I rammed and badly injured? No, there isn't a mark on me.

The month is March 2005. I am twenty years old. The England Under-21 rugby team are training at Franklin's Gardens in Northampton. We're scrummaging. It's my favourite part of the game. I follow the order to crouch and hold and await the command to engage. I'm feeling good. I'm in control. This is my domain. I drive into the scrum with the usual intensity, and within seconds everything has changed. Do I dislocate my neck and trap my spinal cord? You guessed it. Am I condemned to spend the rest of my life wired to a machine? Right again. Why, God? Why was I taken out doing the thing I most loved?

11

Maybe there's no God, maybe it's just fate.

A man steps from a café one morning with a freshly made bacon roll. He peels back the wrapper and is about to take a bite when a dollop of pigeon-shit splats him on the hand. He breaks his stride and drops the roll in disgust, cursing his misfortune as the pigeon swoops and begins feasting on the spoils. A second later, a clinically depressed woman jumps from an apartment overhead and lands at his feet with a sickening thud. She dies on impact. So does the pigeon. The man is in shock. 'That could have been me!' he shudders. 'That's exactly where I was standing when I dropped the roll!' You think that couldn't happen? You think I've made that up? Ask Cusack. He knows.

12

A tribunal of inquiry has been established at a courtroom in London to investigate the injuries sustained by Matt Hampson at Franklin's Gardens, Northampton, on 15 March. Michael Cusack, a 21-year-old loose-head prop from Doncaster, has been called to the witness stand. He looks nervous, wary.

BARRISTER
Mr Cusack, could you please describe to the tribunal the confrontation you had with Mr Hampson on the day in question?

CUSACK
I wouldn't call it a confrontation. We were both training with the Under-21s at Franklin's Gardens. We were both playing for England.

BARRISTER
My understanding is that you were rivals.

CUSACK
Well, yeah, I suppose . . . we were certainly rivals in training: I was the loose-head prop, he was the tight-head prop. He was not playing in my position so to speak, really, but obviously I opposed him in training.

43

BARRISTER
How well did you know him?

CUSACK
The first time I met Hambo would have been with the England Under-19s . . . possibly the 18s . . . He was a tough bloke, a good scrummager, but a top lad to be fair. All the Leicester lads . . . Tom Ryder . . . Matt Cornwell . . . were good lads. I play for Leeds and we played Leicester regularly in 'A' team fixtures, but I didn't really get to know him until that Six Nations campaign.

BARRISTER
Two weeks before the incident, on 25 February, you played against Ireland in Dublin?

CUSACK
Yes.

BARRISTER
Could you tell the tribunal about the game in Dublin please, Mr Cusack?

CUSACK
It was my first start for the Under-21s, and my first try. I'd been on the bench for the two defeats to Wales and France but I was given a start against Ireland and scored — Tom Biggs popped me in the corner. We won easily.

BARRISTER
Did you finish the game, Mr Cusack?

44

CUSACK
No.

BARRISTER
You were substituted in the 49th minute?

CUSACK
Yes.

BARRISTER
Who was your replacement?

CUSACK
Hambo.

BARRISTER
Louder please, Mr Cusack, so everyone can hear.

CUSACK
Matt Hampson.

BARRISTER
You went out that night after the game, I believe?

CUSACK
Yeah, it was a good night, quite a messy night if I recall.

BARRISTER
Messy?

CUSACK
We had a right few beers . . . It was quite a long night as well.

BARRISTER
My information is that you paired off that night
with Mr Hampson?

CUSACK
Yeah.

BARRISTER
My information is that you met two women and
went back to their hotel?

CUSACK
(Laughs nervously) Yeah, I do recall that, yeah.

BARRISTER
Would you mind telling the tribunal what happened please, Mr Cusack?

CUSACK
Not a great deal to be honest. I remember that we
paired off like you say, and went back to the
ladies' hotel — a Travelodge near the airport. It
was miles from the team hotel; cost us an arm
and a leg in a taxi to get back next morning. I still
had a bottle of wine and we finished it in the taxi.
Some of the lads were coming down to breakfast
when we arrived. And then it was a case of just
trying to survive the training session without
throwing up. It was a pretty big night by all
accounts.

BARRISTER
So you had more than your position in common
with Mr Hampson?

46

CUSACK
How do you mean?

BARRISTER
You share a taste for beer and good-looking
women?

CUSACK
Well, that would do it, wouldn't it? No . . . I think
we got on pretty well. I respected him as a player.
I had played against him a few times and he had
been good opposition against me. We had a few
scrapes on the training field and in games but
that's over once you have played. He obviously
likes a beer, I like a beer, and when you win you
just want to go out. I guess Matt and me were the
two best-looking guys in the squad at that time so
it was natural that we teamed up.
(Laughs)

BARRISTER
Your nickname on the team is 'Daddy Cu', I
believe?

CUSACK
(Smiles) Yes.

BARRISTER
This 'Daddy Cu' seems a very different person
from the man facing me now.

CUSACK
How do you mean?

BARRISTER

Bit of a lad by the sound of things, not shy or retiring, likes a night out.

CUSACK

When the beer is talking, it is talking. I don't mind the odd beverage — it might help me now!

BARRISTER

What made you want to be a prop, Mr Cusack?

CUSACK

I don't think I had a choice really, to be perfectly honest. I played number 8 and stuff until I was about fifteen and did not have the body shape as I got older. That was it really. I was at Yorkshire Under-15s, and from there on in I was a prop. Some say it is a good thing; some say it is bad . . .

BARRISTER

What do you say, Mr Cusack?

CUSACK

I say it is tough. Unless you have played there, I don't think anybody really knows what it is like.

BARRISTER

Tell the tribunal what it is like.

CUSACK

Well, it all starts off with the impact of two packs hitting each other and the props are bearing the brunt of it all. There is a lot of force coming together and if you are slightly off, you will be taught a lesson. The opposite prop is trying to bend you in two and get you into a bad position. And if you are in a bad position it is just painful!

BARRISTER
Have you endured much pain, Mr Cusack?

CUSACK
I have had the odd couple of knocks.

BARRISTER
What about collapsed scrums? Have you ever got into difficulty?

CUSACK
What, injured off the scrum? No, touch wood, never.

BARRISTER
Okay, Mr Cusack, I'd like to ask you now about the events of 15 March. What are your memories of the session in Franklin's Gardens?

CUSACK
It was a Tuesday morning, three days before the final game of the Six Nations, against Scotland. I recall that we had both started against Italy on the previous Friday and had gone home for the weekend. We started at about ten, the usual stuff — warm up, a bit of rucking, a few restarts — and then the forwards and backs split and we started scrummaging.

BARRISTER
You haven't mentioned the fight, Mr Cusack.

CUSACK
What fight is that?

BARRISTER
Your punch-up with Mr Hampson during the contact session.

CUSACK
I've no idea what you are talking about.

BARRISTER
Really? That's not what Mr James Haskell recalls. Would you like me to read his testimony? He said, and I quote: 'I don't think we were as physical as we should have been against Italy and we started with a full-on contact session wearing these body suits. It's the first session of the day and we're battering the crap out of each other when it all kicks off between Cusack and Hambo. Normally scuffles are broken up after a couple of seconds but no one broke them up. We were doing lengths (of the field) . . . they started fighting at the top end; we turn around, go to the bottom end, turn around and come back and they are still fighting. They are leaning against each other . . . propping each other up and throwing these windmill punches until Nigel Redman steps in and says: 'Right that's enough.' '

CUSACK
Was that the same day? I'm not sure. I can

remember having a row with someone all right but I don't think it was Matt.

BARRISTER
Do you remember the scrummaging session?

CUSACK
Some of it. We did loads. I think we had about five hits on the scrum machine and then a session of live scrums.

BARRISTER
What do you mean by live?

CUSACK
By live I mean contested scrums; we had enough players for two packs. Spreaders had been brought in to oversee the session.

BARRISTER
Spreaders?

CUSACK
Tony Spreadbury, the international referee.

BARRISTER
And what was the object of these contested scrums?

CUSACK
We'd watched a recording of the game against Italy the night before and analysed the scrum. The coaches weren't happy with the number of resets.

BARRISTER
Resets?

CUSACK
When a scrum collapses the referee will either
reset the scrum or award a penalty. Six of the
seven scrums against Italy had been reset. The
objective of the session was a clean, three-second
scrum: hit, ball in and ball away in three seconds.

BARRISTER
But didn't four of the scrums during the session
collapse?

CUSACK
Well, it's a contest, isn't it? You've got one side
trying to get the ball away in three seconds and
the other side trying to disrupt them.

BARRISTER
What side were you on, Mr Cusack?

CUSACK
Both sides. The packs were reshuffled several
times during the session.

BARRISTER
What side were you on when Mr Hampson sustained his injuries?

CUSACK
It was their put-in. We were trying to disrupt
them.

BARRISTER
What does disrupting them entail?

CUSACK
What it says.

BARRISTER
Is that going in on the angle to bore underneath his chest with your head, Mr Cusack? Were you trying to push him up and out of position? Was the objective to try and bend Mr Hampson in two?

CUSACK
I would never have taken you for a prop, barrister.

BARRISTER
It's called the dark art of scrummaging I believe.

CUSACK
Some might say.

BARRISTER
And you employed that art against Mr Hampson?

CUSACK
Matt knew how to take care of himself, believe me.

BARRISTER
So what happened, Mr Cusack? What do you remember?

CUSACK
Everything and nothing. I've replayed that scrum a

thousand times in my head trying to figure it out. It felt like a regular scrum. We hit and it went down and I got up, expecting to reset but Matt just lay there. The physio and doctor went to him immediately. The coaches stepped in and moved us out of the way and it wasn't until much later that we heard it was serious.

BARRISTER
How did you feel?

CUSACK
Well, knowing that I was against him I felt . . .

BARRISTER
Did you feel guilt, Mr Cusack?

CUSACK
Guilt? No, it was . . . Well, you do wonder about it. Like I say, it felt like a regular scrum, but you do wonder about it. I remember I went back to my room and closed the door and thought about it for hours. Did I feel guilt? No, I felt pain. I thought about what had happened to him and cried my fucking eyes out.

BARRISTER
Thank you, Mr Cusack. There are no further questions.

13

You've got to laugh. Try this.

A genie pops from his lamp and says, 'Hey there, Mr tetraplegic-ventilator-dependent-man, I grant you a wish.'

'Shouldn't that be three wishes?' I reply.

'Sorry, cutbacks,' he says. 'The credit crunch.'

'Okay, then I suppose it will have to be the obvious.'

'You want to walk again, right?'

'No, I said the obvious . . . Tigers to beat Wasps in the final of the European Cup for the next hundred years.'

Okay, so I've no future in comedy, but if I did find that lamp then it really would be the obvious.

I've been thinking about Jennie these past few days and sent her a message this morning using my head-mouse — a laser beamed from a dot on my forehead that enables me to use my laptop. So much to say, so hard to beam it into words. I gave up after two lines: 'How are you doing? I still think about you.'

Not exactly Shakespeare.

14

Some days are tougher than others. Today, a grey October Tuesday, was one of the tougher days. It started with a mix-up at Glenfield Hospital in Leicester over a routine appointment that (unknown to me) was cancelled and rescheduled. Two of my carers, Dean and Ruby, were with me. It had taken us over an hour to drive from my home in Cold Overton and it seemed a shame to drive straight back.

'Starbucks?' Ruby suggests.

'Sounds good.' I smile.

Pauleen Pratt is a senior clinical nurse at Glenfield. We have just left reception and have almost reached the exit when I notice her coming the other way. 'Hello, Matt!' she greets me. 'I didn't know you were in today.'

'Well, apparently I'm not,' I reply. 'There's been some mix-up with the dates.'

'Oh, what a pity. How are you?'

'Yeah, good thanks, Pauleen. We're just heading into Leicester for a coffee.'

'Any chance of a quick word?'

'Sure.'

She leads us back down the corridor to a small consulting room and glances at Ruby and Dean. 'I'd like to speak to you alone, Matt,' she explains.

'Sure,' I reply.

I like Pauleen; she has a great sense of humour

for someone from Norfolk and never objects to my constant ribbing of her surname ('Have you always been a Pratt or did you marry one?'). Her expertise is in patients who require chronic ventilation and we've got along famously since I left Stoke Mandeville. But as she closes the door, there is no disguising her unease. What is it, I wonder? But she is slow to reveal her hand.

'I hear you haven't been sleeping well, Matt.'

'No, not great.'

'Has it anything to do with this book you're writing? You know . . . revisiting it all again.'

'Yeah, maybe.'

'I read the Christopher Reeve book.'

'Was it good?' I ask.

'Yes, it was. The horsey bit was boring but the healthcare aspect was very interesting. It really got me thinking about the way we treat people sometimes — we don't empower them at all.'

'We need a few more like you, Pauleen.'

'How has your chest been lately?' she enquires.

'Not too bad. I had a bit of a fever last week but I'm getting over it.'

'What about the new ventilator?'

'Yeah, it's all right. I've been using the old one at night and the new one during the day . . . They're a bit different. This one is producing air that dries me out a bit.'

'We can give you something for that.'

'Yeah, well, you know what I'm like . . . I want to take as few drugs as possible.'

'Yeah, I know what you're like and I respect

the choices you make, but you give me sleepless nights sometimes. You are so blooming frustrating!'

'Sorry, Pauleen.'

'Okay, well, I've been looking for an opportunity to speak to you alone,' she says, shifting in her chair. 'There are a couple of things we need to discuss . . . things that are not very pleasant.'

'I kind of figured that.' I smile.

'One of the things I admire most about you, Matt, is your drive and ambition — you get out, you socialize, you take risks and you've always made your own choices. I need you to make some more of those choices now.'

'Okay.'

'And if I have asked to speak to you in private it's because I don't want you to be influenced in those choices by your parents or carers or anyone else.'

'Sure.'

'The fact is, Matt, you are dependent on a ventilator to breathe and at some point in time that is going to cause you problems.'

'I understand that.'

'What if you get sick, I mean really sick . . . Would you want to be brought to Glenfield?'

'Yes, I want to be brought to Glenfield.'

'You don't want to stay at home?'

'No, I don't want to stay at home.'

'What if, say, another system is affected and your heart stops or your lungs pack in? Do you want to be resuscitated?'

'Yes, Pauleen.'

'What if . . . '

She pauses, trying to compose herself.

'I am not ready to die yet, Pauleen,' I state with as much assertion as I can muster. 'I have a lot of living to do.'

'I know, Matt,' she replies, almost choking. 'And I am not expecting a problem any time soon but it's better to address this while it isn't pending.'

'I understand.'

'There are some people in your position who would feel that the burden is too great and would want to be left in peace should anything happen. I know you're not one of those people. I knew exactly what you'd say but I had to hear you say it. That's my job. I am now going to document your wishes and copy them into your medical notes.'

'I understand.'

'If at any point you want to change your mind or rediscuss it, there's no problem. The door is always open.'

'Thanks, Pauleen.'

'Okay, last question, what about a will? I don't know if you've spoken with anybody about it, or about writing a living will, but it's something you might consider.'

'Okay, I'll think about that.'

And I have. Almost eight hours have passed since we had the conversation and I've thought of little else.

15

My ghost has arrived for another session of interviews. He's not happy. He seems confused. 'Okay, let's run through this again from top to bottom,' he says. 'You're twenty years old and about to win your fifth cap for England at the 2005 Under-21 Six Nations Championship?'

'Yes, against Scotland.'

'Four days before the game you suffer a catastrophic accident at training?'

'Yes.'

'You almost die by the side of the pitch?'

'Yes.'

'You wake up in intensive care wired to a ventilator?'

'Yes.'

'You spend the next seventeen months at Stoke Mandeville hospital?'

'Yes.'

'During those seventeen months you contract MRSA and C. diff.?'

'Yes.'

'You watch your family almost disintegrate with the strain?'

'Yes.'

'Four of your former team-mates — Haskell, Rees, Varndell and Flood — go on to make full England debuts?'

'Yes.'

'And the day you hit rock bottom, the thing

that almost brings you down is a girl!'

'Jennie.'

'Yes, Jennie.'

'Only love can break your heart.' I smile.

'But it doesn't stand up,' he says. 'The chronology doesn't make sense. You said you met Jennie on the weekend after the French game?'

'Yeah.'

'That's Saturday, 19 February 2005?'

'Yeah, I'm pretty sure of the date.'

'But that's less than a month before your accident?'

'So?'

'How many times did you go out together?'

'I dunno . . . three . . . four . . . three, I think. It was smack in the middle of the Six Nations. I was away with England quite a lot.'

'What did you do on those dates?'

'We went to a bar in Leicester twice for drinks, and met once for coffee in Starbucks.'

'You never went out to dinner together?'

'I'd asked her to come to the Scotland game. We were planning to go out to dinner, but . . . '

'So you had only just met this girl?'

'Yeah.'

'How could you fall in love with someone you hardly knew?' he asks.

'Maybe it was love at first sight.'

'Was it?'

'Not really.'

'So what was it?' he asks. 'And how do we explain it in the book?'

An awkward silence ensues.

'There are some bits I haven't told you,' I concede.

16

The tribunal of inquiry has entered its second day. Matt Cornwell, a twenty-year-old centre from Leicester, has just entered the witness stand. He is calm, assured.

BARRISTER
Mr Cornwell, you are a team-mate of Mr Hampson's at Leicester, I believe?

CORNWELL
That's right.

BARRISTER
And a member of the England Under-21s?

CORNWELL
Yes. I've known Matt basically since the age of nine, when he joined our club, Syston. My father, John, was the coach there. Our parents got to know each other and started socializing together; we'd go to the Hampsons' for dinner and have a kickaround in the garden. I played a lot of football with him in that garden.

BARRISTER
You became friends?

CORNWELL

Yes. The first time I ever got drunk was with
Hambo — a barn party at a neighbour's house.
All the rugby lads were on the bar serving drinks
for the parents. He had this bottle of cider under
the table. 'We'll have a few cheekies,' he says. I
could hardly walk. He thought it was hilarious.
That was typical of him — he was definitely more
of an instigator than a follower. At Syston,
because my dad was the coach, I could not be
seen to be sneaking beer or any of that when we
went away on tour. I'd think: Oh God, I cannot
get caught. Hambo didn't care. 'Just go for it' was
his attitude. He hasn't changed.

BARRISTER

Your friendship was unusual. Forwards and backs
aren't normally that close . . .

CORNWELL

We weren't massively close — not at first. It
wasn't really until we joined the Tigers Academy
that we started to chill out with each other. We
have different characters: I'm probably more
reserved and sensitive, a bit of a soft lad really;
Matt loves a wind-up. It was always just a joke to
him.

BARRISTER

Did you have similar aspirations for the game?

CORNWELL

I never thought I would play rugby professionally,
not at Syston, but I think Hambo always had it in

his head. He loved scrummaging and he had the heart for the game. I can see him now with his scrum hat and gumshield popping out of his mouth, smashing people out of the way. And he could run and handle the ball. He was not one of these props with hands like feet who drop it all the time.

BARRISTER
According to my notes you made your debut for England together?

CORNWELL
Yes, with the Under-18s at a three-week tournament in Scotland, which was cool. We won all four games. That was wicked. I loved playing with him. You would stand next to him for the national anthem and he would start squeezing and get you tight — if you were not up for the game he was going to drag you up. And he never took a backward step. If we needed somebody sorted, Hambo was always in first. He would smash them. If somebody was on the wrong side, he would wade in with his big Nike boots and shoe the fuck . . . sorry, shoe the lard out of them. That's my abiding memory of him as a player. He was always at the front.

BARRISTER
Thank you, Mr Cornwell. Now, if you would kindly address the events of 15 March. You were present that morning at Franklin's Gardens, I believe?

CORNWELL
Yes I was, but I had picked up a dead leg and
didn't train.

BARRISTER
What did you do?

CORNWELL
I watched from the side with my coat and woolly
hat on. It was quite a windy morning and cold. I
remember doing a bit of work with Becky, the
team video woman, and walking around and
watching the play. The backs were pretty much
done; the forwards were still working on the
scrum and doing hits all around the pitch. I was
standing under the posts, chatting with Tom Varndell from about twenty metres away when Hambo
went down.

BARRISTER
The scrum collapsed?

CORNWELL
Yes. I remember looking across and seeing the
doctor behind Matt on his side and thinking: Oh,
there's the doctor!

BARRISTER
I'm sorry, Mr Cornwell, I don't understand.

CORNWELL
The team doctor, Tim Weighman, had packed
down at flanker on that side of the scrum when it
collapsed. It was the first time I had noticed him.

They were obviously missing a man or he was filling in for somebody, which was a bit stupid but . . .

BARRISTER
Stupid?

CORNWELL
The doctor is a nice guy, I like him, but he's not a flanker — half of the prop's power comes from the shoulder of the flanker and maybe it wasn't a factor but it did make me wonder.

BARRISTER
Scrums collapse regularly in the game. At what point did you realize there was a problem?

CORNWELL
At first, it looked pretty normal. I thought: Oh, he's hurt his neck. He'll get up and put some ice on it and it will be fine. But he wasn't moving. The doctor and physio were looking at each other, almost in shock. A couple of the guys moved away and then Tony Spreadbury went flying in.

BARRISTER
The referee?

CORNWELL
Yes. To be fair, the doctor got hold of Matt's head straight away but Tony Spreadbury took control: Call the ambulance, do this, do that, boom, boom, boom. I remember walking over and peering over the top and that was when it hit me:

66

Jesus! This is fucking bad!

BARRISTER
How much time had elapsed?

CORNWELL
Not much . . . ten . . . twenty seconds.

BARRISTER
What did you see?

CORNWELL
Matt had stopped breathing. I looked down and
he was literally blue in the face. It was brutal. I
couldn't believe it. I didn't know what to do. The
guys were saying, 'No, stay back, stay back.' Then
he took some sort of a turn and Spreaders started
pumping his chest: doosh, doosh, doosh.

BARRISTER
He was administering CPR?

CORNWELL
Yes. And as soon as I saw that I broke down. I
was in bits . . . all of the Leicester boys — me,
Tom Ryder, Tom Varndell — we were really cut
up. Spreaders was great, I owe him a few pints. In
my eyes, he saved Matt's life. I'm not saying the
other guys were not qualified, but in the heat of
the moment he dealt with it. He was the boy.

BARRISTER
What happened when the ambulance arrived?

CORNWELL
The session was ended and we went back to the team hotel, but I couldn't bear it. I thought: I have got to go to the hospital. I was still in my gear, but I jumped in my car and drove to the hospital.

BARRISTER
What hospital?

CORNWELL
Northampton General. I couldn't find it at first; had to go down the M1 and cut back in. When I got there, they had brought him straight into emergency so I didn't see him, but the team doctor and physio were there. They were white as sheets. It had never happened to them before; it had never happened within the England set-up. Everybody was in complete shock. The next day we had a meeting to decide what we were going to do about the Scotland game. It was just the players. No management. I said, 'Look, I think Hambo would have wanted us to play', but looking back it was a mistake. There was no atmosphere; it was too emotional. I cried my eyes out during the national anthem, other guys were the same, especially Cusack. We played like a bunch of twats . . . Not that it mattered.

BARRISTER
How long was it before you saw Mr Hampson again?

CORNWELL
It would have been on the Monday or the Tuesday . . . I think it was the Tuesday, exactly a week after it happened.

BARRISTER
And he had been moved to Stoke Mandeville?

CORNWELL
Yes. I remember there was something wrong with my car so I borrowed my dad's van and drove down with Jennie.

BARRISTER
Jennie?

CORNWELL
Matt's girlfriend. It was the first time I had met her. She had got my number somehow through a friend of a friend and called me: 'Can you pick me up and take me down to see Matt?' We drove down together. I think we stopped for something to eat on the way. I thought she was a nice girl, quite funny; quite a good-looking girl as well.

BARRISTER
And you had not met her before?

CORNWELL
No, I had heard about her, but Hambo was unusual like that . . . we used to go and get with chicks as you do — young lads leading the bachelors' life — but Hambo would never 'stick' as such. He would never do stuff, if you like.

BARRISTER
Stuff?

CORNWELL
Relationships . . . girlfriends . . . shagging; the lads
in rugby live off that, all you talk about is chicks
and cars and computer games, but Hambo was
different. You would never hear him talking about
it. He had gone out with a few girls, but never
seemed that interested until maybe two months
before the accident when he was on fire with the
chicks. Unbelievable! He was pulling them left,
right and centre. All the boys were like: 'Yeah, go
for it, Hambo.' I had never seen him like that
before. That was when he met Jennie.

BARRISTER
How did they meet?

CORNWELL
I've no idea, but she obviously made an impression on him because on the night before he was
injured he was on the phone for ages to this bird
in the corridor of the hotel. I remember laughing
about it. 'Hambo! This isn't you, mate. What are
you doing? Tell her to get lost and we'll mess
around.'

BARRISTER
What happened when you arrived at Stoke
Mandeville?

CORNWELL
Matt was in intensive care. He was blown up like

a balloon with all the fluids and stuff in him. There was no response apart from blinking. That was all he could do. He could not move a muscle.

BARRISTER
That must have been difficult?

CORNWELL
Well, I knew I'd be a bloody mess and tried to prepare myself by going to see Paddy Mortimer, the sports psychologist we use at Tigers. He gave me a couple of techniques to make it easier.

BARRISTER
Techniques?

CORNWELL
Yeah, you know, ways of coping. He told me 'Go in, be really bubbly, tell him what was going on with the boys at Leicester; be really enthusiastic and say, 'It is great to see you, mate.' Even if he is not responding, just tell him everything. After ten minutes make an excuse to go to the toilet and compose yourself. Then go back in again.'

BARRISTER
Did it work?

CORNWELL
Yes and no. It was hard watching him lying there. He was on life support, hanging on, and looked dreadful. I came out after ten minutes and completely broke down. We hardly spoke on the journey home . . . No, sorry, Jennie stayed with

71

him; I am pretty sure she slept by his side. She stayed around for a few months, six months, maybe a bit longer.

BARRISTER
What do you mean by around?

CORNWELL
Sorry, I mean the relationship lasted for about six months. I don't know how it ended. He has never spoken about it and I have never asked. He keeps stuff like that close to his chest.

BARRISTER
Thank you, Mr Cornwell.

17

I lost my virginity on a Saturday afternoon in front of 17,000 Tigers fans at Welford Road . . . Or at least, that's how it felt. The following morning, and for the next week at training, it was coming at me from every angle and playing on every tongue.

'Heard about Hambo?'

'No.'

'Lost it, hasn't he?'

'What?'

'He's finally popped his cherry.'

'You're joking.'

'No, gone in twenty seconds.'

'Really? Who's the lucky girl?'

'You know her.'

'Not . . . '

'Yeah.'

'Oh Christ! She must have serviced half the squad!'

'Yeah, some of them together!'

'I hope he remembered to dip it in Listerine.'

It was mortifying, one of the worst weeks of my life. It was also a massive relief. You see, I wanted my team-mates to know, needed their approval; it was the solution to a problem that had been dogging me for weeks.

It wasn't that I didn't like girls or was indifferent to sex — I just wasn't in any hurry to explore it. I enjoyed female company and had

73

lots of friends who were girls, but rugby was my priority. I lived for the battles on the field, the banter in the dressing room and the craic of being one of the boys. I was also a bit old-fashioned, I suppose. I believed in love and marriage and commitment; if I was going to have sex, it would be with the right girl.

It wasn't an issue at school or during my formative rugby years at Syston, but from the moment you enter a professional academy, everything gets noticed: the size of your nose, the cut of your hair, the make of your car, the label on your clothes, the playlist on your iPod and, most importantly, the length and circumference of your organ. Shagging was part of the lexis. Some of the guys had been sexually active since their early teens and never missed an opportunity to brag about it . . . or pick up on when you didn't. You were moody? They noticed. You were thrifty? They noticed. You were dopey? They noticed. Stale breath, snore, fart, bite your nails, pick your nose. They noticed. You didn't have a girlfriend? They noticed. And when they noticed, you had a problem. By my eighteenth birthday, the ribbing had become merciless.

'Has anyone ever seen Hambo with a bird?'

'No, can't remember.'

'He's obviously gay.'

'Do you think so?'

'Yeah, I bet he's a willy watcher.'

'Naaaaah.'

'Have you noticed how long he spends in the shower?'

'Yeah, that's true.'

74

'I bet he still has his cherry.'

'He couldn't have!'

'I bet he's the oldest virgin in rugby.'

'You mean the *only* virgin in rugby.'

Yep, that was me. I was Hambo, 'the Virgin King'.

★ ★ ★

Life was a lot more comfortable once I had proven my manhood (I'll spare you the gory details), and for the next two years I was free to get on with the business of just being myself. A Saturday in December, three months before the accident, still brings a smile.

Tigers were at home to Gloucester the following day and omission from the squad meant a ball-breaking session with Phil Mac at the training ground. Now Phil had many qualities as a bloke and a conditioning coach, but an ability to count isn't one of them and tempers began to flare during the 100 m sprints.

'That's it, Phil, that's twenty.'

'No, I make it seventeen, guys.'

'Fuck off, Phil, we're done.'

'No, no, three more.'

'Get an abacus! You stupid Aussie bastard!'

By the end we wanted to lynch him. Legs aching and blowing through my arse, I limped off the pitch with James Buckland, a hooker who had joined Tigers in 2002 from Northampton. Buckland, or 'Cabbage' as he is affectionately known (he has a face like a Cabbage Patch Doll), was four years older than me but we got on like a house on fire.

'I tell you what, Hambo,' he says. 'We need a good drink tonight. Do you fancy coming down to my place?'

'What? Aylesbury?'

'Yeah, I'll drive. One of my mates from the local gym is having a Christmas do. We can come back up tomorrow.'

'Yeah, why not?'

I had never been to Aylesbury. I knew it was in Buckinghamshire and that Cabbage had grown up there, but I had no idea that the hospital on the edge of the town was called Stoke Mandeville, or that I was about to spend the next two years of my life there. No, the only things on my radar that night were beer and carousing. And boy did we carouse.

The next morning I woke up in this room and it was as if I had been sucked through a time warp. The furniture and furnishings were ancient; the TV at the end of the bed must have been thirty years old! I blew the dust off an old photo album in the cupboard but gleaned nothing from the portraits.

Who are these people?

No idea.

Whose bed is this?

No idea.

Where am I?

No idea.

How did I get here?

No idea.

Where's Cabbage?

No idea.

I remembered the drive down from Leicester and being introduced to his mum. I remembered meeting his mates, going to a curry house and doing some serious drinking at a bar. And I had a vague recollection of going on to this smoky R'n'B club. But after that, nothing.

The floorboards creaked in a distant room. 'Is that you, Cab?' I shouted, warily. A moment later, he staggered through the doorway, bollock naked and pale as a ghost. 'Oh fuck, Hambo,' he wheezed. 'Call the cops!'

'Why? What happened?'

'I think we've been date-raped!'

The perpetrator of the crime, an old flame from his college days, was a smashing girl. She made us breakfast and then she drove us back to Cabbage's house, where his mum was not best pleased.

An hour later, as we were driving back to Leicester, he had a go at me. It was a familiar theme.

'Not fit enough, was she?' he needles.

'Who?'

'That bit of treacle last night in Chicago's?'

'Treacle?'

'The blonde that was coming on to you.'

'Was she?'

'Listen, mate, when they tell you they're off to the toilet and will be back in a minute, believe me, they're coming on to you.'

'Yeah, well . . . I wasn't that bothered to be honest. I was having too much craic with your mates.'

★　★　★

77

December rolled into January. Cabbage put down the deposit on a new house in Leicester and I agreed to move in as a tenant with Tom Varndell, after the Six Nations. There were five Tigers players — me, Matt Cornwell, Ross Broadfoot, Tom Ryder and Varndell — named in the England squad. A sixth, Dave Young, was selected for Scotland.

We started badly with defeats to Wales and France and returned to Leicester for a week before preparing for the match in Dublin. The date was 19 February. It was my first Saturday at home in almost a month and it began almost perfectly with a brutal game at Sixways against the Worcester Under-21s. 'Perfect' because Dusty Hare had made me captain; 'perfect' because I had shoved the Worcester prop, Dylan Hartley, around the park; 'perfect' because we won; 'almost' because I picked up a dead leg and was forced to come off with ten minutes to go.

Spirits were high on the drive back to Leicester and we rocked the coach with a familiar chant:

'*There was a girl called Sally Brown*
THERE WAS A GIRL CALLED SALLY
  BROWN
Who claimed no man could lay her down
WHO CLAIMED NO MAN COULD
  LAY HER DOWN.
Over the hill shot Pistol Pete
OVER THE HILL SHOT PISTOL PETE
With ninety pounds of swinging meat.

WITH NINETY POUNDS OF SWING-
ING MEAT.
He laid Sally down on the green, green
grass
HE LAID SALLY DOWN ON THE
GREEN, GREEN GRASS
And shoved his . . . '

Showered and gelled and thirsty for beer, we were heading for Showrooms — one of the swankier Leicester bars — and a night of classic revelry.

It was almost closing time when my attention was drawn to this good-looking blonde in a dress. I hobbled (my leg was heavily bandaged) through the crowd and decided to introduce myself: 'I just want you to know that I'll wait.'

She was confused. 'You'll wait?'

'Yeah, you know . . . If you want to go to the toilet, I'll be here when you get back.'

'What have you been drinking?' She laughed.

'You're right, I'm just a twat, ignore me.'

But she didn't and we started to chat. Her name was Lisa and she had the most gorgeous green eyes. She also had company. 'This is my friend Jennie,' she announced.

18

'What if you get sick? I mean really sick? Would you want to be brought to Glenfield?'

I'm lying in the back of an ambulance heading for Glenfield. Twenty-eight days have passed since the meeting with Pauleen Pratt and I'm being haunted by her words as I drift in and out of consciousness. I've been sick for almost a week now, struggling with a battery of ailments — chest infection, urinary infection, raw throat, insomnia — that have reduced me to a feverish wreck. The insomnia has been hardest to deal with: lying in bed tossing and turning and . . . Well, obviously, I haven't been tossing or turning, but you know how it is when things are playing on your mind. And things have definitely been playing on my mind. Dean blames it on the strain of writing the book; Cornish blames it on the strain of watching England (they have just lost the World Cup final to South Africa); Dad blames my new ventilator and insists the settings aren't right. But that doesn't explain the panic attacks. I'm worrying about everything. I'm terrified something will go wrong.

'What if you black out or your lungs pack in?'

The tipping point was a recent trip to Birmingham; my sister, Amy, was home on a mid-term break from her teaching job in London and suggested we go shopping for the day. In hindsight, it wasn't a great idea — I was struggling with a bit of a stomach bug and my schedule had been manic for weeks — but I hate conceding anything to my disability, so off we went with a friend, Tom Armstrong, and a carer, Jacqui Pochin, who is more like a second mother to me. I like Birmingham, a modern, wheelchair-friendly city with some great shops. I bought some shirts and a couple of DVDs and chose Nando's for a late lunch, where Jacqui changed the battery on my ventilator. She had just ordered some food when the alarm tripped.

'It's the battery,' she announced.

'But you've only just changed it,' Amy observed.

'I know, but it mustn't have been properly charged. There's another spare in the van.'

We abandoned our meal and were halfway down Broad Street when the battery went flat. The ventilator stopped. There was nothing going into my lungs and I was suddenly gasping for breath. Think of a fish a moment after it is plucked from the sea; watch it thrash up and down on a harbour wall and imagine how that might feel. Except that you can't; not the shock or the vulnerability or the sheer fucking terror of it, not even when there's a plan B. As Tom was dispatched at speed to the van for another battery, Jacqui whipped the tube from the cuff on my neck and replaced it with a small rubber bellows stored permanently in the emergency bag. Then, cupping the device with her hands, she began pumping air into my lungs. As we waited for Tom to return, each minute felt like an hour. I did my best to appear calm but

81

couldn't avert my gaze from Jacqui's fingers. It must feel very odd indeed to hold a human life in your hands, and though she applied herself with steely concentration there was no disguising the strain.

Meanwhile, it was business as usual for shoppers on Broad Street. Nobody offered to lend a hand. Nobody offered to call an ambulance. There we were, stranded on one of Britain's busiest streets, and it was as if a paralysed man being given a blow-job was the most natural thing in the world!

* * *

I did not sleep well that night. It's the seventh time I've been 'bagged' since leaving Stoke Mandeville and it doesn't get any easier. The following day my throat was raw and the internal tube in my neck kept plugging with mucus. I had a chest infection and was struggling to get enough air into my lungs. And then the worrying started. At night, I am wired to an alarm that monitors my breathing and heart-rate and my carers usually spend the shift cleaning or reading in an adjoining room, but I insisted they sit by my bed. I was scared of the dark. It was like being a kid again.

'*The fact is that you are dependent on a ventilator to breathe and at some point that is going to cause you problems.*'

* * *

The ambulance has reached Glenfield. I catch a glimpse of the late-evening sky and protest that I want to go home. I detest hospitals. The stench of Stoke Mandeville has never left my nostrils and I'm feeling very short-changed when they wheel me inside to a (plastic) bed in the Clinical Decisions Unit. The respiratory specialists have all clocked out for the night. There's a raving alcoholic in the bed to my right who keeps shoving his face through my curtains: 'Got any fags? Got any booze?'

'No, sorry, mate.'

A moment later, he is back again.

'Got any fags? Got any booze?'

The old man to my left is wired to a monitor and sleeping soundly.

beep, beep, beep

The same rhythm as my ventilator.

beep, beep, beep

An hour drifts by.

beep, beep, beep

I wonder, has he been counting.

beep, beep, beeeeeeeeeeeeep

The alarm on the monitor trips.

A team of doctors come crashing into the ward and pound his chest with a thousand volts but can't bring him back. One of my carers, Amy Smith, has been listening by my side. 'Oh my God! He's died!' she shrieks, bursting into tears. I don't cry; I don't even blink; in fact, I am almost starting to envy him. I haven't slept for three days; my tubes keep plugging and every breath is a struggle. And the whiny pest to my right is driving me fucking crazy.

83

'Got any fags? Got any booze?'
'FUCK OFF.'

★ ★ ★

My mood blackens with each passing hour. I'm exhausted and irritable and prickly as a briar. There's a song by Faithless called 'Insomnia' playing constantly in my head:

Deep in the bosom of the gentle night
Is when I search for the light
Pick up my pen and start to write
I struggle, fight dark forces
In the clear moon light
Without fear . . . insomnia
I can't get no sleep.

Dean arrives with some comforts from home — my mattress, my shower chair, my wheelchair, my laptop — and I'm moved to a private room.

My brother, Tom, has given him a couple of DVDs for us to watch but I can tell he isn't keen. Dean is a pussy when it comes to horror films. He is also a firm believer in God. We are halfway through *Vacancy* when I notice he has turned down the sound.

'What are you doing?' I snap.
'You were almost asleep,' he says.
'Turn it up.'
'It's just screaming.'
'Turn it up.'
'You will wake the other patients.'
'TURN IT UP, YOU POOF.'

84

And soon the madness almost consumes me. I can't breathe. There's a crushing tightness in my chest and it's killing me. Is it psychological, I wonder? No, I can definitely feel it . . . But that's impossible! I'm the guy who watched as his (big) toenails were pulled at Stoke Mandeville. I can't feel anything from the neck down!

'Dean?'

He's dozing.

'DEAN?'

'Sorry,' he mumbles. 'What is it?'

'I've got these terrible pains in my chest. It's really bad.'

'Do you want me to get a doctor?'

'Yeah.'

Twenty minutes elapse. The doctor hasn't shown. I start to cry. I've reached breaking point. 'Dean, I can't do this. I just can't. It's horrible. Why isn't anybody coming?'

'I'm sorry, Matt. He said he'd be right over. I'll ask him again.'

A doctor finally arrives and explains that they can't prescribe any drugs or do anything with the ventilator until the specialists arrive in the morning.

It feels like a sketch from *Monty Python* . . .

'What if you get really sick? Do you want to be brought to Glenfield?'

'Yes, of course.'

'Well, get sick early because we knock off at five.'

But I'm in no mood to laugh. I feel complete despair.

'Dean?'

'Yes, Matt.'

'This God of yours.'

'You mean this God of ours.'

'Yeah, this God of ours.'

'What about him, Matt?'

'He's a wanker!'

19

Scene 8: INTERIOR — COURTROOM — DAY

Tony Spreadbury, a 43-year-old international referee, has been summoned to the tribunal. He is wearing a crisp grey suit and appears relaxed and affable.

BARRISTER
Mr Spreadbury, what did you know of Mr Hampson before the morning of 15 March?

SPREADBURY
Not a lot to be honest. I can't remember ever sending him off, but I'm sure I refereed some of his games. He was obviously pretty talented or he would not have been playing for England, and it was clear that he was a real rugby man . . .

BARRISTER
And what, Mr Spreadbury, is a real rugby man?

SPREADBURY
Well, he was at Tigers, wasn't he? Special breed. They're not known for being touchy-feely, now, are they? They remind me of an old Victorian family at times. But great people, and fantastic for rugby. I love going to Welford Road because they are real rugby people. They haven't a clue about the laws of the game, mind, but they are real rugby people, they really are.

BARRISTER
Are you a real rugby person, Mr Spreadbury?

SPREADBURY
Depends who you ask. The late Bill McLaren would say, 'If Tony Spreadbury is refereeing, I always get haemorrhoids in my ear.' I've been known to talk, you see, part of my character. It is also my outlook on life — if there is a bit of humour or a smile it makes the day. I can give you an example if you like.

BARRISTER
Please do, Mr Spreadbury.

SPREADBURY
I refereed Wales and Australia at Cardiff Arms Park in 1992. Those were the days you wore your white England shirt and 70,000 people hated you — a tremendous feeling! It was a very good game: Campese scored a great try and Phil Kearns, the Australian captain, said some wonderfully complimentary things about me — probably the first time I had ever been praised! So the next day, at three o'clock, I return to Bath where I was working and . . .

BARRISTER
Working?

SPREADBURY
Yes, I'm a paramedic.

BARRISTER
You're not a professional referee?

SPREADBURY
I've been an employee of the RFU since 2001 but back then I had a full-time job with the Avon Ambulance Service.

BARRISTER
Thank you. Please continue, Mr Spreadbury.

SPREADBURY
Anyway, I've got a shift in Bath on Sunday, the day after the international, and we're called to this house — a bloke with bad chest pain. I put a needle in his wrist, give him some oxygen and put the monitor on. There's a portable TV in the corner. Rugby Special is just starting. They're showing the Wales v Australia game from Cardiff Arms Park and Bill McLaren has just introduced me as the match referee in his wonderful Scottish accent. Well, the poor bloke looked at me, looked at the telly, saw my face — and died. So clearly, I'm not everybody's cup of tea.

BARRISTER
How did you become a paramedic, Mr Spreadbury?

SPREADBURY
I always wanted to be in the ambulance service. It wasn't the blue lights or the sirens; it was . . . I don't know, the challenge I suppose: you arrived at the scene with your colleague and had to work out what was right for the patient — and

hopefully improve their outcome. I joined in 1984 and did two years of what they call patient transport services — taking old ladies into day hospitals. It was a great way of learning to speak to people. I mean, people think being a paramedic is all about lights, action, cameras, motorways ... It ain't! It's about people falling down. It's about little old ladies falling over and breaking their hips. It's about talking to people and listening to people.

BARRISTER
How long did it take to qualify?

SPREADBURY
I did two years of patient transport services and then a six-week training course in basic ambulance aid in 1986. There was then an exam process that consisted of three months in school and three months at Frenchay Hospital, working in theatres, putting needles in veins and tubes down throats, under anaesthetists. So my skill base was gold standard. And in 1995 I was promoted to divisional commander in the ambulance service.

BARRISTER
You are also a gold standard referee by all accounts?

SPREADBURY
Thank you, that's very kind, but it has also been said that I was the first disabled person to referee.

BARRISTER
How so?

SPREADBURY
Well, excuse the intemperate language but it went
something along the lines of 'You're fucking blind,
Spreadbury!'

BARRISTER
Was it difficult to combine the two roles?

SPREADBURY
It was just about manageable until they introduced
twelve-hour shifts. With the eight-hour shift, I'd
work through the night in Bristol; get on a train to
Wigan; referee Orrell and Leicester; send Chas
Cusani off; get back on the train for an 11 p.m.
start, and deliver a baby at two in the morning.
So, eight-hour shifts you could do it. You were
shattered but you could do it.

BARRISTER
How many international games have you refereed,
Mr Spreadbury?

SPREADBURY
Let me see . . . Forty internationals and thirty-five
European Cup games.

BARRISTER
How many domestic games?

SPREADBURY
Oh, shed loads.

BARRISTER
How many players have suffered serious injury in those games?

SPREADBURY
What do you mean by serious?

BARRISTER
An injury comparable with Mr Hampson's?

SPREADBURY
None; it was the first time I had ever experienced it on the rugby field. As a paramedic, I had been called out to quite a few games at junior level where there were concerns about a player and the game was stopped but they were all breathing and conscious and feeling their limbs. We did the spinal care to a gold standard and took them in for X-ray but . . . No, nothing like Matt.

BARRISTER
Mr Hampson was injured during an England training session; you're an international referee. What brought you to Northampton that morning?

SPREADBURY
I was invited by the team management to officiate during the session. Chris White — another international referee — and I had worked with the Under-21s the previous season when they won the Championship, and they wanted to continue it, to watch what they were doing and give some advice.

BARRISTER
What sort of advice?

SPREADBURY
Just general advice on how to engage with the referee basically. I gave them a talk and said, 'Be nice to a referee because during a game you might get that 60/40 call. Be smart. Don't get under his skin. Call him 'sir'.' Nowadays they call me 'Spreaders' at every level, but that's fine.

BARRISTER
Mr Cusack mentioned something about a problem they were having with resets?

SPREADBURY
The reset is more scrums. Why? Well, there are several reasons: slippery conditions, loose footing, people losing their bind, illegalities . . . you know, people collapsing it. When a scrum goes down, the easy way for a referee is to reset it.
I don't take the easy way. I regard myself as a confident referee of the scrummage. If I see a player collapsing the scrum, I won't reset, I'll award a penalty. I reward — I hope — the dominant scrum, provided they are legal. But if you are not sure who is at fault, you reset.

BARRISTER
How many scrums were there before Mr Hampson sustained his injury?

SPREADBURY
I called the engagement process on all ten scrums on the scrummaging machine. Then we went on to the field and I called the engagement process at ten opposed scrums at various positions, without incident.

BARRISTER
What do you mean by the engagement process?

SPREADBURY
Well, first I show the mark to the hookers — in other words, 'This is where I want you to be over' — and I make sure the scrum is square and stationary and that they are all in the right position to push. Then I say 'crouch and hold', give a pause, check they are the same height and give the command to 'engage'. Now, as soon as you say, 'Crouch and hold' they are up on their toes and twitching. It's a trigger mechanism — cough and they are gone. And if you don't vary the 'pause' they will try to take over and go early. So I always say, 'Look, lads, please wait for the first 'e' on engage — not the last 'e' on pause!' It's so important that you are vocal, so that everybody can hear, because of all that force when the packs come together.

BARRISTER
So there were ten contested scrums?

SPREADBURY
Yes.

BARRISTER
And during those contested scrums you penalized Mr Hampson twice, I believe?

SPREADBURY
No, I awarded the penalties against Matt and his hooker, Neil Briggs.

BARRISTER
Why?

SPREADBURY
If memory serves me correctly it was for going in on an angle and taking the scrum down.

BARRISTER
Isn't that cheating?

SPREADBURY
It was very competitive. They were all fighting for their places. They all bend the rules and suffer from collective deafness: 'I didn't hear you, Spreaders.' 'Rubbish.' They are characters. We are talking here about the next generation of Lawrence Dallaglios and Martin Johnsons.

BARRISTER
What about the fatal scrum, Mr Spreadbury?

SPREADBURY
On the eleventh scrum I called the engagement process. The engagement was normal and then the far side of the scrum collapsed. I blew my whistle loudly. Matt remained on the ground. He

was curled up with his head tucked on to his chest and I knew there was a problem and just got into the mode . . .

BARRISTER
The mode?

SPREADBURY
By the mode I mean that I reacted instinctively: I am a paramedic, this is my scene. Doctor Tim Weighman was playing wing-forward and immediately lay on the ground and held Matt's head in the position he lay in, to provide manual alignment. A 999 call was made by the physiotherapist, Phil Duffell, for an emergency ambulance. I called for my paramedic kit and started ticking the boxes: his airway, his breathing, his circulation. His airway was compromised. He was struggling to breathe. I took the decision to log roll him on to his back to put an airway in . . .

BARRISTER
I'm sorry to interrupt, Mr Spreadbury, but can you explain that, please?

SPREADBURY
I inserted an oro-pharyngeal airway — it holds the tongue forward, helps them breathe — while Doctor Weighman maintained cervical alignment. We then assisted ventilations to Matt via a self-inflating resuscitation bag connected to oxygen. After approximately two minutes, I couldn't find a pulse so I commenced cardiac massage at a rate of fifteen compressions to two inflations for six

cycles to get his pulse back. The emergency ambulance arrived. We connected Matt to a cardiac defib/monitor. He was in normal sinus rhythm. I then inserted a venflon into the back of his left hand for venous access and flushed the cannula with 5 mls of sodium chloride. Matt continued to breathe spontaneously. A cervical collar was applied and with the assistance of the ambulance crew, we log rolled Matt on to a spinal board and he was transferred to Northampton A&E department. It was only when the ambulance was driving away that I gasped and thought: Crikey!

BARRISTER
What do you mean, Mr Spreadbury?

SPREADBURY
When he stopped breathing, there was a moment when I thought we were going to lose him.

BARRISTER
I would imagine, as a paramedic you've seen some pretty gruesome things, Mr Spreadbury?

SPREADBURY
Yes.

BARRISTER
Are you ever affected by it? Were you affected by what happened to Mr Hampson?

SPREADBURY
I parked it. I did what I had to do and moved on.

I am 'old school' in the way I deal with it. I'll usually go and referee a school match. I do the same on the Wednesday after an international — I will referee a school match. Why? Because they don't know or care who Tony Spreadbury is and it keeps you grounded. You no longer feel the high of how well you have done, or the low if it has gone badly. You are back on the pathway. You learn to park it.

BARRISTER
My question was, did it affect you?

SPREADBURY
Well, when he was in the ambulance and had gone off, what was distressing was the number of players that were crying — just totally upset and distraught. When you see someone being ventilated or receiving CPR you know there is severe trouble; there are severe consequences.

BARRISTER
Did it affect you, Mr Spreadbury?

SPREADBURY
Yes, of course it did. When it happened, I didn't know whether or not he was going to survive and it was . . . There's a different aspect to it when you are dealing with your own family.

BARRISTER
I'm sorry, Mr Spreadbury, I don't understand.

SPREADBURY
What I am trying to say is . . . My son had a fit when he was one year old. My wife is an Accident & Emergency nurse. She was hysterical, totally hysterical. Why? Because you know the patient where, if an ambulance crew arrives, it is just a child. I dealt with a four-month-old cot death recently. I hadn't a clue who the baby was; I was not attached to it. I did my job. I parked it. I knew the Under-21 lads; I knew Hambo and that group and they were a great bunch of lads.

BARRISTER
So the point you are making is that Mr Hampson was almost family.

SPREADBURY
He is the extended family.

BARRISTER
What happened after the ambulance had left?

SPREADBURY
The coaches brought the players into the changing rooms and they went back to the hotel. I was going to go home but I stayed on that night.

BARRISTER
Why?

SPREADBURY
To support the players. Some of them were very upset and wanted to chat. They said 'Spreaders will he be all right?' I said, 'Hang on a minute; he

is in a critical condition.' That was the other thing, being honest with them. This was not a five-minute wonder. This was not a quick concussion check-over. This was critical. The impact was obvious. They had deep thoughts with Hambo. They had known each other. They had played with each other. I know Matt Cornwell had a special relationship with him but there was, I believe, a general feeling of 'family'. I thought it was outstanding.

BARRISTER
Thank you, Mr Spreadbury.

20

A simple tale of boy meets girl; a simple tale of boy likes girl; a simple tale of boy falls in love with girl; a simple tale that complicates when boy damages his spinal cord and is paralysed. What if girl hears the news and comes rushing to boy's side? What if girl helps boy come to terms with what has happened? What if girl becomes the light at the end of boy's tunnel? Would there ever be a finer monument to love?

But what if girl decides to end the relationship? What if, having offered boy her life, she decides to take it back? What would the monument say then? Where would our sympathies lie? With the poor, ventilator-dependent tetraplegic who may never find love again? Or with the heartless bitch who has abandoned him to his plight? But what if the tale wasn't that simple?

21

Scene 9: EXTERIOR — RUGBY GROUND — DAY

Dave Young, the young Tigers prop, is walking from the Leicester training ground at Oadby and glancing at his mobile phone. There are twenty missed calls. Most are from his house-mate, Tom Ryder, who is training in Northampton with the England Under-21s. He calls Ryder's mobile.

YOUNG
Tom? It's Dave. What's the craic with Hambo? Dusty's just told us that he thinks he has fucked his shoulder.

RYDER
Nah, mate. Nah.

YOUNG
What happened?

RYDER
He has done his neck.

YOUNG
What do you mean he has done his neck?

RYDER
They've taken him to hospital.

YOUNG
It's obviously precautionary. If he has hurt his
neck, then it's obviously precautionary.

RYDER
Nah, mate, nah.

YOUNG
What is it? What are you not telling me?
A long pause ensues. Ryder is struggling to com-
pose himself.

YOUNG
(Firmly) Tom, what is it? What happened?

RYDER
It's bad, Davey.

YOUNG
How bad?

RYDER
Well, at one point he stopped breathing.

YOUNG
Oh fuck!

RYDER
Yeah.

YOUNG
Do you know the extent of his injury?

RYDER
No.

YOUNG
Okay, well, phone me as soon as you get any feedback. No one at Leicester has been informed.

22

Jennifer Marceau. She had a name like a French movie star and looks to match: short blonde hair, deep brown eyes and a figure that ticked all the boxes. Jennifer — or Jennie, as she preferred — was born in Reading and spent most of her childhood in Abingdon before moving to Leicestershire. We were an odd match: I was set on what I wanted from life but Jennie, who was two years older than me, was still trying to figure it out. She had a degree in psychology but didn't want to be a psychologist. She was studying law but didn't want to be a lawyer. She loved acting but wasn't sure she would make an actress. She disliked rugby but was continually drawn (she had just ended a three-year relationship with a college player) to rugby men. The contradictions were fascinating. She was unlike anyone I had ever met before . . . That we managed to hook up at all was a miracle.

We met the night of my 'almost perfect' performance at Worcester and the team had repaired to a Leicester bar. I had a dead leg, a cut lip, a skinful of alcohol and had just started to click with Lisa, her friend. It was almost closing time. We were moving on to a nightclub called Life and I invited them to join us. My leg was killing me, and as I hobbled up Charles Street to the entrance of Life I discovered I was out of cash.

'Have you any money?' I asked, sheepishly. 'I promise I'll pay you back.'

Jennie was not impressed: 'Oh my God! Is this guy serious?' she hissed. 'I thought he invited us?'

'It's okay, I've got it,' Lisa said.

We went inside and ordered a drink and some old flame asked Lisa to dance. Suddenly I was alone with Jennie. It was loathe at first sight . . .

'Your lip is revolting,' she observed.

'Yours are quite nice,' I replied.

'I bet you were in some ridiculous fight?'

'No, I did it playing rugby.'

'You play rugby?'

'Yeah.'

'I should have known.' She sighed.

'Why?'

'I can't stand it.'

'You've lovely eyes,' I countered, undaunted. 'I've always been attracted to blue eyes.'

'That's a pity.'

'Why?'

'I'm wearing contact lenses. My eyes are really brown.'

'Oh.'

And for the first time she smiled.

The three hours that followed went swimmingly. We caught a taxi to her apartment, shared a nice bottle of wine and proceeded amorously to the bedroom, where events took a cataclysmic turn: I pulled off my shirt, dived into bed and was comatose almost before my head hit the pillow. Jennie, to be fair, could have slept

106

with that. What she could not sleep with was the thunderous rumble of the jumbo jet on a holding pattern around her ears. She pulled a pillow over her head. It got louder. She slammed my injured leg with her fist.

'Uhhhh! What's up?' I groaned.

'Will you pleeeeease stop snoring?' she implored.

. . . but the walls were soon vibrating again.

'Oh my God, you're hideous!' she fumed.

Relations were somewhat cool next morning. I apologized profusely but she was cross-eyed and irritable. 'No, it's my fault for inviting you back,' she insisted. A croissant seemed out of the question, so I took a taxi back to the house I was sharing with Tom Varndell to shower and pack a bag.

It was Sunday morning, five days before the international in Dublin, and we were leaving almost immediately to join up with the squad in Bath. Matt Cornwell drove. I crashed on the back seat and slept until Cheltenham with Jennie in my head. I sent a text: 'What are you doing?' There was no reply. I sent it again — still nothing. I peppered her inbox until we had almost reached Bristol when she finally texted back: 'You're weird.'

'Why?'

'What sort of message is that?'

'What?'

'What are you doing?'

'Well, what are you doing?'

' 'Hello' would be nicer or 'Sorry about last night' or 'Maybe we could hang out again.' '

'Hello.'

'Hello.'

'Sorry about last night.'

'You should be.'

'Maybe we could hang out again.'

'Maybe.'

We met at a bar in Leicester, three days after the Ireland game. It was a strange and somewhat unnerving experience. I had never been on a proper date before or had to converse with a girl when I wasn't half-cut and though we had already spent an evening dancing and laughing and even sleeping together, it was as if we were meeting for the first time. There was a lot to learn . . .

'Your hair is much longer,' I observed.

'It's grown.' She smiled. 'You haven't seen me for over a week.'

'It's grown a lot in a week,' I insisted.

'They're extensions, you idiot.'

'Oh.'

My timidity was a surprise to her. She had never dated a boy who had asked permission for a kiss, but she seemed to enjoy the experience. We went out again a few days later and then I was off to prepare for the England game with Italy.

The last time we met before my accident was for coffee in Leicester. I had rushed back for a day after the Italy game but had to rejoin the squad in Northampton. The following evening we spoke for over an hour on the phone. I was rooming with Dan 'Test Match' Smith and remember sneaking out to take the call. She sent a text the following morning as I was being lifted into the ambulance and was surprised when I didn't reply. If it had ended there, if I had never seen her again . . . the pain might have been bearable.

PART 2

PROXIMO'S RULES

1

This is the sound.

whoooooooosh

The sound of morning.

whoooooooosh

The sound of winter.

whoooooooosh

The sound of 29 November 2007.

whoooooooosh

It is 6.30 a.m.

whoooooooosh

I am lying in bed and have just opened my eyes.

whoooooooosh

Twenty-eight days have passed since I returned home from Glenfield.

whoooooooosh

Twenty-eight days I wasn't sure I'd have.

whoooooooosh

My chest infection has cleared.

whoooooooosh

The doctors have sorted the glitches in my ventilator.

whoooooooosh

I feel so good I could almost play for England.

whoooooooosh

Thank you, Glenfield.

whoooooooosh

Thank you, God.

whoooooooosh

Sorry for that little misunderstanding.

2

Today is my birthday.

whooooooosh

The third since my accident.

whooooooosh

I am twenty-three years old.

whooooooosh

For two and a half of those years, I have been wired to this ventilator.

whooooooosh

For two and a half of those years, my life has been on hold.

whooooooosh

There have been few great memories.

whooooooosh

Few moments to cherish and love.

whooooooosh

Like the thrill of dating a girl.

whooooooosh

Or the fun of holidaying with friends.

whooooooosh

Or the buzz of a great game.

whooooooosh

It's as if time has stopped ticking for me.

whooooooosh

I feel exactly the same age.

whooooooosh

How can that be when so much has changed?

3

Beyond the bedroom window.

whoooooosh

In the cold and damp and dark of morning.

whoooooosh

There is another sound.

whoooooosh

The crunch of my father's boots in the yard.

whoooooosh

The clang of trowels and shovels and picks being loaded into a trailer.

whoooooosh

The clump of a scratched Tupperware lunchbox being tossed on to a dashboard.

whoooooosh

The yelps of a black Labrador pawing at the door.

whoooooosh

The sound of my father swearing.

whoooooosh

'Bloody hellfire, Bruno! Calm down!'

4

The first time I ever heard my father swear was on the site of a house he was building near Oakham in 1998. I was fourteen at the time and had been pressed into service during a mid-term break from school: I spent the day making tea and ferrying slates and bricks like a mule. Every morning he would wake me with the slap of a wet flannel on the face and a sergeant-major's roar: 'Come on, lard arse! Time for work.' And I can think of gentler ways to bond but that was Dad. He could be moody and gruff at times and guarded with his affections but there was no malice in him and he had a curious sense of fun. Sometimes I would open my lunchbox and find a dead sparrow in it, and he could never stir his tea without scalding my arm with the spoon. A man's man I suppose is what you would call him, and like most boys I gravitated towards my mum. I didn't want to be a builder. I didn't want to be like Dad. It's only now, looking back, that he makes any sense to me.

5

In 1948, ten years before my father was born, my grandfather, Fred Hampson, returned to his home in the Manchester suburbs after the greatest day of his life. He had just played right-back for Everton reserves and the club were talking about signing him. 'Can you believe that, Dad?' he gushed, euphoric. 'I might be turning professional.' But his father, Frank, who worked in the local cotton mills, dismissed it out of hand. 'Forget it, son,' he warned. 'You need a proper job.' And with those words, his football career was ended. He found a proper job, and a proper wife, and raised three proper boys in the Bolton suburb of Farnworth, burdened by a lingering regret . . .

What if I had followed my dream?

★   ★   ★

My father, Phil, the second of Fred's three sons, played for Bolton Boys. In 1973, shortly after his fifteenth birthday, he returned home one day breathless with excitement after a game with Mancunian Juniors. 'You're not going to believe this, Dad,' he gushed. 'Two of their coaches came up to me as I was walking off the pitch. They want me to come to the Cliff this week for a trial! What do you think?'

But Fred was never going to deny him. A few

117

days later they travelled together to Manchester and he watched as his son entered the Promised Land. He was playing in the same kit as Bobby Charlton, soaking in the same baths as George Best and shaking hands at functions with the legendary Sir Matt Busby. And for the next three years that's mostly how it was. Three years of being blinded by the allure of Old Trafford; three years of being nurtured by one of the world's greatest clubs; three years of being propelled by his father's stolen destiny . . .

What if I had followed my dream?

And then, on the morning of 26 October 1975, it was all taken away when his right knee and tibia were shattered by an opponent's brutal lunge. 'Don't even think about playing football again,' the surgeon observed.

He thought of nothing else. He had set his heart on becoming a footballer. He had committed his life to Manchester United. He had followed his dream. It wasn't supposed to end like this.

★   ★   ★

It was my grandfather who took me to my first football match — a Bolton Wanderers game at Burnden Park. Embittered by his experience, Dad showed no interest in the game and was slow to warm to my burgeoning passion for rugby. He'd play waterboy or hold the tackle bags at training sometimes but had no understanding or feel for the game. The turning point was the final of a schoolboy championship

118

at Twickenham, when he gifted me a framed piece of the hallowed turf and hung it on my bedroom wall. He encouraged me to train harder, reach higher and started winding me with the same intensity as he had been wound. He was proud of me, no doubt, and when I made my debut for the England Under-18s it was as if a destiny had been fulfilled — his destiny: 'One of the proudest moments of my life.' He beamed. But the fun was only beginning. He was convinced I would play for England at the 2007 World Cup.

whooooooosh
I hear the sound of his feet in the corridor.
whooooooosh
I feel his presence at my bedroom door.
whooooooosh
'You awake, Matt?' he enquires, peering through the darkness.
whooooooosh
'Yes, Dad.'
whooooooosh
'Happy birthday, son.'
whooooooosh
'Thanks, Dad.'
whooooooosh
'I'm off to work, mate. I'll see you later.'
whooooooosh
'Okay, Dad.'
whooooooosh
And he waves and forces a smile but his face is cracked with pain.

6

A phone is ringing at the headquarters of Spinal Research in Surrey.

rinnnnng rinnnnng
rinnnnng rinnnnng

The camera moves towards the sound through a series of empty corridors until we arrive at the deserted office of Jonathan Miall, the Chief Executive Officer. The phone is continuing to ring and becoming louder and more piercing.

RINNNNNG RINNNNNG
RINNNNNG RINNNNNG

INDY (voiceover)
Einstein once defined madness as doing the same thing over and over again and expecting different results. How would he define pain? What would he say about the phone calls?

RINNNNNG RINNNNNG
RINNNNNG RINNNNNG

INDY (voiceover)
It was in March 2005, about a week after Matt's accident, that Phil made his first call to Jonathan

120

Miall. He called again a week later . . .

RINNNNNG RINNNNNG
RINNNNNG RINNNNNG

INDY (voiceover)
. . . and a week after that . . .

RINNNNNG RINNNNNG
RINNNNNG RINNNNNG

INDY (voiceover)
. . . and a week after that.

RINNNNNG RINNNNNG
RINNNNNG RINNNNNG

INDY (voiceover)
In fact, he has called once a week, every week,
since Matt was injured. He always asks the same
question: 'Any new developments, Jonathan?' And
often gets the same answer:
'Not since we last spoke, Phil.' But he keeps calling because one of these weeks they are going to
tell him what he wants to hear: that science has
made a breakthrough, that his son will breathe
and walk again.

7

I don't know much about love or marriage or commitment or . . . Actually no, that's not quite true.

The year is 1975. Phil Hampson, his leg wrapped in plaster, his dream as shattered as his limb, has returned home to Farnworth. For three years, football has been the essence of his life but he must now reinvent himself. He joins the sixth form at Bolton Grammar School, shows a flair for geography and art and catches the eye of a pretty classmate called Anne Wilkinson. On their first date after a swim at a local baths, he is walking her home and they pause for a kiss. Phil hasn't done much kissing during his three years at the Cliff, and feeling suddenly light-headed, he loses his balance and pitches them backwards over a low-cut wall. Anne fractures her collarbone and the date ends in Casualty. Her parents are not impressed. 'Who is this long-haired buffoon?' But Anne kind of likes him and survives a second date.

The Wilkinsons live in the Bolton suburb of Heaton. Anne is the younger of two girls. Her father, Bill, works for an aluminium company. Her mother, Barbara, is a gifted head teacher. Anne inherits her mother's drive and pursues a teaching degree at Liverpool University. Phil is drifting through an Arts degree in Bradford still dreaming of what might have been. For two years, they phone from time to time and agree to be 'just friends' but the fire is rekindled one afternoon when Phil hitchhikes across the Pennines to the halls of residence.

★　★　★

Anne's first teaching job is at a secondary modern school in one of the toughest areas of Leicester. Her class — a year 5 tutor group that nobody wants to teach — are Sex Pistols fans but she finds a way to connect. Phil follows her to Leicester and takes a job with a local builder. Their first home together is a small Victorian terrace house. They marry in 1982, and the following year a daughter, Amy, is born. Eighteen months later, in November 1984, Anne gives birth to a son. The boy is a massive nine and a half pounds and spends his first waking hour trying to climb from his crib. 'What a strong little neck he has!' the midwife observes. 'I've never seen that before, usually they are all floppy!' They call him Matthew.

I am trouble from day 1 . . .

8

Scene 11: INTERIOR — RUGBY CLUB — NIGHT

It is the evening of Matt's twenty-third birthday. A surprise party has been thrown in the main function room of the Leicester Tigers rugby ground at Welford Road. The scene opens with a shot of Matt, laughing and joking with a group of former team-mates and then the camera moves to a table in the corner where Phil Hampson is sitting with a friend, Roy Jackson. He is staring across the room at his son.

PHIL HAMPSON
It sounds ridiculous but it's moments like these that I find hardest.

ROY JACKSON
Why is it ridiculous?

PHIL HAMPSON
Look at him . . . look at how happy he is . . . it's a party . . . he's surrounded by friends and really enjoying himself and it's great but . . .

ROY JACKSON
What?

PHIL HAMPSON
Look at them . . . look at how healthy and strong they are. Most of them are playing for the first

team now; Tom Rees and James Haskell are playing for England. I know their parents — we trailed around Ireland and Scotland and Wales together, watching our kids play. We were all on the same circuit, sharing the same dream, but it's never going to happen now. And I know it's selfish but I want what they have for my son.

ROY JACKSON
That's perfectly understandable, Phil.

PHIL HAMPSON
They've been great with him. They call to the house and ask him out but he cannot do what he used to do. And he never will. That hits you hard, knowing he cannot do normal things again. He cannot have kids! He cannot have a family. Things like that upset me. Everything upsets me. I have to really try not to be so bitter and angry about it, but you just don't know where to turn sometimes. You keep looking for a reason, something or somebody to take it out on.

ROY JACKSON
How soon after the accident did you start feeling angry?

PHIL HAMPSON
Not long to be honest, probably two or three months. At first, you're just in shock and you don't know what is going to happen. Is he going to get some movement back? Will he ever get off the ventilator? You don't know. And the doctors don't tell you anything because they don't really

know. And as time goes on, you realize it is less and less likely that things will improve. And then bitterness starts. You hear people say, 'Oh, my son is going there this year and then he is doing that.' And you know Matthew cannot do anything like that and it eats you up.

ROY JACKSON
Is there nobody with the expertise to help you through that?

PHIL HAMPSON
I feel I am improving a little bit but I don't know if Anne would agree, probably not. It is hard. It has affected our relationship in a lot of ways. I get really angry and frustrated and take that frustration out on Anne, which I am pretty ashamed about. I don't mean to take it out on her but there is nowhere else to go with it. It is terrible really.

ROY JACKSON
I'm sorry, Phil, I had no idea. I obviously knew it must be hard, but from the outside looking in you seemed to be coping so well.

PHIL HAMPSON
Well, instinctively you put up a shield, don't you? But I'm being totally honest with you, Roy. It has been terrible, really devastating. Matthew knows what I'm like. He has seen me lose the plot and that's not good for him. If I am negative and miserable about the whole thing, I am not doing him any good, or myself, or Anne. And it is not fair on Tom.

ROY JACKSON
How old is Tom now?

PHIL HAMPSON
Nineteen. He has had a tough time. We were
away to Stoke Mandeville every weekend for
almost two years and he was at home on his own.
So if I went to pieces, how would it affect Tom?
You cannot do that. It would not be fair to him
and his prospects in life. Anyway, Anne would not
allow that to happen. She is strong and very positive. I'm a worrier, more negative, I find it hard.

ROY JACKSON
When is it hardest?

PHIL HAMPSON
Well, like I say, moments like these or when I'm
away from him.

ROY JACKSON
Away from him?

PHIL HAMPSON
Whenever I'm at work, I find it harder. When I
come home and see him, I feel better. I don't
know why, I think that is just his personality. He
never feels sorry for himself and that makes me
think: Why are you feeling sorry for yourself? But
it's hard. Every single physical movement that I
make, I know Matthew cannot do. Sometimes I
will be shovelling sand from my trailer and think:
Jesus! Matthew used to help me do this — and
he never will again! Or I might be chucking the

ball in the garden with Tom. It is everything. It is every day. You never get away from it.

ROY JACKSON
But you say it's easier when you're with him?

PHIL HAMPSON
Yeah. Talking to him is a compensation of sorts for the physical things I am doing without him. But there's not a day goes by when I don't think about his situation. Sometimes I wake up in the middle of the night and think: Shit! What if there's a power cut and his ventilator stops working? And there was something else that probably hasn't helped.

ROY JACKSON
What was that?

PHIL HAMPSON
One weekend when Matthew was still in hospital, we got a call from a couple in Nottingham who had read his interview in the Sunday Times. They explained that they had a son with a similar injury and were offering us the use of a tilt table.

ROY JACKSON
What's a tilt table?

PHIL HAMPSON
It's a table that tilts — they are used in physiotherapy. Anyway, I drive over to the house and meet this really nice couple in their sixties. Their son was thirty-two years old and had damaged his

spinal cord in a car accident twelve years ago. They introduced me to him but he had brain damage — not from the accident but from negligence.

ROY JACKSON
Negligence?

PHIL HAMPSON
Three or four years after the accident he was in hospital for a check-up and his phrenic nerve pacer — a box with electrodes that forces your diaphragm to expand — had popped off during the night. Nobody noticed until it was too late. His brain had been starved of oxygen. It was awful! I came home and it was all I could think about: Imagine if that happened to Matthew? What if his ventilator popped off during the night and his carers were asleep? I couldn't deal with that. It worries me more than anything. I wake up regularly in the middle of the night and wander over there to check up on them. But you can't keep living your life like that.

ROY JACKSON
No, you're right, but I can empathize with how you feel.

PHIL HAMPSON
It's my biggest worry — at least I can have a bit of banter and an intelligent conversation with Matthew, but if that happened . . . The brain is the most important thing. Your brain is who you are. Lose your brain and you are just a piece of meat. I

see it with my father — he's had a form of Alzheimer's for months. And then my mother had to have a bypass.

ROY JACKSON
Jesus, that's tough.

PHIL HAMPSON
Yeah, we've had a bad two or three years of it.

ROY JACKSON
What was the lowest point emotionally?

PHIL HAMPSON
When the reality of his injury hit me it was devastating. I drink more now than I used to. I drank a lot down in Stoke Mandeville. It's self-indulgent. You create a cocoon of self-pity. I drank too much the other night and had a big argument with Anne. It has happened a few times. Next day we try to get over it and start again.

ROY JACKSON
What is the root of the argument?

PHIL HAMPSON
It's the frustration and anger and bitterness. I am just an angry person. If you can bury yourself in work it helps but my work is not as absorbing as Anne's. Hers is a challenging job. She is on the go all day. I'm self-employed and have a couple of guys working for me but I still spend quite a bit of the day thinking about Matthew.

130

ROY JACKSON
If it was me — and again I can only imagine this, Phil — I think the source of my anger would be: Why did it have to happen to my son?

PHIL HAMPSON
Yeah, you do think that but I try not to go down that route because it makes you feel depressed. And I still retain some hope. I call Spinal Research every week. I still think, with the advance of technology, that some day he might be able to breathe for himself. They are making great progress in stem cell research. There is always hope.

9

My first childhood memory is bombing round the living room with a Thundercats sword and a little blue devil called 'My Pet Monster' that went absolutely wild when you undid its handcuffs. Handcuffs weren't an option for a hyperactive boy and I gave my parents some serious grief. When I wasn't falling out of my mother's car or driving my sit-and-ride toy through the patio doors, I was crawling across our new cream carpet with black paint on my hands, or being sent home from the mothers and toddlers class for biting Iona Moore, or sliding down the bath and cracking my front tooth on the tap; or kicking the dentist in the head as he tried to 'have a little look'.

In my first year of reception, I was Joseph in the school Nativity play and had to sit on a bale of straw but it didn't take long for my inner monster to rebel. I plucked a piece of straw and pretended I was smoking and floored Mary, my still-virgin wife, with a shove. The audience loved it; my parents despaired; there had to be some outlet to channel the boy's energy.

It was a neighbour, Clint Thewlas, then editor of the *Rutland Times*, who found it. 'Why don't you take him down to Oakham rugby club, Anne,' he suggested to my mother, after I had been caught trampling on the shrubs in his garden. 'They'll know what to do with him.'

It sounded like a trip to the dentist.

'Come on, Matthew, get your gear on,' my mother implored.

'No, I don't want to play rugby.'

'Matthew, you will love it.'

'I want to stay at home.'

'But this is your kind of game.'

'I want to watch television.'

'MATTHEW, PUT YOUR GEAR ON NOW!'

And I wailed all the way to the ground.

* * *

Steve Beanland coached the minis at Oakham and decided almost immediately that he had found a new prop. That's pretty much how it works in rugby.

Short and fat?

'You're a prop.'

Tall and meaty?

'A second row.'

Fast?

'A wing.'

Skilful?

'A centre.'

Good awareness and kicking skills?

'A fly-half.'

Aggravating little gobshite?

'You'll make a great scrum-half.'

I took to the sport with relish and quite fancied myself during those formative years — it's stamped across my face in an old photo at home as I race away from Tom 'Jif' Lemon and a

133

pack of eager boys with the ball under my arm. 'Look at me,' it says. 'Look how special I am. Stop me if you can.'

And then, just before my twelfth birthday, I heard about this wonderclub called Syston that had just won the biggest mini-tournament in Europe. A couple of the guys at school played there and I plagued my father to drive me down. The good news was that I was welcome to join. The bad news was that I was no longer top dog. Matt 'Badger' Shaaf was the best player I had ever seen and in Matt Cornwell, Ollie Mills, Joe Wheeler and Greg Burnham, he had good company. The Syston coach, John Cornwell, set very high standards and was a strict disciplinarian. 'I don't care how good you are,' he warned, 'mess about and you're out!' I quite liked to mess about, messing about was in my nature, but John had a way of keeping you focused and after a while I was even impressing his son.

Matt and I were chalk and cheese personality wise — he was Chief Librarian, I was Jack the Lad — but we became really good friends. Alex Pochin, a rival prop, was another good friend and we won everything during my first two seasons at the club.

In 1998, we were invited to play the Gloucester club Spartans in a curtain-raiser to the annual Tigers v Barbarians game at Twickenham. It was my first ever visit to the shrine of English rugby and a massive thrill for a fourteen-year-old. But it is for another reason that I most remember the year.

10

Home in 1998 was a splendid country house my father had built in Cold Overton, a small, remote, village five miles west of Oakham on the border of Rutland and Leicestershire. Not a lot happens in Cold Overton; there are no pubs or commerces. Main Street consists of a thirteenth-century church, St John the Baptist, an adjoining graveyard with some fascinating tombstones (like John Poynbee, who died on 5 March 1855 at the age of eighty-two and buried three wives, all called Mary) and a string of period cottages. There is also the magnificent Cold Overton Hall, the best place in the world to play hide-and-seek, which is home to the only other kids in the village — Alastair, Rose, Hugh and Violet Wilson — and their lovely nanny, Jannine.

My father was working on an extension to a house that summer, just outside the village on the Knossington road. It was my first prolonged stint as a lackey for P.H. Building Services and, if it wasn't for the support of Will Trower, it might have been my last. He was seventeen, four years older than me, and I had been hanging on to his shirt-tails for years. The younger of two boys, he had never known his father and had been raised by his mother, Jean, who absolutely doted on him. Everybody loved Will, and my mother often laughed at how similar we were. Like me, he was blond; like me, he was dyslexic; like me, he was clumsy; like me, he was accident prone; like me, he was . . . well, like me. But I just wanted to be like him.

He liked rugby and we often spent hours playing with the Thewlas brothers in the garden. Or sometimes we would sit in his bedroom listening to Kurt Cobain belting out 'Smells Like Teen Spirit' . . .

> *With the lights out, it's less dangerous*
> *Here we are now, entertain us*
> *I feel stupid and contagious*
> *Here we are now, entertain us*

. . . on Will's favourite album, *Nevermind*.

'What's teen spirit, Will?'

'Haven't a clue, Matt.'

He started boxing that summer and my father, who was still trying to turn me into the next Jonny Wilkinson, used to encourage him to take me jogging on the roads because 'Matthew could do with a bit of stamina'.

And then, one Saturday morning, shortly after eight o'clock, we were shaken by a frantic call from my father, who had just left to collect Will for work.

'He's not here!' he exclaimed.

'What do you mean?' my mother replied.

'The front door is open and the lights are on but there's no one here!'

'What about Jean?'

'She's away this week on holiday.'

'Maybe he stayed with one of his friends last night.'

'I don't think so. There's a can of beer and a half-eaten pizza on the table. And Jean's car is gone.'

'You said she was on holiday.'

'She didn't take the car. It has been here all week. I don't like it. Something is wrong.'

They found the car, and what remained of Will's body on a small back road, later that morning. Jean was devastated. My father was burdened by an irrational guilt ('If I hadn't taken him on, he would not have had the money for the pub') that lingers even today. Me? I just cried, and I still cry when I think of him. It was the most shocking, painful experience I had ever endured. It was also my first stern lesson in life: bad things happen to good people.

11

Scene 12: INTERIOR — STRIPCLUB — PARIS — NIGHT

Matt has travelled to Paris on pre-Christmas break with his sister's fiancé, Adam Wheatly, and four of his carers, Dean Clarke, Jacqui Pochin, Ruby Kullar Rai and Angela Clarke. Two years and nine months have passed since the accident. It is his first trip abroad. They spend the day visiting the Louvre and shopping at Galeries Lafayette and finish up at Crazy Horse, the celebrated girlie show on Avenue George V. The scene opens with Matt being served a glass of champagne as a dozen girls take to the stage singing 'God Save Our Bare Skin', a high-camp, satirical take-off of the changing of the guard at Buckingham Palace. The dancers are wearing busbies and very little else.

MATT HAMPSON
Adam?

ADAM WHEATLY
Yes, Matt.

MATT HAMPSON
Have I a hard-on?

ADAM WHEATLY
No, mate, looks pretty calm down there.

MATT HAMPSON
Good.

ADAM WHEATLY
(Laughs) . . . but give it another chorus.

MATT HAMPSON
I've a question for you. Do you see the bird on
the end to the right?

ADAM WHEATLY
Yeah.

MATT HAMPSON
How far apart do you reckon her nipples are?

ADAM WHEATLY
Whaaaat?

MATT HAMPSON
You heard me.

ADAM WHEATLY
Can I phone a friend?

MATT HAMPSTON
No.

ADAM WHEATLY
I dunno . . . Fourteen inches?

MATT HAMPSON
In centimetres, this is France.

ADAM WHEATLY
Okay, hmmm . . . thirty-two centimetres.

MATT HAMPSON
Final answer?

ADAM WHEATLY
Final answer.

MATT HAMPSON
Wrong. Twenty-seven centimetres.

ADAM WHEATLY
How do you know?

MATT HAMPSON
I've always had a head for figures.

ADAM WHEATLY
Yeah, right.

MATT HAMPSON
Okay, another one: how far from her belly button
to her pubis?

ADAM WHEATLY
You are joking.

MATT HAMPSON
Come on.

ADAM WHEATLY
I'm starting to worry about you.

MATT HAMPSON
How far?

ADAM WHEATLY
Fifteen centimetres?

MATT HAMPSON
Not bad. Thirteen centimetres.

ADAM WHEATLY
And you're sure about that as well?

MATT HAMPSON
Absolutely. Did you not learn that in biology? It's
called the firm buttock theorem: 'The larger the
gap between the belly button and pubis, the more
droopy the butt.'

ADAM WHEATLY
Your mum always said you have a policeman's eye
for detail but that's ridiculous.

MATT HAMPSON
Why is it ridiculous? It's a scientific fact that as
you lose some faculties, others sharpen and
improve.

ADAM WHEATLY
Bollocks! Your eyes are not that good.

MATT HAMPSON
No, you're right. There was a piece about it last
week in the Sunday Times. Dad came over with it
tucked under his jumper: 'Have you heard about

141

this place, Crazy Horse in Paris?' he says. 'To become a dancer, the girls must be between 1 m 68 cm and 1 m 72 cm tall, measure not more than 27 cm between the nipples and 13 cm from the belly button to the pubis. There are no tattoos or silicone implants allowed and they have their weight checked every week.' He was well impressed.

ADAM WHEATLY
So you booked it?

MATT HAMPSON
No, he booked it.

ADAM WHEATLY
Did he really? Good old Phil. I was wondering how you heard about it.

MATT HAMPSON
Yeah, and I've told Dean to pack a measuring tape. We're going backstage after the show to check that none of the girls are cheating.

12

I was not wired like my father. I did not want to be famous. There was no sporting hero I ever aspired to be. I never dreamt of winning the Ashes or scoring at Wembley or playing for England. I was a fifteen-year-old boy who enjoyed playing rugby and stuffing his face with Double Decker bars. Will's death marked a turning point. I would picture his lifeless face lying next to Kurt Cobain, and for the first time in my life I felt the flicker of ambition. Fuck teen spirit! I was not going to waste my life; I wanted to be someone. I wanted to succeed. But at what? I was bright but never destined for Cambridge and the idea of working for Dad had never turned me on, so that left rugby, the one thing in life that always had. Two years had passed since Martin Johnson had stormed South Africa with the Lions, and at a time when Shakespeare continued to elude me, and my classmates were majoring in porn, I could recite almost every scene from *Living with Lions*: Neil Jenkins retching in the changing room . . . Jim Telfer groaning in the stands . . . Martin Johnson having his eye stitched . . . John Bentley chuckling at a fat-bottomed girl in the gym ('One for the front five') . . . the poetry of Jason Leonard . . .

'Every single scrum is a different fucking challenge. We take it on board every single time.

143

The South Africans think that's their fucking livelihood . . . an affront to their manhood — if you fucking stuff 'em there, they don't like it.'
. . . wonderful.

*　*　*

I was making good progress at Syston and in July 2001, four months short of my eighteenth birthday, I joined the Leicester Tigers Academy. To facilitate the sitting of my 'A' levels, the club had an arrangement with Queen Elizabeth College and my average day consisted of a thirty-minute train ride to Leicester, four hours of classes at QE, a break for lunch, a bus ride to the training ground at Oadby, a one-hour weights session, a two-hour contact session and the reverse journey home if I couldn't cadge a lift. All for the princely stipend of £2000!

But it was the physicality that jolted most. Stuart Redfern and Tom Smith coached the forwards at the academy. In one of my first sessions, they sent me out with some 'A' team players and some Under-21s for a game of ruck and maul. I had been playing for almost ten years and enjoyed the occasional dust-up and butting heads with my peers but this was something else. There were guys spitting blood and retching on the sideline; they were battering each other and relishing the confrontation.

'You wanker, that was shit!'

'This is Tigers, put some fucking effort in!'

144

It was a barely controlled brawl. I did my best to run and hide and escaped with a few bruises but went to bed that night with just one thought in my mind: What have I got into here?

13

Some of you are thinking that you won't fight. Others, that you can't fight. They all say that until they're out there.

— Proximo (Oliver Reed) in *Gladiator*

14

Proximo? Well, let's see now . . . Yes, I suppose that would have to be Daz. We were there about a week when he arrived one morning on the training ground. 'All right, lads, how is it going? I'm Daz,' he announced. The introduction wasn't necessary. Darren Garforth was an England international and the cornerstone of the 'ABC' club, the most acclaimed and abrasive front row in England. A scaffolder by profession, he had joined Leicester Tigers in 1991, when the sport was still amateur, and often drove to games straight from the building site, just before he played. A month previously, I had travelled to Paris and watched him lift the Heineken Cup and now, here he was, leading us towards the scrum machine to show how it was done. His manner was the first surprise — I expected a sergeant-major, but he was affable and softly spoken. And his love for the craft was obvious. 'Okay, I'm going to start by watching you hitting into the scrum machine individually,' he announced. 'You won't be able to push it back on your own but I just want to check that you're hitting with the correct technique.'

He watched a couple of guys hit and suddenly it was my turn.

'What's your name, son?'

'Matt Hampson.'

'Okay, Matt, when you're ready.'

I stepped up to the scrum machine and started to tick the boxes; feet shoulder-width apart . . . weight on my toes . . . arched back . . . chest out . . . head up . . . eyes glaring through the tops of my eyelids . . . hand out . . . triggered . . . ready . . . waiting for his call to . . .

'ENGAGE!'

I slammed into the pads.

'KEEP YOUR BODY SHAPE.'

I tried to shove that old machine out of the ground.

'UP ON YOUR TOES . . . CHASE YOUR FEET.'

He seemed reasonably pleased. For the second lesson, he got us to bind with a hooker and hit the machine as a twosome, and then as a front row, before the session ended with a series of full scrums. It was tough but hugely enjoyable and his clinics were soon the highlight of the week for me. I had always had good hands and fancied myself as a runner and was pleased when he noticed one afternoon.

'You carry the ball well, son,' he observed.

'Thanks, Daz.'

And then he said, 'I'm a good ball player, was offered a trial at Coventry City once. Yeah, always been good with the ball, and always had good skills but I never get any credit for it at Tigers. Why do you think that is, Matt?'

'I don't know.'

'Because I'm not paid to carry the ball — that's not my job. And it's not your job, Matt. What is your job? What position do you play?'

'Tight-head prop.'

'That's right. And the primary duty of the tight-head prop is?'

'To perform in the scrum.'

'That's right. The scrum is the most important part of the game and if the tight-head prop is doing his job, his team is going forward. So remember that, Matt. You don't have to touch the ball; leave the running to the girls.'

'Okay, Daz.'

★ ★ ★

In March 2002, ten months after entering the academy, I was selected for an England Clubs v England Schoolboys game at Welford Road which doubled as a trial for the England Under-18s. The ground was almost empty but imbued with the spirit of Daz, I was rampant in the scrum and was invited to make my representative debut at a quadrangular tournament in Scotland. We assembled at a crummy hotel near the RFU development facility in Wolverhampton where my room-mate was a surprisingly engaging toff from Wellington College in Berkshire. James Haskell was a big unit who talked as well as he played and we spent hours dissecting the training sessions and wondering who would make the team.

The tournament consisted of games against Italy, Wales and Scotland. I was benched for the opener, but started against Wales on an absolutely foul afternoon. And it wasn't just the weather. In the first scrum, I was head-butted twice by their hooker and prop; a minute later, I was whacked at the bottom of a ruck. It was the most brutal game I had ever played but I was happy to respond in kind until being sent to the sin-bin for some over-exuberant footwork. A few days later, we clinched the tournament with a win over Scotland and I returned to Leicester with my England kit, feeling very proud indeed. I was a young international rugby player. I was learning my trade at the greatest club in England. Life was good. And then Dusty Hare, the Tigers chief scout and development co-ordinator, sat me down for an end-of-term appraisal. Had he heard that the Welsh front row had done a number on me? Was I confusing the game with chess? That seemed to be the theme of his impassioned speech.

'Matt, I want you to be fucking ruthless,' he said, fixing me with a glare. 'I want you to dominate your opposite number — not just beat him, dominate him. Look at Darren Garforth, he's ruthless, never takes a backward step. That's what we expect from you, Matt. I don't want to hear about anyone messing with you.'

I swallowed hard. There was still much to learn.

15

Scene 13: EXTERIOR — PLAYING FIELD — DAY

It is a cold but pleasant winter's afternoon in Leicestershire. A group of seventeen-year-old boys are playing rugby on the splendidly manicured playing fields of Oakham School. Ian 'Dosser' Smith, a former Leicester captain and the director of rugby at Oakham, is supervising a first XV training session and has invited Matt to assist with the coaching.

MATT HAMPSON
I see you won on Saturday. How was the scrum? Were you happy?

IAN (DOSSER) SMITH
No, we scraped it 15-7. Shocking. We made mistake after mistake. You can't fault their commitment but they are still a bit naïve, especially the loose-head. James, the tight-head, is immensely strong and the hooker, Lambert, is great around the field but his throwing-in was awful.

MATT HAMPSON
Well, we need to work on that, obviously.

IAN (DOSSER) SMITH
Yeah, we'll do a bit this morning.

MATT HAMPSON
Get the front row to have a hit on the scrummaging machine and I'll have a quick word.

IAN (DOSSER) SMITH
(Shouts) Okay, just the front row, please.

The three players, Aiden Newby (loose-head), Chris Lambert (hooker) and James Iman (tight-head) step forward.

MATT HAMPSON
Okay, lads, bind.

CHRIS LAMBERT
(Shouts) Oakham!

MATT HAMPSON
Crouch.

CHRIS LAMBERT
(Shouts) Set!

MATT HAMPSON
Touch . . . pause . . . engage!

FRONT ROW
(Shouts) Hit two-three . . . keep it on . . . keep it on . . . keep it on.

MATT HAMPSON
Keep your feet going, lads . . . Right, come off . . . come off.
The players separate and stand, breathing heavily.

MATT HAMPSON
It's not bad . . . Lambert, you've just got to boss it a bit more.
Remember, you're the man. And try and get a bit tighter when you are scrimmaging. Iman, if you're nice and tight to Lambert, then their loose-head has no space to move and you can come across him.

IAN (DOSSER) SMITH
He still has a lot to learn about the front-row mentality. He's still a bit nice.

MATT HAMPSON
You can't be too honest, mate. You've got to try and push the boundaries of what you can get away with. You've got to dominate.

IAN (DOSSER) SMITH
Right, let's go now as a full pack.

MATT HAMPSON
Okay, Lambert, boss it.

CHRIS LAMBERT
(Shouts) Oakham!

IAN (DOSSER) SMITH
Bind.

SECOND ROW
(Shouts) Two's in!

IAN (DOSSER) SMITH
Crouch!

CHRIS LAMBERT
(Shouts) Set!

IAN (DOSSER) SMITH
Touch . . . pause . . . engage!

PACK
(Shouts) Hit two-three . . . keep it on . . . keep it on . . . keep it on.

IAN (DOSSER) SMITH
Whoah! And away . . .
Smith turns to Hampson as the players disband.

IAN (DOSSER) SMITH
The problem we had on Saturday was . . . three times we kicked the ball through, so it looked like they had taken it against the head at vital times. But also, we were dominating. We were getting our metre and a half really quickly and the referee was like 'Slow down, slow down', and from having them under the cosh, our players were now in a position where they had to readjust.

MATT HAMPSON
So you are penalized for getting a big hit!

IAN (DOSSER) SMITH
Yeah.

MATT HAMPSON
A lot of referees don't know what they are talking about. If it happens again, try and narrow the gap so you're not hitting as far.

IAN (DOSSER) SMITH
Did you hear that, guys? Do you appreciate the difference? If we get too big a charge we look too good, but if we shorten the gap we just get that little bit of a nudge and that unsettles them. Okay, let's try a couple more.

The forwards regroup and prepare to hit the machine again.

MATT HAMPSON
(Shouts) Lambert! Keep your height down. Iman! Your back heel shouldn't be touching the ground! On your toes!

IAN (DOSSER) SMITH
We are nowhere near tight enough! You've got to set yourself square and get the bind. It's the jab, that's what we're after, short and sharp. Let's go again.

CHRIS LAMBERT
(Shouts) Oakham!

IAN (DOSSER) SMITH
Bind.

SECOND ROW
(Shouts) Two's in!

IAN (DOSSER) SMITH
Crouch.

CHRIS LAMBERT
(Shouts) Set!

IAN (DOSSER) SMITH
Touch . . . pause . . . engage!

PACK
(Shouts) Hit two-three . . . keep it on . . . keep it
on . . . keep it on.

IAN (DOSSER) SMITH
And away, good work.

MATT HAMPSON
Iman, that's better, mate.

IAN (DOSSER) SMITH
Okay, we'll do one more. This is the one we're
going to take into Saturday against Stowe. They
are big and abrasive up front but this is where
you put the marker down — the scrummage.
First encounter, we let them have it. Right?
Especially if it's on their ball — if it's our
ball we're as tight as can be and we don't
move an inch. You put that marker down and
for the next seventy or eighty minutes, we
know we'll be on the march. If we don't get it
right first off, it becomes an uphill struggle so
make sure you're ready for it. Here we go
then . . .

156

CHRIS LAMBERT
(Shouts) Oakham!

IAN (DOSSER) SMITH
Bind.

SECOND ROW
(Shouts) Two's in!

IAN (DOSSER) SMITH
Crouch.

CHRIS LAMBERT
(Shouts) Set!

IAN (DOSSER) SMITH
Touch . . . pause . . . engage!

PACK
(Shouts) Hit two-three . . . keep it on . . . keep it on . . . keep it on!

IAN (DOSSER) SMITH
And one, two, three, squeeze!

PACK
(Shouts) Squeeze!

IAN (DOSSER) SMITH
One, two, three . . .

PACK
(Shouts) Squeeze!

IAN (DOSSER) SMITH
Stop! Chris, with each little bit you are getting higher and higher, you've got to keep down. They'll be underneath and your ribs will go and the referee will penalize us. Not good. We won't finish on that one . . .

JAMES IMAN
(Shouts) Let's make this one right, boys!

MATT HAMPSON
Hey, Lambert, even if it is not going back . . . Just keep it down, the height . . .

CHRIS LAMBERT
(Shouts) Oakham!

IAN (DOSSER) SMITH
Bind.

SECOND ROW
(Shouts) Two's in.

IAN (DOSSER) SMITH
Crouch.

CHRIS LAMBERT
(Shouts) Set!

IAN (DOSSER) SMITH
Touch . . . pause . . . engage!

PACK
(Shouts) Hit two-three . . . keep it on . . . kept it on . . . keep it on.

IAN (DOSSER) SMITH
And one, two, three.

PACK
(Shouts) Squeeze!

IAN (DOSSER) SMITH
Okay, and away, that will do us.

The players disband and march towards the changing room.

IAN (DOSSER) SMITH
What do you think?

MATT HAMPSON
He still looks a bit unsure, doesn't he? He needs to boss it more. The second-rows are coming in and he's not bollicking them.

IAN (DOSSER) SMITH
Yeah.

MATT HAMPSON
And the loose-head . . . His right leg is going in front of his left leg. He hits all right but he is too straight when he is moving his legs.

IAN (DOSSER) SMITH
Have a look at the second team and I'll speak to you after.

MATT HAMPSON
Okay, mate.

One of Matt's carers, Dean Clarke, has watched the session in silence. He adjusts the chin control on Matt's wheelchair and they cross the field to watch the second team.

DEAN CLARKE
Iman was the tight-head, right?

MATT HAMPSON
Yeah.

DEAN CLARKE
How would you have reacted at his age if someone like Matt Hampson, who had had this catastrophic accident, turned up to supervise your training one day?

MATT HAMPSON
(Shouts) I'd have paid attention, mate.

DEAN CLARKE
No, be serious. What kind of impact would it have had? Would it have registered with you? Were you aware of the danger?

MATT HAMPSON
I think it has opened a lot of my friends' eyes but I don't know ... It depends on whether you worry about things and what kind of personality you are. When I was fifteen, Andy Blyth, the Sale player, broke his neck in a tackle and was very bad for a while. I remember seeing it on Sky and stuff like that.

DEAN CLARKE
And?

MATT HAMPSON
And what?

DEAN CLARKE
Did you ever consider it might happen to you?

MATT HAMPSON
No. When you are that age you just think you're invincible, don't you?

16

There were two changing rooms at the Tigers training ground in Oadby, one for the established stars and one for the wannabes, but we were separated by more than plasterboard and paint. The big-timers didn't have to haggle constantly for towels or kit and their conversations ranged from the latest game to cars and politics and current affairs. The mongrels weren't quite as cerebral; *chez nous* it was all about the bird you were shagging or how pissed you were at the weekend. But we did use the same showers and it was here in November 2002, five months into my second term at the academy, that I was offered another vivid reminder of this brutal passion we shared. Johno was there with Neil Back. They had just returned from a record 53–3 thrashing of the Springboks at Twickenham and were covered in bloody stitches and bruised from head to toe — the legacy of one of the most violent games in memory. I had seen plenty of blood before on *Living with Lions* but it looked different up close and I wondered, not for the first time, how I'd have performed.

Would I have stood my ground like Johno? Am I tough enough for this?

★   ★   ★

162

Having relished the experience of my debut for England, I made selection for the Under-19 World Cup in France my objective for the season. Tosh Askew and Dosser were the coaches and we prepared with a week-long training camp in Coventry, where I joined up with Haskell again. I was still a cub at Tigers, a small cog in a very big wheel, but to wear the red rose was to step into the spotlight and the ten days that followed were the most enjoyable of my rugby life.

We opened with an easy win against Russia in Paris and then travelled to Epernay for the champagne fixture against South Africa. It was the first time my parents had watched me play for England and I stood listening to the sound of our national anthem with tears running down my face. The South Africans were incredibly skilful. In an early line-out, their hooker threw it over the number 8 at the back, but he stretched and brought it down with one hand and then flicked it to the scrum-half. We had a couple of aces too in Rees and Haskell and gave our best but it wasn't enough. There was a reception afterwards at Moët & Chandon, but even the best champagne in the world tastes flat in defeat. With no chance now of making the final, we entered the play-offs for the minor placings, beating Wales (when I scored my first international try) and then losing narrowly to Ireland. It was my fourth match in ten days and I was absolutely shattered but walked off the field to some glowing praise from Askew. 'Matt, I've got to be honest,' he said. 'I probably wouldn't have picked you if David Wilson hadn't been injured but you proved me wrong. You were awesome. Well played.'

★ ★ ★

Battle-hardened and confident, I felt a lot more comfortable at Tigers when the new season — my third at the club — began the following August. A new Under-21s Development League had just been announced and I was training and playing with some great lads: James Buckland, Jim Hamilton, Dan Hipkiss, Jo-Jo Ajuwa, Tom Ryder, Will Skinner and Daniel Montague, to name but a few. 'Big' Jim Hamilton, our leader on and off the field, was the founding member of the legendary 'Tour de Cov' — the cycling classic in Coventry that entailed dressing up in Tour de France Lycra and racing from pub to pub. I don't know how he thought them up!

We beat Gloucester in the final of the league that season and were celebrating with a crate of beer in the changing room at Welford Road when he whipped out a bottle of Tabasco sauce. 'Okay, this is the challenge,' he says. 'Nobody gets out of here until we've all had a swig of hot sauce.'

He handed me the bottle and I almost coughed my tonsils out, much to the amusement of Jo-Jo Ajuwa, our massive Nigerian winger. 'That ain't hot sauce,' he scoffed, reaching for the bottle. 'My moma has hotter sauce than that!'

And to prove it, he downed it in one. I have never seen a black man turn so green in my life.

His eyes almost popped from his head. We laughed so hard we thought we were all going to die.

There were other challenges like 'Shooooe!', which entailed swallowing a mouthful of beer from the sole of one of Jimbo's mouldy runners, but the ultimate test was 'the Jommy', in honour of Yomi Akinyemi, our other impressively built Nigerian. For 'the Jommy', we had to position ourselves between his legs with our mouth open as a thimble of beer was poured on to his chest and catch each droplet as it rolled down his arse crack and off the end of his knob. Brings tears to my eyes just thinking about it but it was fun . . .

★ ★ ★

There was, of course, another World Cup played that year. I was up early on the morning of the final in November and watched the game unfold with my parents at a friend's house in Oakham. The tension was almost unbearable until Jonny Wilkinson's dropped goal and we jumped out of our seats, proud to be English and thrilled for Martin Johnson. Was there a finer England player in the history of the game? He was back playing for Tigers a week later and was invited to a reception with the Queen a few days after that. I remember seeing the pictures and wondering how it must feel . . . to lift the Webb Ellis trophy . . . to meet the Queen. I never imagined I'd find out.

17

Scene 14: INTERIOR — BEDROOM — NIGHT

Eight months have passed since the trip to Paris. It is the evening of Tuesday, 22 July 2008 and Matt has returned home from a garden party at Buckingham Palace and an audience with the Queen. One of his carers, Jacqui Pochin, has made a pot of tea and is sitting by his bed.

JACQUI POCHIN
Okay, how was it? Come on! I want every single detail.

MATT HAMPSON
Well, quite strange to be honest. I mean, you see the Queen every day, don't you? Take a £10 note out of your pocket and she's there smiling up at you. She must be the most famous person on the planet.

JACQUI POCHIN
I'll say . . . Were you nervous?

MATT HAMPSON
A little. I mean, obviously it wasn't a private audience and a bit more relaxed but it was still pretty formal. We were given instructions about where to stand and what to say. 'You will call her Ma'am,' they said. 'It will be fine,' they

said. 'She is great at speaking to people and will put you at ease.'

JACQUI POCHIN
How many people were there?

MATT HAMPSON
A few hundred. We were instructed to form two lines on the lawn and she came out at four o'clock and started moving from side to side.

JACQUI POCHIN
What? At random!

MATT HAMPSON
The Queen doesn't do random. We had all been selected and briefed. She was presented to about twenty people — war heroes and various achievers. Dean was standing beside me. My parents were just behind. She came over and said, 'Oh, you are a rugby player then?' 'Yes, Ma'am,' I replied. Then she said, 'It's a rough sport, isn't it?' I said, 'Yes, Ma'am, if you're not careful you could break your neck.'

JACQUI POCHIN
(Laughs) You didn't!

MATT HAMPSON
No, but I was tempted. I wanted to make her laugh. I said, 'Your lawn is great. It would make an awesome rugby pitch.' It was odd, I felt I had to put her at ease.

JACQUI POCHIN
Really?

MATT HAMPSON
Yeah — and not just because I'm in a wheelchair. I mean, it must be very difficult having to talk to twenty sets of people about twenty different things. And what do we have in common? She must be eighty! I'm the same age as her grandchildren! At the end, I could see she was starting to dry up and had nothing else to say. It must be very difficult for her.

JACQUI POCHIN
What happened then?

MATT HAMPSON
Well, Mum felt it was our duty to stay and mingle but I wasn't overly keen. The grounds were impressive . . . massive . . . it was a bit surreal really. I thought: Wow! I've just met the Queen. She is just a human being! And then, as we were leaving, something really odd happened.

JACQUI POCHIN
What was it?

MATT HAMPSON
We had just left Buckingham Palace and I noticed this shop, a short walk from the gates. I thought: Imagine, the Queen has never been in there! She lives just a couple of hundred yards away but has never walked into that

shop! And it occurred to me that we are both prisoners of sorts. She must have looked at me and thought: Strewth! I wouldn't want to be him. And I was driving home thinking exactly the same about her.

18

There were big changes at Tigers when pre-season training began in July 2004. John Wells had replaced Dean Richards as head coach. Pat Howard and Richard Cockerill had returned after two years at Montferrand to become his assistants. Martin Johnson had retired from international rugby and was playing in his final season. Darren Garforth had played his final season and was coaching at Nuneaton. And Matt Hampson had just been promoted to the first-team squad. Three years at the academy had taught me the Leicester traditions: if someone threw a punch during a game, I did not take a backward step; if my team-mates weren't doing it in training, I would abuse them and tell them they were shit. But training with the first team was like starting over again. How do you square up to a guy like Martin Johnson? How do you tell Neil Back to put more effort in? And I was so nervous and anxious to prove myself that I was constantly messing up. It didn't help that I was prohibited from contact work until the scars from a recent surgery on my left shoulder healed, and I was the butt of every joke as I jogged up and down and shadow-boxed on the sideline as the boys piled into the tackle bags.

'Who's that lazy bastard?'

'Hey, it's Ricky Fatton!'

Lewis Moody was also injured that summer and we spent a lot of time in rehab together before being cleared to resume full training in October. Our first session back finished with a game of touch rugby. I was picked on a side with Johno and Alex Tuilagi; Lewis was on the opposing team. The game started and was flowing nicely when Alex made a break that sliced through their defence and was clearly easing up when Lewis came out of nowhere and almost buried him with the tackle. Johno was incensed. 'What the fuck are you doing, Moods?' he roared, grabbing him by the throat. And when Lewis responded by trying to swing his arm he was dropped by a straight left that absolutely flattened him. I couldn't believe it. I thought: Fuck! What a madhouse! How do I compete with that? But you do, you learn, because that's the Leicester way. And there was no place to hide when your boss was Richard Cockerill.

His *modus operandi* — 'I don't expect you to do anything I wouldn't do myself' — sounded pretty reasonable until you saw him in the gym with the veins popping out of his neck, buckling under the strain of some ridiculous weight. 'Every time I'm struggling on the last rep [repetition],' he'd say, 'I close my eyes and think of Mark fucking Regan!' It's fair to say that he disliked his Bristol rival with a passion.

In one of my first games back — a reserve-team match against Sale at Heywood Road — Cockers picked himself at hooker and we packed down together for the first time. He was thirty-four years old and had played in over 260 games for Leicester but his passion had not waned. He was like a pit-bull in the changing room. 'Just remember, Hambo,' he said, fixing me with a glare. 'Forwards win games — backs just decide by how much. We take the game to this lot from the first scrum.' Then he clipped Tom Ryder around the head, 'Come on! Follow me!', and led us into battle.

He gave me hell on the training ground and hell in the gym . . .

'You're a fucking lazy bastard, Hambo!'

. . . but I kept coming back for more; more weights, more press-ups, more scrum sessions, more contact work, and after four months of training with the stars and playing with the reserves I began to earn his respect.

★ ★ ★

On the third Wednesday of November, John Wells announced the team for the Premiership game against Wasps at Adams Park. The autumn internationals were being played at Twickenham and six of the first-team regulars — Graham Rowntree, Julian White, Ben Kay, Lewis Moody, Martin Corry and Harry Ellis — had been called up for England. I listened with the usual detachment as Wells began his speech.

'The team is Vesty, Varndell, Cornwell, Gibson, Healey, Goode, Bernard, Holford, Buckland, Morris, Johno, Louis Deacon, Henry Tuilagi, Backy, Will Johnson. The subs are

Taukafa, Hamilton, Montagu, Skinner, Hampson.' My heart skipped a beat.

Was I hearing things? Had he just called out my name?

Then Cockers walked over and gave me a playful dig. 'Don't worry.' He smiled. 'You're ready.'

But I'm not sure I slept that night.

We left for a hotel near High Wycombe on the day before the game and I was allocated a room with Darren Morris, the Welsh international and British Lion. I was comfortable with Darren — we had played a couple of times together for the reserves — but it felt surreal to be so close to Johno. Exactly a year had passed since I had watched him lift the Webb Ellis trophy at a friend's house in Oakham and here we were, sharing the same changing room, as we strapped our fingers and wrists. A waft of Ralgex singed my nostrils. I pulled on my boots and started to feel uncomfortable. The presence of Matt Cornwell and Tom Varndell in the starting XV was compounding my anxiety; both had earned rave reviews after a seamless transition from the reserves and I couldn't help but envy them. Why them and not me? Had they been scared? Was it different for the girls? The intensity was suffocating. There were guys banging heads and retching in the toilets and soon Johno would begin his speech and there would be nowhere to hide. And I wanted to hide. Cockers was wrong. I wasn't ready for this. And as I ran out and took my place on the bench I was shaken by an unforgivable thought: I hope I don't get on.

A few yards away, on the opposite side of the dugout, Haskell was sitting with the replacement Wasps. He had his own World Cup icons to contend with in Matt Dawson and the antichrist Dallaglio and I wondered if he was having similar thoughts. The game started. Darren Morris locked heads with Craig Dowd in the first scrum and the doubt continued to haunt me . . . 'Imagine that was you, Hambo.'

'No problem, mate.'

'Dowd would fucking destroy you.'

'No, I'd be okay.'

'You're scared out of your wits, man!'

'That's not true.'

'You don't even want to play!'

'No, it's not that . . . I just don't want to hurt the team.'

'Here pussy, pussy.'

'Fuck off.'

'You're a coward, Hambo.'

'No! I'll go on! Put me on.'

The battle between the two great rivals of English rugby was pulsating. Wasps were the better team for most of it and led 17-7 with thirteen minutes to go, but were held to a draw by the boot of Andy Goode, the guile of Austin Healey and an exhibition of defiance from Johno. I followed them into the dressing room with my jersey unsoiled, unsure whether to laugh or cry.

It was the same a week later against Saracens at Welford Road, when I spent another eighty minutes watching from the bench, torn between desire and fear.

Two days after the Saracens game, the

174

'England' boys returned from the autumn internationals and the natural order was restored. The date was 29 November 2004 — my twentieth birthday — and a decision had been taken to send me to Bedford on a short-term loan until Christmas. 'They've got some injury problems down there,' Cockers explained, 'and the experience will do you good. You need to get some matches under your belt before the Under-21 Six Nations.'

'Sure,' I replied, 'no problem.'

I pulled on my jersey and prepared to go to work. Training began with a tough scrummaging session and some line-out work and, as I grabbed Johno's thigh and hoisted him skyward, I was feeling pretty good about life and was convinced my time would come. I was wrong. It was as close as I would get to touching greatness.

19

The tribunal has reached its sixth month. Richard Cockerill enters the witness stand wearing a sports jacket and jeans and is presented with a copy of Me and My Mouth, an autobiography by Austin Healey. He glances at the book and smiles. 'What happened to the Bible? I hope you don't expect me to swear on this?'

BARRISTER
Mr Cockerill, are you familiar with this book?

RICHARD COCKERILL
No. I'm afraid I've never been a great reader . . . and I'm not going to break the habit of a lifetime for Austin Healey!

BARRISTER
I would like to draw your attention to the following passage, please: 'Leicester were the biggest and the best rugby club in the British Isles long before our Heineken Cup triumphs. I know that because Richard Cockerill told me the first time I met him. He also punched me in the face. It was the summer of 1996 and Cockers, the small and imperfectly formed Tigers hooker, thought I was a smart-arse. I'd just joined the club from Orrell and was taking part in my first training session out of

176

the gym with my new team-mates. At least, I thought they were my team-mates. My introduction to the lads was a game of touch rugby. My introduction to Cockerill was a knuckle sandwich. I made a half break and touched him and he swivelled round and caught me in the jaw. After I had stopped laughing I asked him what the hell he was doing. 'There are no superstars here,' he yelled, in that over-dramatic way of his. In his pea-sized forward's mind, he thought he was doing it for the club (he was known as Captain Club Man, because he'd have died for Leicester Tigers). He obviously thought he had to show me the Leicester way.'

RICHARD COCKERILL
That sounds like Austin's style.

BARRISTER
What exactly is the Leicester way?

RICHARD COCKERILL
Where would you like me to start?

BARRISTER
At the beginning, please.

RICHARD COCKERILL
I'm not from Leicester. I grew up in a place called Leamington-Hastings, about halfway between Leamington and Rugby. Working-class background. My father, Robert, spent most of his working life at Rolls-Royce in Coventry. My mother, Janice, worked in a hotel for most of

her life in various guises. I had one brother. We didn't really get on.

BARRISTER
Why not?

RICHARD COCKERILL
We were chalk and cheese. He's the intelligent one in the family. He went to grammar school and worked in a bank and sometimes used his intelligence to wind me up and get out of situations. I didn't have that intelligence so my first reaction was to belt him. Not a bad trait to have for a front-row forward.

BARRISTER
What about your education?

RICHARD COCKERILL
Harris Church of England Comprehensive School . . . hated it. Hated writing, hated reading, hated students.

BARRISTER
That's a lot of hate?

RICHARD COCKERILL
Well, hate is probably too strong a word for it but it just wasn't my thing. I'm a doer. I learned to do things. I left school at sixteen and did an apprenticeship as a cabinetmaker and French polisher. I always wanted to do stuff. I'm not an academic in any way, shape or form and people who are academics intimidate me a bit. I

178

feel . . . I dunno, a bit inferior because they are better educated than me.

BARRISTER
Even now?

RICHARD COCKERILL
Not so much now, but . . .

BARRISTER
Initially?

RICHARD COCKERILL
Yeah, in my younger days. I'm a very ordinary person. I come from a very ordinary background and I hope that comes across. Some people might say, 'Oh, but you've played rugby for England', but I just see myself as the next bloke on the street.

BARRISTER
Have you children, Mr Cockerill?

RICHARD COCKERILL
A boy and two girls: Stanley, Ann and Olivia.

BARRISTER
So what happens when Stanley comes home one day and says, 'Dad, I hate education. I hate school. I hate reading.' What are you going to say? 'That's my boy'

RICHARD COCKERILL
(Laughs) I'm going to say, 'Go and tell your mother.' No, I think everybody is different. My

parents saw that my brother was quite intelligent and they pushed him in that direction. I was very good with my hands. I could make things, do things. Rugby suited my personality. I first started playing the game at Newbold, a really basic club where one of the first lessons we learned was: it doesn't matter how good the bloke standing opposite to you is — beat the shite out of him and you'll see how much he wants to play.

BARRISTER
And that appealed to you?

RICHARD COCKERILL
Absolutely. I loved the game. I loved the training. I enjoyed the physicality. I had this trait where I could go from being relatively calm to relatively insane quite quickly and all the good players — the Martin Johnsons, the Julian Whites — have that. And it's not that I'm a particularly hard person. I'm no Queensberry Rules champion. I am not a great fighter but I've a lot of grit in me. Brave people, for me, aren't the ones that are born tough; they're the ones that do things they are actually scared of but they will do them because they need to be done. I'm probably one of those rather than a natural hard man.

BARRISTER
When did you join Leicester?

RICHARD COCKERILL
Summer of 1992. They were looking for a hooker. It was a big move. They were a big side. I had

180

played Under-16s with their loose-head, Graham Rowntree, and knew the tight-head, Darren Garforth, by reputation. Graham was very dedicated; Darren was just hard, and there was me in the middle.

BARRISTER
And you got on?

RICHARD COCKERILL
Famously. We trained together, drank together, socialized together. Training was violently brutal. We used to do defence on Wednesday mornings and it almost always finished with an all-out brawl. Carnage. But that was a good sign. It meant we were up for it at the weekend. We'd have this huge brawl and there would be blood and stitches everywhere and then we'd sit in the bath together and have a cup of tea. It sounds a bit mindless but, well, parts of the game are mindless, aren't they? And a good smack in the gob didn't do any harm. It bred a good mentality because we didn't get bullied very often. If you weren't prepared to sign up to that, you didn't last here very long. Or it got beaten out of you quite quickly, especially as a young player.

BARRISTER
A young player like Mr Hampson?

RICHARD COCKERILL
Yes. If you wanted to be part of this squad, you needed to understand what it took to play at this level. Matt did get the odd clip around the ear, not

because people didn't like him, it was a testing ground to see how he would react.

BARRISTER
Part of his apprenticeship?

RICHARD COCKERILL
Well, in the old-fashioned way, yeah.

BARRISTER
Weren't you once quoted as saying that good players are born with a hard streak? That you cannot coach hardness into a player?

RICHARD COCKERILL
No, I don't think you can. It's genetics. I think you are born with it . . . Take Julian White, a fantastic bloke, but he has the ability to turn from normal Julian into almost psychopathic Julian (clicks fingers) like that. And that's the difference with good front-row forwards. They can turn from being sensible and quite thoughtful to 'Fuck! I'm going to bash this bugger now.'

BARRISTER
Did Mr Hampson have that ability? Was it in his genes?

RICHARD COCKERILL
Yes, I believe it was. Matt had huge potential as a rugby player, huge. He had that little glint in his eye that, you know, he could do some damage.

182

BARRISTER
There was a bit of bastard in him?

RICHARD COCKERILL
(Smiles) Yes, that's the expression.

BARRISTER
Do you get many young players who haven't got it?

RICHARD COCKERILL
We get them all the time.

BARRISTER
Really?

RICHARD COCKERILL
Yeah. It all comes down to how much you want it. Do you want it? Training is hard and physical. Sometimes you don't play well. People are criticizing you. Do you have the guts to take it? Do you have the will to train harder? Matt had that.

BARRISTER
You worked with him for two separate periods at Leicester, both as a player and a coach, I understand?

RICHARD COCKERILL
Yeah. I don't remember much of him when I was playing because he would have been only fifteen or so when I left to play in France for two years. I came back as assistant forwards coach to John Wells and obviously had a fair bit to deal with

183

him because he was under my tutelage, so to speak, for the period up until his accident.

BARRISTER
What are your memories of that period?

RICHARD COCKERILL
The thing that sticks out most is that you could throw anything at him and he would keep coming back for more. I am a hard taskmaster, especially with the younger kids. It's important they understand what it takes to play at this level and Matt understood. I mean, if you watch the DVD, there's a clip of him bossing the scrum and knocking heads together. It's like listening to Darren Garforth. Same attitude. Darren was his role model.

BARRISTER
What DVD is this, Mr Cockerill?

RICHARD COCKERILL
The DVD of the training session when Matt had his accident. His parents asked myself and Graham Rowntree to take a look at it. Obviously, we are all looking for an answer — I presume that's the purpose of this tribunal. Why did this happen? Whose fault was it?

BARRISTER
Did you reach a conclusion?

RICHARD COCKERILL
No. He just got himself into a bad position.

BARRISTER
Can you explain what a bad position is, please?

RICHARD COCKERILL
The most critical time for any front row comes at engagement. Get it wrong and it's not funny — you are taking four to five hundred kilos up through your backside and into your head and if the scrum collapses, and the second row are still pushing, you are literally driven into the ground.

BARRISTER
Is that what happened to Mr Hampson?

RICHARD COCKERILL
The camera view is from the other side so it's hard to tell exactly. As a tight-head, to cause maximum disruption to their scrum, the trick is to go in at an angle and get the loose-head to scrummage outside of you. I think Matt went in and tried to lose the loose-head and . . .

BARRISTER
Are you saying he did not bind properly?

RICHARD COCKERILL
Well, as I said, the camera view is from the other side so it's hard to . . .

BARRISTER
I'm asking for your opinion, Mr Cockerill.

RICHARD COCKERILL
I think they were both cheating like buggery to be

honest, as old and young blokes do. If you are asking me whose fault it is . . . I don't think it's anybody's fault. He just got himself into a bad position and was really unlucky. And to his credit he has never denied that. He has never said, 'The game is shit' or 'They should ban scrummaging.' In fact, he's quite the opposite. The scrum is still his favourite part of the game.

BARRISTER
Where were you when it happened?

RICHARD COCKERILL
The training ground at Leicester — we got a call from one of the England guys saying he had hurt himself training. Well, everybody hurts themselves training. We thought it was his shoulder or a broken collarbone or something. Then we heard that it was serious and that he had almost died on the pitch. It was horrendous, just horrendous. You think: Fuck! What's it all about? You think of all sorts of things.

BARRISTER
Did you visit him in hospital?

RICHARD COCKERILL
Yes. I went down to Stoke Mandeville with Graham Rowntree about a week or so later when he was stable. But what do you say? 'How are you doing, Hambo? Are you all right, mate?' You try to be as normal as possible but it's such a shock. And the only thing he was bothered about was

his contract. I said, 'Don't worry about that. When you are better we will talk about that.'

BARRISTER
Would he have got a new contract? Would he have made it?

RICHARD COCKERILL
No question. I mean . . . this probably sounds a really crass thing to say but the biggest disappointment . . . Well, not the biggest disappointment but the biggest shame for me is that he could have made a first-class prop. No doubt about it. And I don't say that out of kindness. We don't do kindness at Leicester.

BARRISTER
Really? My understanding is that you have been exceptionally kind.

RICHARD COCKERILL
It's not about being kind. It's not about feeling sorry for him. The courage he has shown in the last four years has been extraordinary and I feel that the club has a responsibility to look after him. He was with England when he was injured but he was a Tigers player, our player. He is still our player. And he will be our player until the day he is no longer with us.

20

I made two appearances for Bedford in December 2004 — a National League 1 game at Bristol and a Powergen Cup game at Goldington Road — but can't really say I enjoyed the experience. My new team-mates were a mix of predominantly ex-Northampton players who hated everything Leicester (I was 'the Leicester boy') so we were never going to gel. And I found the club's director of rugby, Rudolph Straeuli, strange and hard to understand.

A year previously, while still coach of South Africa, Straeuli had been the architect of the infamous Kamp Staaldraad — a military-style boot camp designed to build team unity before the 2003 World Cup. Six weeks before the finals, he had marched his players into the South African bush and watched as they were ordered by armed guards to strip and crawl naked over gravel. They were then dropped into a foxhole and made to sing the national anthem while icy water was poured over their heads. And then a clearing was made for a boxing ring and they were made to fight each other. In his book, *The Right Place at the Wrong Time*, the captain, Corné Krige, describes the opening bout between Werner Greef and Thinus Delport:

Werner and Thinus started very meekly, tapping each other a few times, but not much more. The guards stopped the fight and said that if they messed around any more, they would have to spend the rest of the day running. 'Either hit each other properly or get punished,' the two were told. Prompted by this warning, Thinus really climbed into Werner, getting in a few good shots. When it was over, Werner took off his gloves and threw them at his 'instructors' in disgust. He told them 'This is really fucked up.' His sentiments were shared by all of us.

Straeuli had made a fundamental error — everybody knew that kind of brutality only worked at Leicester!

*   *   *

My loan at Bedford expired (thankfully) at Christmas. I spent the New Year at home and was welcomed back to Leicester with a volley of abuse from Cockers and some good news and some bad news. The 'bad' was that he was sending me away on loan again to Nuneaton, a club eight points adrift at the bottom of Division 2. The 'good' was that he was certain I was going to get on with the coach, Darren Garforth. A few days later, the *Coventry Evening Telegraph* carried details of the move:

NUNS TURN TO TIGERS FOR FORWARD POWER

Nuneaton have procured the services of two more forwards on loan from Leicester Tigers as they attempt to play their way off the bottom of National Division Two. Tight head prop Matt Hampson, who has gone straight into the 19-strong squad for today's home game against Newbury, will be available for Nuns until required by England Under-21s next month. He is joined at Liberty Way by open side flanker Joe Wheeler, the youngest son of Leicester's chief executive and former England hooker Peter. Hampson has already had a loan spell at Bedford this season and is rated an excellent prospect by forwards coach Darren Garforth.

Almost four years had passed since my first lesson from Daz at the academy but he hadn't mellowed with age. 'I want you to fucking hit every ruck and maul that you get to,' he bellowed on the training ground. 'I don't want you to even think about touching the ball.' And I didn't. Not once. Daz picked himself for the 8-6 defeat of Newbury and I watched, disappointed, from the bench.

A week later, we travelled to Launceston in Cornwall — a five-hour drive from Nuneaton by coach — and I was benched again. The game was held on a cold and wet Saturday afternoon and was scoreless at half-time and turning into a dogfight — meat and drink to Daz, who was playing out of his skin. The teams ran out for the second half. Launceston went ahead with a converted try and then, to the delight of the home fans who had been abusing him since the start, Daz was sent to the sin-bin. He ordered one of the backs to come off and gave me the nod.

I peeled off my layers and ran on, feeling nervous and heavy-legged. The pitch was like a swamp. Everyone was caked in shit. The Launceston front row were big and abrasive and we struggled to contain them. My fault. I was blowing out of my arse and needed a bit more time to settle but we didn't have more time and Daz called me ashore and put himself back on as soon as his penalty had expired. It was the right call. He was clearly stronger and more experienced than me (and effectively won the game for Nuneaton with a brilliant last-minute scrummage) but it felt like a slap in the face.

He didn't fucking rate me!

. . . I felt degraded and almost betrayed.

The coach journey home was interminable. We opened a crate of beer and were shit-faced before Bristol. I sat at the back with the other forwards, listening to Daz telling stories about his extraordinary career. He was thirty-nine years old and had won two European Cups and twenty-five caps for England but that final minute against Launceston . . . the crowd jeering him . . . his scrum edging closer to their line . . . turning the screw until he had battered them into submission . . . had brought him as much pleasure as any of them. It was obvious. He was buzzing. And though I was still feeling sore it was hard not to worship him.

'Daz! Tell them about the battle for the back seats at Leicester,' I laughed.

He took a swig from his beer and smiled.

Every week at Leicester, when the team took to the road, the back seats were occupied by the team's enforcers, Cockerill, Garforth, Rowntree and Johnson. And every week, when the team took to the road, a couple of challengers would be selected to displace them. Most ended up with split eyes and busted jaws and having their clothes ripped off and chucked out of the skylight, but it was considered cowardly to refuse.

I was sitting with Daniel Montague, another Leicester expat, as Daz was finishing the story.

'Why don't we start that here?' I grinned.

'What?' Monty replied.

'Why don't we start that tradition at Nuneaton?'

'You've got to be joking,' he said.

I jumped out of my seat and into the space beside Daz.

'Right! Who are the challengers? We're not going to let anyone on the back seat of this bus. Are we, Daz?'

And just when I thought things couldn't get much worse, they did.

'No,' Daz replied. 'I'm with them.'

He didn't fucking rate me!

I launched myself at him but he caught me with a punch that almost broke my jaw. I

192

grabbed his shirt and we fell backwards across the seat, wrestling and trading blows. He was pummelling me and cruising to an easy win on points when I stopped him with a punch that split his left eye and caused a tremor that rocked the Leicester training ground for days.

'Hey, Johno, did you hear about Hambo?'

'No.'

'He knocked out Skin!'

'What?'

'He gave Daz a smack after a game with Nuneaton and knocked him out.'

'Always knew that kid had something!'

I arrived home from Launceston in the early hours of Sunday morning, pissed and dishevelled and with just a day to sort myself out before the first Six Nations training camp with England at Bath. I wasn't feeling confident. My career had stalled. I'd gone from almost making my Premiership debut with Tigers, to a bad month at Bedford, to (literally) a slap in the jaw at Nuneaton. Where was the progress? What had I achieved? No, wait! But, of course . . . I was the man who twatted Darren Garforth!

21

Scene 16: INTERIOR — COURTROOM — DAY

Graham Rowntree has been called by the tribunal.
He is wearing a crisp navy suit and appears calm and
affable.

BARRISTER
Mr Rowntree, I'd like you to cast your mind back
to the autumn of 2004, please. You were thirty-
three, I believe?

GRAHAM ROWNTREE
Yes, that's right.

BARRISTER
And still playing?

GRAHAM ROWNTREE
Yes, it was my fourteenth season at Leicester and I
was still getting capped for England.

BARRISTER
Loose-head prop.

GRAHAM ROWNTREE
Yes, loose-head prop.

BARRISTER
It was also Mr Hampson's first season with the
Leicester elite?

GRAHAM ROWNTREE
Well, we don't do elite at Tigers but, yeah, it was his first season as a senior squad member.

BARRISTER
What were your impressions of him?

GRAHAM ROWNTREE
I had heard a bit about him at the academy and had kept an eye on him the season before but had not seen him play. I was certainly impressed with how he trained.

BARRISTER
Why so?

GRAHAM ROWNTREE
Well, Richard had rejoined the club from Clermont that season and . . .

BARRISTER
Richard?

GRAHAM ROWNTREE
Richard Cockerill. He had returned to the club after two seasons in France as an assistant forwards coach and one of his remits was to nurture the players who were coming out of the academy. He used to punish them but in a good way, making them stay behind for extra fitness training and running. He bullied Hambo, no question, but I admired how well he took it. But the thing that really stands out was how quiet he was.

BARRISTER
How quiet he was?

GRAHAM ROWNTREE
Yes, wouldn't say boo to a goose. It was a running joke at the club. 'For God's sake shut up, Hambo!' And he would just smile . . . But a good work ethic and a real determination to play. He was fitting in nicely, was very . . . Leicester. Quiet. Got on with it. Loved to drink. Loved to fight. Loved the ethic, the training. 'Shut up, Hambo!' I'd say it to him every day, 'Hambo, shut up gobbing off!'

BARRISTER
Now, correct me if I am wrong, Mr Rowntree, but you established a reputation as one of the best props in England as a member of the 'ABC' club? Would you mind explaining to the tribunal exactly what that was?

GRAHAM ROWNTREE
Well, for a number of years at Leicester we played with letters in place of numbers on our shirts. The front row were A, B and C.

BARRISTER
And you were Mr A?

GRAHAM ROWNTREE
That's right. Richard was B and Darren Garforth was C.

196

BARRISTER
It has also been noted here that the player Mr Hampson admired and aspired to be was not you or Mr Cockerill but Mr Garforth?

GRAHAM ROWNTREE
Darren was the player we all aspired to be. Toughest bloke I ever played with, but also the most down-to-earth, with the biggest heart, a real gentleman . . . but not a man you would ever want to cross. Him and Dean Richards both had special qualities, but Darren set the standard at Leicester of how you acted as a rugby player, on and off the field. He was a special talent. I mean, I work with Martin Johnson and the England forwards now and the number of times we look at players and say, 'I wish he had a bit more Garforth in him' is just . . .

BARRISTER
How would you articulate 'a bit more Garforth'?

GRAHAM ROWNTREE
Desire. He had a never-ending passion in him. He liked and was good at the rough stuff and he played on the edge all the time . . . the edge of the referee . . . the edge of the law . . . and constantly in the face of the opposition. But not mouthy; Richard was mouthy, but Darren would just get this look in his eye and you knew when he was going to kick off.

BARRISTER
Any particular incident spring to mind?

197

GRAHAM ROWNTREE

Our first European Cup game in 1996. We had to go to Pau in the Pyrenees. It's always daunting when you come out to a pitch from underneath a stand and we knew running out it was going to be bad. A roughhouse it was . . . cage around the pitch . . . spitting at us . . . screaming at us. The game started and there was a lot of gouging — one guy had his finger in John Wells's eye socket, up to his knuckle, until Dean sorted him out. It was a battle. We were under the cosh. The crowd were going mental. They tried this short-tap penalty move near our line and would have scored but Darren came from nowhere and buried the bloke carrying the ball. Just buried him! The guy couldn't get up. He knocked the ball on, we cleared our lines and that was the turning point.

BARRISTER

How?

GRAHAM ROWNTREE

It changed the game and that was Darren. There was always a moment in a game where he would boot somebody or have a fight and set the tone: 'We are Leicester. You don't mess with us.' We built this great aura away from home and Darren was one of the instigators, with Dean and Martin Johnson of course. We would sense the crowd wanting our blood — and I mean wanting — and we used to love it. And the more the game went on, and the tighter it got, the better it was for us.

198

We would sense the opposition thinking: We're going to lose this. Leicester will squeeze us. And we did and .. I'm sorry, I'm going off on one now, aren't I?

BARRISTER
No, please continue, Mr Rowntree . . .

GRAHAM ROWNTREE
Yeah, well, like I say, we had this aura and if we were ever struggling we would just start a fight. We loved it. The 'ABC' club had this fierce reputation and it was bloody great. They were glory days, fantastic days. We were this fearless trio, but you could get away with a lot back then. I mean, half the stuff we used to do you would get banned for these days. We were dirty. We loved a scrap.

BARRISTER
Did you have a mentor, Mr Rowntree? How did you acquire the dark arts of scrummaging?

GRAHAM ROWNTREE
I learned a lot as a nineteen-year-old playing in the Leicester youth team. We used to all train together — the first-team pack, the second-team pack and the youth-team pack — on Monday nights at Mandela Park behind the Welford Road Stadium. I remember tackling Peter Wheeler as a seventeen-year-old — you would never get that now! So I learned a lot that way and from playing in the second and third teams. But I learned the most from getting my head shoved up my backside and

from guys like Dean and John Wells. They taught me a lot.

BARRISTER
Mr Cockerill has gone on record as saying that you cannot coach hardness — that aspiring young players either have it or they don't. What's your opinion?

GRAHAM ROWNTREE
I think the club has been very good at weeding out the guys who haven't got it, and nurturing those who have. There's a special talent to be a Leicester player, a special mindset, and I think you can coach it. But it comes more natural to some people than it does to others.

BARRISTER
Did it come natural to Mr Hampson?

GRAHAM ROWNTREE
He was a Leicester man. He had earned his stripes.

BARRISTER
Do you remember the day he was injured?

GRAHAM ROWNTREE
I remember it well. I was with England. We were training at the Pennyhill Park Hotel on the Tuesday before playing Scotland. Andy Robinson pulled us all together after the session. 'I'm sorry to say that there has been a terrible injury,' he said. 'A young prop with the England Under-21s has hurt his neck in training and has been taken to hospital.

We don't know how bad it is.' I knew straight away that it was Hambo . . . Well, I didn't know but sometimes you just get an inkling. I thought: Crikey! It's not Hambo, is it? I hope it's not Hambo. You stand there waiting for him to say someone else's name — not that I would wish it on anybody — but you don't want it to be him. And then he said it, 'Matt Hampson.' It shocked me. Terrible. I thought: Shit! Is he all right? How bad is it? Where is he? I started scrambling and trying to call people. 'Oh it's early days . . . He's in hospital . . . We don't know . . . The scrum collapsed . . . There was a paramedic there.' It was terrible. I remember going down to the hospital to see him.

BARRISTER
How soon after was it?

GRAHAM ROWNTREE
I was keen to go down asap but that wouldn't have been right. It was maybe a month or two months later — we had to wait for the green light from the family and the club. I went down with Richard and just seeing him in that ward was . . . terrible. Richard is good in those situations — if there's a sombre moment, he's good at saying something to change the mood. But you could see the strain on his mother's face . . . I had never met his mother before. And his girlfriend, I forget her name . . .

BARRISTER
Miss Jennifer Marceau?

201

GRAHAM ROWNTREE
Yeah, tough times.

BARRISTER
It is my information that you watched a DVD of
the incident with Mr Cockerill?

GRAHAM ROWNTREE
Yes, we were asked as expert witnesses to take a
look at it. It was like being asked to watch a
horror video or something you don't want to see.

BARRISTER
What did you see?

GRAHAM ROWNTREE
You see them training. You see a couple of scrums
collapse and then they stop for a drinks break and
he makes this speech about the Scots and the
upcoming game. 'If they try to come around the
outside,' he says, 'we are going to fucking drive
through them and keep them straight.' Typical
Leicester chit-chat. And then they start scrummaging again and it happens. Harrowing. He lost his
shape immediately and his head went under him.
I'm watching it thinking: No!

BARRISTER
How did it happen?

GRAHAM ROWNTREE
I've seen a lot of scrums collapse but this was a
freak. Normally you will go to your knee first or
your arm, but to go straight down on your head!

And it happened so quick. Normally the impact is staggered . . . somebody will go down, and somebody else will go down and kind of car crash in behind them. But this was instant. There was only one place for all the pressure to go. Awful.

BARRISTER
Did Mr Garforth attend the viewing of the DVD?

GRAHAM ROWNTREE
No, it was just me and Richard.

BARRISTER
Did he visit Mr Hampson in hospital?

GRAHAM ROWNTREE
I'm not sure whether he did or not.

22

4 February 2005. A cold and wet Friday evening at the Gwent Dragons ground in Newport. I'm sitting in a corner of the visitors' changing room with my head between my hands listening to the torment of defeat.

'Fucking hell!'

'How the fuck did that happen?'

'We were clueless!'

'Shit!'

'Fucking hell!'

The opening game of the Under-21 Six Nations Championship has just ended. We have been thoroughly outplayed by Wales. No Grand Slam glory for us this year and my season of woe continues. Just five out of ten for me tonight; like the team I must do better.

An empty beer can comes flying through an open window and crashes on to the floor. A bunch of yobs have rushed down from the terraces to offer their commiserations . . .

'Have a drink on us, boyos!'

'English wankers!'

'Fuck off back to London!'

'That will fucking teach you!'

Charming.

We shower and change and return to the team hotel — a Hilton on the outskirts of Newport. It has been a week since we came together for the game and my room feels like a prison cell. I float the idea of a few beers in Cardiff. Richard Blaze, the Worcester second row, and James Welwood, the Wasps centre, are up for it. So is Michael Cusack.

We take a taxi into the city, flirt briefly with Charlotte Church (unfortunately I hadn't waxed my chest) in a club and return to the hotel shortly after two. Nigel Redman, the forwards coach, is not impressed: 'Clearly you weren't that bothered about losing or you wouldn't have gone out,' he says. What bollocks! It wasn't about losing or lacking passion for my country . . . I had to get out, I needed a release. I felt *trapped* . . . I don't yet understand the meaning of that word.

A week later, we lose our second game of the Championships to France at Franklin's Gardens. Seven out of ten for me — I've played better, we've played better and probably deserve to win, but it's another defeat, another *disaster* . . . I don't yet understand the meaning of that word.

23

Scene 17: INTERIOR — COURTROOM — DAY

Darren Garforth has entered the tribunal. He is wearing jeans and a casual blue jacket and shirt and appears sullen.

BARRISTER
Mr Garforth, a man of few words by all accounts.

DARREN GARFORTH
Yes.

BARRISTER
But of great deeds on the rugby field.

DARREN GARFORTH
Thank you very much.

BARRISTER
And Mr Hampson's all-time hero according to a recent interview in the Sunday Times.

DARREN GARFORTH
Yes, I saw that . . . Very kind of Matt.

BARRISTER
You are from Coventry?

DARREN GARFORTH
Yes, that's right, Coventry kid.

BARRISTER
A 'Cov Skin'.

DARREN GARFORTH
That's right. Cov Skin.

BARRISTER
You described yourself once as a 'tubular executive'?

DARREN GARFORTH
(Smiles) Cracking line, that one, but I'm afraid it was someone else's. Still, it made me sound very important, so I was quite happy to associate myself with the description.

BARRISTER
And what would your description be, Mr Garforth?

DARREN GARFORTH
I'm a scaffolder. My father's business. I was in it straight from school.

BARRISTER
How did you start playing rugby?

DARREN GARFORTH
My father, Jim, was a good footballer and was on the books for Coventry City but broke his leg at eighteen. Football was also my preferred sport. I played for Folly Lane in Coventry and was quite decent. One week the game was called off because of a frozen pitch and I was walking home — a walk of about a mile and a half — when this

207

minibus full of lads pulled up and asked if I wanted a game. I had all my kit so I said 'yeah' and that was it. They put me in at tight-head and I have played rugby since.

BARRISTER
You abandoned your football career?

DARREN GARFORTH
Yeah. I rang them up the following day and said, 'Look, I don't want to play football no longer. I'll start playing rugby and see how I get on.'

BARRISTER
How old were you?

DARREN GARFORTH
Seventeen.

BARRISTER
What was it about rugby that appealed to you?

DARREN GARFORTH
They put me in at tight-head against a side called Barker Butts, who were the best side in Coventry. Their whole front row were Warwickshire players and they gave me a bit of a roughing up . . . Well, a bit of mouth. At the end of the game, the prop came over and I thought he was going to give me a slap but he put his hand out and said, 'Well done.' We went and had a bath together and a few pints afterwards. I thought: Bloody hell! My type of game.

BARRISTER
You joined Leicester in 1991?

DARREN GARFORTH
That's right, yeah.

BARRISTER
And played in 300 games for them?

DARREN GARFORTH
Three hundred and forty-eight.

BARRISTER
Three hundred and forty-eight.

DARREN GARFORTH
Not that I am counting.

BARRISTER
And twenty-five caps for England.

DARREN GARFORTH
That's right, yeah.

BARRISTER
And you were a member of the 'ABC' club?

DARREN GARFORTH
Yes, with Richard and Graham.

BARRISTER
Do you remember your first game together?

DARREN GARFORTH

Well, I didn't really know Graham at all. We'd played together in training sessions and what have you, but I knew Richard because he had played with my brother, Joe, at Warwickshire and the Midlands and they were good mates. So I knew Richard quite well. I knew what to expect of him.

BARRISTER

Did you expect this of him?
The barrister holds up a copy of In Your Face — Cockerill's controversial (he never played for England again after it was published in 1999) autobiography.

GARFORTH

(Smiles) You expect everything with Richard.

BARRISTER

If it would please the tribunal I will read a short extract:

Playing for Newbold was all about physical intimidation. Most junior rugby is no different, and I loved it. We could mix it with the best at Coventry Colts as well. One day we played Mosely Colts and a scuffle erupted, involving me and Joe Garforth, Daz's brother, among others. Joe's dad, Jim, was watching and he came on to the pitch to split us up, whereupon the Mosely number 8 ran over and smacked him one. That was the signal for a mass brawl involving players and spectators. Joe Garforth is a handful at the best of times but once he saw his father being hit, he got hold of this

Mosely bloke — who was a big bugger — by the hair and started whacking his head against the wire fence that surrounded the pitch. Anyway, the game eventually resumed and we won. Everyone trooped back down the tunnel, in the middle of the stand, towards the dressing rooms; ours was on the right and the visitors' on the left. Mosely went in first, as the visitors, and I was following Joe Garforth down the tunnel. We were soulmates, he'd follow me anywhere and I'd follow him, sort of thing. What does Joe do? Instead of turning right into our dressing room, he turns left and follows Mosely into theirs. I go with him, and see him go straight up to this number 8 and drop a head-butt on him! It all kicks off again in the changing room. The story even made the Daily Telegraph and The Times. Joe is a smaller version of Daz, a scaffolder, a rough diamond, salt of the earth. We'd have taken on the world.

The barrister finishes reading and places the book on his stand.

BARRISTER
Would this be an accurate portrayal of your brother, Mr Garforth? He seems a rather . . . fiery man?

GARFORTH
(Smiles) He was a little bit, yeah.

BARRISTER
You wouldn't be as fiery, would you?

DARREN GARFORTH
I don't know . . . It depends, really.

BARRISTER
It depends?

DARREN GARFORTH
It's a difficult question to answer, isn't it? I can be quite fiery. But I can be quite mellow at times as well.

BARRISTER
Did you have a mentor, Mr Garforth? Someone who taught you the game?

DARREN GARFORTH
The lads who picked me up the first time I played were from Coventry Saracens. There was a chap there called Brian Hancocks who ran the club and looked after the Colts team. He was a legend of a man, a prop forward, and he showed me a lot of tricks. He used to drive us all over the place and his enthusiasm was inspirational. He was old school, a great bloke, and that's probably what I got my love of the sport from.

BARRISTER
How did you become a Leicester player?

DARREN GARFORTH
I played with the Colts for a couple of seasons and then spent three years at Nuneaton in Division 2, where Dean Richards's father was one of the coaches, and that's how the contact was

made. Dean rang me up one Sunday lunchtime when I was down the pub having a drink. I got home and my missus said, 'You'll never guess who has been on the phone! Dean Richards wants you in for training on Tuesday night after work.'

BARRISTER
You were working? The game was still amateur then?

DARREN GARFORTH
Yes, it was. I played for four years as an amateur at Leicester and eight years as a professional.

BARRISTER
Your career was winding down when Mr Hampson joined the club?

DARREN GARFORTH
Yeah. He was there two years, I think, before I retired.

BARRISTER
He described you in that Sunday Times interview as his mentor. He said he got the impression that you liked him, and took a shine to him?

DARREN GARFORTH
It's true.

BARRISTER
What did you like about him?

DARREN GARFORTH
I liked him because he was a fairly quiet kid but could do what was needed. And I'm a bit like that. I'm the same.

BARRISTER
So you saw a bit of yourself in him?

DARREN GARFORTH
Yeah. He was aggressive when he needed to be — not stupidly aggressive, which some people are — but when he needed to be. He stood up and dished it out, which is probably what I would have done.

BARRISTER
Now you didn't actually retire after leaving Leicester, did you?

DARREN GARFORTH
That's right. I left Tigers and went coaching at Nuneaton.

BARRISTER
And Mr Hampson joined you at Nuneaton shortly before his injury?

DARREN GARFORTH
Yes, he did. Richard was keen to get him some game time. The problem with these academies is that they don't play enough games against blokes and, when I heard there was a chance of him coming over, I said, 'Yeah, he needs that if he wants to improve.' It's no good playing against

kids week-in, week-out. But the problem with all these big clubs now is that they don't bring the players through.

BARRISTER
They will go and buy someone?

DARREN GARFORTH
Exactly. When I left they bought Julian White. There is so much depending on it now, isn't there? So much money involved. So they just go and buy from overseas and the kids don't get nurtured as well as they could do.

BARRISTER
What do you remember of Mr Hampson's spell at Nuneaton?

DARREN GARFORTH
I remember him joining. I used to play on the bench to help out and what have you . . . If there was any sticky games and we needed to do something I used to play on the bench. He was doing all right. He knew what he was doing. He could have made a good professional I think.

BARRISTER
He was doing all right?

DARREN GARFORTH
Yes, he was.

BARRISTER
But if he was doing all right, why didn't you play

him more? I refer to the league game at Launceston in January when you played and started Mr Hampson on the bench?

DARREN GARFORTH
I can't remember that game or what happened. It's difficult because . . . you know, I had been there and done it all, hadn't I? And it was probably a game we needed to win.

BARRISTER
You didn't rate him, did you, Mr Garforth? That's the bottom line.

DARREN GARFORTH
No, that's not true. The thing is . . . I didn't want to play again when I joined Nuneaton, I just wanted to be a coach. But you got forced . . . Well, not forced, but I am a bit of a soft git at times and we were under pressure to avoid relegation. So I played more than what I wanted to, to be honest, but because I didn't rate him . . . Crikey! No. And what age was he then, twenty-two?

BARRISTER
He had just turned twenty.

DARREN GARFORTH
See! It's very young, especially for a tight-head. I never joined Leicester until I was twenty-five. I had six or seven years of kicking around in the lower divisions, meeting people and learning about it.

BARRISTER
There was an altercation after that game, wasn't there, Mr Garforth?

DARREN GARFORTH
An altercation?

BARRISTER
A fight. Mr Hampson gave you a punch.

DARREN GARFORTH
(Laughs) Well, you know what it's like when you have a few beers. We used to do some right silly things at Leicester on the bus after games and this was the same. I was holding the back seat with a couple of the Nuneaton lads and having a fight for it, and what have you, and he just came over and gave me one straight in the eye. A good punch as well, my eye was nearly closed by the time I got home. But it was nothing. I blamed it on too much booze.

BARRISTER
Do you remember where you were when you heard about his injury?

DARREN GARFORTH
Yes. I had just come in from work and somebody rang me — I think it was Dorian West, or it might have been Dusty.

BARRISTER
How did you feel about it?

217

DARREN GARFORTH
For the first twelve months I found it really difficult to . . . I didn't want to go to any of his
dinners . . .

BARRISTER
The fund-raising dinners?

DARREN GARFORTH
Yes . . . And in fact I didn't. It was bad. I just felt
sick.

BARRISTER
Have you seen the recording of what happened?

DARREN GARFORTH
No, I don't think I could watch that.

BARRISTER
Did you visit him in hospital?

DARREN GARFORTH
No. I knew he would be asking about me because
I was his bloody idol but that made it harder . . . I
just felt that I couldn't face up to him really . . . I
don't know what it was . . . I mean, I had nothing
to do with the accident but I just felt that I
couldn't go and see him. And it took me a long
time to get over it . . . It was probably eighteen
months before I saw him again.

BARRISTER
And how did you feel about it then?

218

DARREN GARFORTH

Well, he's an inspiring bloke, isn't he? People moan about this and that, but when you look at what he has had to deal with . . . Christ! He has obviously had some great support, but ultimately it is all to do with him because you can go one way or the other, can't you? And he has obviously decided to roll up his sleeves.

24

Night fever in Dublin. I'm sprinting through the streets of Temple Bar wearing black leather shoes and a blue Hackett suit, chasing a rickshaw carrying Haskell and two birds. 'Keep going, you fat bastard,' he guffaws. My feet are starting to blister, I've a dead leg, a cut lip and my hair is matted with sweat but pain has rarely felt so good.

Three hours have passed since our Six Nations win against Ireland at Donnybrook and we've stormed every bar from the team hotel to the river Liffey. The city is buzzing. Haskell flags down a rickshaw. I chase him through a web of cobbled streets to a club in Temple Bar. Matt Cornwell and Tom Varndell are chatting in a corner. We pull up some chairs and are joined soon afterwards by Blaze, Cusack, Mark Hopley, Sean Cox, Ryan Davis and Neil Briggs — the hell-raising heavyweights. Toby Flood is made to drink an absinthe for each of the six penalties he missed and is soon *hors de combat*. A round of vodkas is followed by a round of strawpedos and showmungos and flaming sambucas. Everywhere you look, there's a blue Hackett suit with a smile on his face and his eye on some skirt. There's a lot of drinking and a lot of sniffing. Only the strong survive. I leave with Cusack and two smashing-looking Bolton girls. We have rucked our teammates off the park.

★ ★ ★

Two weeks and three days later, on the morning of Monday, 14 March, I'm in my car driving north to the Hilton in Northampton to rejoin the squad for our final game of the Championship, against Scotland. I've played well in the defeat of Italy and had four dates with Jennie since the blowout in Dublin and I feel . . . different, sharper, emboldened. 'Time to Grow', a favourite song by Lemar, is playing on the radio.

My time has come.

25

Scene 18: INTERIOR — COURTROOM — DAY

Matt Hampson has been called to the tribunal. He is wearing a crisp black suit and is accompanied by his carers, Dean Clarke and Jacqui Pochin. His parents, Phil and Anne, and siblings, Amy and Tom, are also in attendance.

BARRISTER
Mr Hampson, it is the morning of Tuesday, 15 March 2005 and you are just about to leave the Hilton Hotel in Northampton for the training ground at Franklin's Gardens with the England Under-21 rugby team. Can you explain to the tribunal, please, how the morning unfolds?

MATT HAMPSON
(Smiles) Do I have to?

BARRISTER
Well, that is why we are here.

MATT HAMPSON
Yes, of course, I'm sorry, it's just . . . Hindsight is a great thing but it can also be a bad thing and it's healthier for me to look forward rather than back. But I understand you have a job to do and will endeavour to do my best to aid you in that task.

BARRISTER
Thank you, Mr Hampson.

MATT HAMPSON
That was the good news. The bad news is that my memories are pretty sketchy. I have been following the testimony of the other witnesses ... Tony Spreadbury ... Matt Cornwell ... and I find their perspective interesting. And I was particularly interested in what Daz and Wig and Cockers had to say ...

BARRISTER
For the record, that's Mr Garforth, Mr Rowntree and Mr Cockerill?

MATT HAMPSON
Yes, I'm sorry ...

BARRISTER
Please continue, Mr Hampson.

MATT HAMPSON
I was shocked at how it affected Daz. Why should he feel any guilt? And I was thrilled that Wig and Cockers rated me. One of the harsher lessons you learn when you spend two years in a hospital ward is that you are really just a number ... All those highly qualified doctors and nurses, they look on you as just a number. And I always thought that was the way rugby players were produced. We didn't matter. They didn't care. We were just numbers ... But I was not just a number. They did care and they were affected by

223

what happened to me. And to hear them say, 'He was a good player' means the world to me because I never thought of myself as a good player. I just wanted to earn their respect.

BARRISTER
What do you remember about that morning?

MATT HAMPSON
I think I was rooming with a guy called Dan Smith. He was a second row at Bath. They used to call him 'Test Match' because he used to have to do everything at Test Match standard. He was really keen.

BARRISTER
What do you mean by really keen?

MATT HAMPSON
Well, you would go out and play a game of touch rugby as a warm-up. You would drop the ball and he would be like 'Urrrggghhh!' You know? Really over the top.

BARRISTER
He was intense?

MATT HAMPSON
Yeah, nice lad, though. We got on well.

BARRISTER
So you would have chatted to him in the room the previous night?

MATT HAMPSON
Well, I think I spent most of the night on the phone to my girlfriend, Jennie. I would have slipped out to the corridor and he would have gone to bed early . . . as you would before a Test Match.

BARRISTER
What time did your day begin next morning?

MATT HAMPSON
Out of bed probably . . . half-seven . . . eight . . . Go down and have breakfast . . . Maybe have a bit of a meeting for half an hour with the coaches before going to the training ground.

BARRISTER
What was the meeting about on the morning in question?

MATT HAMPSON
I can't remember. It was our final game of the Championships. We had been together on and off for about six weeks and, you know, one training session rolls into another when you have been away for that long.

BARRISTER
How did you get from the hotel to the training ground?

MATT HAMPSON
(Smiles) I think I drove . . . Yeah, I'm pretty certain I took the car.

BARRISTER
Why are you smiling?

MATT HAMPSON
No, it's nothing.

BARRISTER
Why are you so certain you took the car?

MATT HAMPSON
(Laughs) Because for weeks afterwards, when I was lying in intensive care, it was all I could think about — there was a porn video in my portable DVD player in a bag with some other stuff and I was worried my mother would find it.

BARRISTER
(Smiles) And did she?

MATT HAMPSON
First thing she put her hand on.

BARRISTER
Have you watched the DVD that Mr Cockerill referred to?

MATT HAMPSON
Of the accident? Yes, I've watched it once with my father . . . I think I was in a good mood that day.

BARRISTER
Would you mind talking us through it now?

MATT HAMPSON
I'll do my best.

A large white screen is wheeled into the courtroom.
A clerk places an RFU recording of the training session into a machine and the viewing commences.
The morning is cold and grey and overcast as the
squad take to the field and begin to warm up. Matt
Hampson is wearing shorts and an orange-coloured
track top adorned with the logo (O2) of the team
sponsor. The barrister pauses the tape and identifies
James Haskell who is wearing the same coloured top,
Matt Cornwell, who is injured and watching from the
sideline; and Michael Cusack, who is flying into a
tackle bag. He also identifies Nigel Redman, the
team's forward coach, and Tony Spreadbury, the
international referee who will supervise the session.
After ten hits on the scrum machine, two packs (A
and B) are formed for a series of contested scrums in
different areas of the field. 'That's your mark,'
Spreadbury announces, scraping a line with his boot
as the front rows prepare to bind and engage.

BARRISTER
Can we just hold it there for a moment, please?
Thank you. Now, Mr Hampson, can you explain
what is happening here? Mr Spreadbury has called
the mark so you first have to bind, is that right?

MATT HAMPSON
Yeah, the referee makes a mark where the
knock-on has been and we have to bind and get
ready to go. I always liked to get there first and
get bound up quickly because there is nothing

227

worse than seeing the other front row crouched and ready to go.

BARRISTER
So you move quickly into position and then you bind. Is that correct?

MATT HAMPSON
Yeah. At Tigers, Daz always taught us that the tight-head was to bind with the hooker before the loose-head came in, but it was the opposite at England — the loose-head had to bind with the hooker first, and that used to unsettle me a bit. I never thought I got as good a bind, but that was the way it was.

BARRISTER
Okay, so we are watching you bind here with the pack A front row.

MATT HAMPSON
Yeah, Neil Briggs is the hooker and Martin Halsall is the loose-head. So, as you can see, Briggsy binds with Halsall, then me, and then he gives the signal for the second row to come in. Sometimes they'll start pushing and you'll have to give them a bollicking because you need to be nice and steady before you crouch and if they are moving you around you're fucked basically. You need to be poised and ready to go, ready to fire like a sprinter . . . on my toes . . . arse in the air . . . head up . . . arching my back and looking up through my eyebrows.

BARRISTER
And you are looking at the other prop? You are looking at your rival?

MATT HAMPSON
No, you are looking at the gap where you are going to hit. And the other prop is the same — he is looking at the gap where he is going to hit. The start is the most important bit — it's like a 100 m sprint. If you don't get out of the blocks quick you are fucked basically.

BARRISTER
Who is packing down with Mr Cusack in pack B?

MATT HAMPSON
Wayne Thompson is the tight-head and Dave Ward is hooker. Now watch what happens when we engage . . . Bang! Did you see that? I've beaten him on the hit.

BARRISTER
Can you explain that please, Mr Hampson?

MATT HAMPSON
The tight-head's job is to lead the scrum in and to dominate his opposite number so the scrum goes forward. In this one, I've beaten Cusack to the hit. I've got there first and have the upper hand.

BARRISTER
You didn't like Mr Cusack, did you? Tell me about the altercation you had earlier that morning? There was a punch-up according to Mr Haskell?

MATT HAMPSON
I'm not sure that was the day of the accident. It might have been the week before.

BARRISTER
But the enmity between you is pretty obvious from the recording. You are not exactly blowing kisses at each other.

MATT HAMPSON
No, that's true. Haskell would often complain about that. 'We're training,' he'd say. 'We shouldn't be going at each other like this. You're a fucking nause, Hambo!' But training for me was almost as important as playing games. It was a place to earn respect and show what you could do.

BARRISTER
I'll repeat the question. You did not like Mr Cusack, did you?

MATT HAMPSON
Not true. I thought he was a good lad. We had a good night out in Dublin together but we were competitive and always at each other in games. We both wanted the same thing, we both wanted to be top dog, but I always thought I was better than him . . . And still do.

The barrister orders the clerk to play the final frame of the recording. The two packs have engaged fifteen times during the session; four of the scrums have collapsed; several have been reset; Hampson has been penalized once by Spreadbury for not binding properly but is scrummaging well. The barrister orders the clerk to play the final frame of the recording. Redman has called a drinks break. The coach is commending the players on their work and reminding them of how well they played against Ireland. Richard Blaze, the second row, is worried about the Scottish scrum and their habit of 'crabbing' prior to engagement. 'Then we'll hit in and fucking pile through them,' Hampson says. 'If they are coming around, put the ball in and we'll go all the way through them. Let's fuck them up, yeah?' The session resumes. Spreadbury calls the mark, 'Crouch and hold.' Neil Briggs lifts his hands above his head and drops his arms over the shoulders of Halsall and Hampson. Tom Ryder and Dan Smith have slotted in behind. Haskell and David Seymour are linked on the flanks. Mark Hopley stands at number 8. Pack A is ready. Dave Ward lifts his hands above his head and drops his arms on the shoulders of Cusack and Thompson. Sean Cox and Richard Blaze have slotted in behind. Dr Tim Weighman and Tom Rees are linked on the flanks. Will Skinner stands at number 8. Pack B is ready. Spreadbury gives the order and the packs engage but the scrum collapses almost immediately. The sixteen players pile into a heap and slowly regain their footing, but one hasn't moved. Tom Ryder reaches down to pull his team-mate off the floor but then straightens and backs away. There is a look of complete horror on his face . . .

BARRISTER
Thank you. You can stop it there, please.

MATT HAMPSON
I can't remember if my bind slipped or if his bind slipped or if we both slipped . . . Anyway, we went down. Bang! I hit the ground and I'm suddenly in this position where everybody is on top of me. I can't breathe! I'm on the floor! Everybody is on top of me! I feel like I am standing on my head! I can't feel my legs! I thought I was going to die . . . Everybody says you see your life flash in front of your eyes, but it doesn't work like that. It happens too quick. You cannot even think. I could not breathe. That was it. The next thing I remember was the dark in intensive care.

BARRISTER
You say you can't remember if your bind slipped?

MATT HAMPSON
Yes.

BARRISTER
But you remember taking a bind?

MATT HAMPSON
I would always take a bind — it's dangerous not to and the scrum can collapse at any time. If you watch it again, as I hit in my right hand goes across to bind with Cusack, but I must have missed his shirt, or he missed mine, and we went down.

BARRISTER
What if, say, the tight-head made a conscious decision to slip his bind, Mr Hampson? Would there be any advantage to be gained?

232

MATT HAMPSON.
It's illegal.

BARRISTER
I'll repeat the question: would there be any advantage to be gained?

MATT HAMPSON
Sure. It would allow him to bore in on the hooker and go straight through the middle. If you could get away with it, you would try it, but there would be no point.

BARRISTER
Did you ever try it?

MATT HAMPSON
I can genuinely say that I would never . . . I have done it before, but it was too risky because generally the scrum would collapse. There was no point in doing it.

BARRISTER
But you have done it before?

MATT HAMPSON
Yes, I think all props have tried it.

BARRISTER
But if there was no point in doing it, why did you try?

MATT HAMPSON
I did it because I got away with it, but I would

not get away with it with Tony Spreadbury. He's too good a referee.

BARRISTER
But weren't you penalized at least once during the session for failing to take a correct bind?

MATT HAMPSON
Yes, I was.

BARRISTER
(Smiles) So he's not that good a referee?

MATT HAMPSON
Well, like I say to the young lads at Oakham — you do what you can get away with. You bend the rules to your own advantage.

BARRISTER
Because that's what you were taught?

MATT HAMPSON
Yes, it was.

BARRISTER
To be hard and ruthless and dominant?

MATT HAMPSON
Yes.

BARRISTER
To never take a backward step?

MATT HAMPSON
Never.

BARRISTER
I put it to you, Mr Hampson, that when you faced
Mr Cusack in that almost fatal scrum, your mind
wasn't filled with charity.

MATT HAMPSON
No, it wasn't.

BARRISTER
I put it to you, Mr Hampson, that you were prepared to use every trick in the book to gain an
edge and were both cheating like buggery?

MATT HAMPSON
Cheating is a strong word.

BARRISTER
What word would you use, Mr Hampson? Be
honest now. Tell the tribunal your exact thoughts
as you looked Mr Cusack in the eye.

MATT HAMPSON
My exact thoughts? That's easy, Mr Barrister. They
were the same for every opponent and the same
for every scrum. I would have looked at Michael
Cusack and thought: I'm going to drive your head
through your fucking arse.

PART 3

LEGALLY BLOND

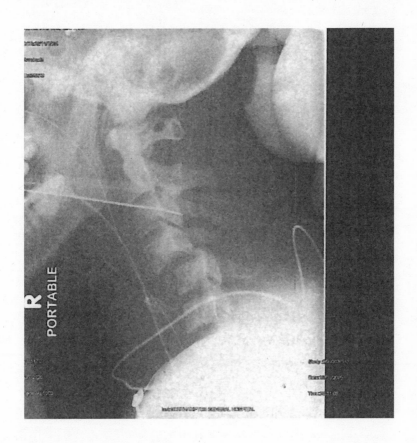

1

This is the sound.
  'ENGLAND.'
  The sweetest sound.
  'CROUCH.'
  The sound of the scrummage.
  'TOUCH.'
  The sound that gave meaning to my life.
  'PAUSE.'
  The last sound I heard.
  'ENGAGE.'
  And then there was darkness.

2

Darkness and then the haze; and then the dreams through the haze.

The dreams were weird. I'm in an airport somewhere in France and people are running towards me, screaming about a bomb that's about to explode. A crack SAS team burst through the door and order me out of the building. There are women carrying machine guns and dressed as nurses. 'I'm Hambo. I can help you with this,' I tell them. They lead me to the bomb and I defuse it.

What do I know about bombs?

I'm in a lift heading for the bedroom of my French hotel when the light suddenly flickers and the lift stops between floors. I press the button to go up but nothing happens. I try to contact reception and press the alarm but there is no response. The doors are jammed. It's pitch dark and eerily silent. I'm trapped.

Why is it always France?

We've just beaten Wales in the Six Nations. I'm at the post-match reception, enjoying a beer with Cornwell, Haskell, Ryder and Varndell when this crazed fan appears at the top of the room and starts singing 'Bread of Heaven'.

'Put a sock in it, Taff,' we scoff. 'Did you not see the score?'

And then the bullets start flying.

The crazy fuck has a gun!

I dive under the table but am hit in the arm. Blood is gushing from an artery between my fingers. I'll be dead in minutes without help. 'You gotta save me, Cornish,' I cry. 'I'm dying.' A bullet flies over our head and splinters the table. Cornish unpacks a medical kit and starts stuffing the wound with Kerlix. 'This is what they do in *Saving Private Ryan*,' he says, knuckle deep in my arm.

What's Kerlix?

They put me in an air ambulance and whisk me to a hospital in France. I'm slipping in and out of consciousness and soaked in blood as they wheel me into the operating room. The chief nurse is sobbing hysterically. 'You couldn't stop yourself, could you?' she cries. 'I told you rugby was a dangerous sport.' It's Jennie!

How did Jennie become a nurse?

3

Darkness and then the haze, and then the dreams through the haze and then the sound following the dreams. The sound was recurrent, rhythmic, like the *whish* of a train coming down the tracks. Or a *whoosh*. Yeah, it was more of a *whoosh*. Sometimes the morphine kicked in and the dreams took over again — the dreams were terrifying. And then it would come back . . .
whooooooosh
whooooooosh
. . . as regular as clockwork.
whooooooosh
whooooooosh
. . . as constant as a watch.
whooooooosh
whooooooosh
What did it mean?

4

Scene 19: EXTERIOR — CEMETERY — FALKLAND ISLANDS — DAY

A cold winter's day near Darwin in East Falkland. A short, balding, well-dressed man is studying the inscription on a marble plaque at the entrance to a cemetery.

EL PUEBLO DE LA NACIÓN ARGENTINA
EN MEMORIA DE
LOS SOLDADOS ARGENTINOS
CAÍDOS EN ACCIÓN EN 1982

A fierce howling wind is buffeting the island. The man steps slowly across the gravel and up and down the lines of small white crosses. There are tears running down his face.

Dr ALI JAMOUS
Why did you die in this godforsaken place?

FADE TO
Scene 20: INTERIOR — COURTROOM — DAY

Phil Hampson has been called by the tribunal. He is wearing a steel-grey suit, blue shirt and yellow tie.

BARRISTER
Mr Hampson, will you tell the tribunal where you

were when you were informed of your son's accident, please?

PHIL HAMPSON
I was in the village of Whissendine, not far from where we live. I was doing a job for the author Billy Ivory — he wrote the BBC drama A Thing Called Love — very good writer and a really nice guy.

BARRISTER
What sort of job?

PHIL HAMPSON
I'm a builder. We were doing some internal renovation work on his cottage. I was upstairs plastering a wall when I got the call from my wife, Anne.

BARRISTER
What time was it?

PHIL HAMPSON
Elevenish. She was at work in Peterborough. Anne is a teacher.

BARRISTER
What did she say?

PHIL HAMPSON
She told me Matthew had had a serious accident and that he had been taken to Northampton General Hospital. She said that we should go to the hospital and that they would tell us more once we were there.

BARRISTER
You travelled to Northampton together?

PHIL HAMPSON
Yes. I arranged to meet Anne at home and we
then drove up together. We didn't know where the
hospital was. The only time I had been to
Northampton in my life was to watch Matthew
play rugby at Franklin's Gardens. We didn't say
much in the car. We were both very anxious.

BARRISTER
What time did you arrive at the hospital?

PHIL HAMPSON
We arrived just before 1 p.m. We parked the car
and, as we approached the main door of the hospital, I saw a friend of Matt's, Matthew Cornwell,
waiting for us at the entrance. He was waiting
there with Dr Weighman, the RFU doctor who had
been involved in the opposing scrum. He was still
wearing shorts and in his training gear. While
Anne was talking to Matthew Cornwell, I went
inside and was met, I think, by the registrar. I said
that I was Matt Hampson's father and I asked
what the situation was.

BARRISTER
What did the registrar say?

PHIL HAMPSON
He said 'I'm ever so sorry but your son has had a
serious neck injury.' I immediately said, 'Will he
be in a wheelchair?' The registrar said, 'Yes.' It was

shocking. I am sort of half understanding what he is saying but not really believing it. I can't take it in.

BARRISTER
I'm sorry for interrupting, Mr Hampson . . . You're saying that the registrar informed you that Matthew would not walk again.

PHIL HAMPSON
It wasn't categorical. He did not say, 'He will never walk again.' The question I asked was, 'Will he be in a wheelchair?' He said, 'Yes.'

BARRISTER
Where was Mrs Hampson at this stage?

PHIL HAMPSON
She was still outside talking to Matt Cornwell. She then came in and the registrar took us to meet Mr Kerr, who was the doctor looking after Matt. Anne's a very logical, methodical person. She is not the sort of woman who starts screaming or throwing her hands up. Her attitude was 'Right, let's have the facts. What can we do now to benefit Matthew?'

BARRISTER
And what did you do, Mr Hampson?

PHIL HAMPSON
We spoke to Mr Kerr. He told us that the X-ray showed that Matt had a dislocation, but he was now stable. He had also been sedated. I remember

Anne asking if we could see him and Mr Kerr said that we could, but that we should be aware that Matt could not talk. We were taken to this trauma unit and Matthew was there. They had cut his training gear off him; he was unconscious, sedated and breathing through a tube in his mouth. The doctors told us that there was nothing more we could do that day. They said they were going to start traction and would keep him sedated. They said there was no point in us being there and that we would be better off going home and coming back the next day.

BARRISTER
And did you go home?

PHIL HAMPSON
Yes, but even that was complicated. Matthew's car, the silver Polo, was still at the training ground in Northampton. John Cornwell — Matt's father — arranged to get it to Market Harborough, which was on our way home, and we picked it up there. The phone kept ringing. People had heard on the news and were trying to get in touch. I didn't sleep that night, neither of us did. In the morning we got up and went straight back to Northampton General and of course it was the same crap again.

BARRISTER
You're saying that nothing had changed?

PHIL HAMPSON
We arrived at about 9.30 a.m. The doctors had told us not to rush in as Matt would be still

sedated. When we arrived there seemed to be a lot of cameras and reporters outside. I did not realize it at the time but Sky TV was there. However, they did not know we were Matt's parents and we had no contact with them. We first went to have a look at Matt. He looked no different but he had a huge calliper-type thing on his head with what looked like pincers that were cutting into his temple. There were weights hanging on the end.

BARRISTER
He was having traction?

PHIL HAMPSON
Yes, they had been trying different weights to reduce the dislocation. We were then taken into a room for a meeting with Mr Kerr and Tim Weighman and a gentleman who, I think, was the chief executive of the hospital. We asked what was happening. The doctors said they were still applying traction and that it had not worked overnight. They said that there had been no positive effect and that it had not moved the dislocation whatsoever. I was not surprised. I am not a medical person but it just seemed obvious to me that a few weights would not relocate Matt's neck given the massive forces involved to cause the dislocation in the first place. They said it was 'standard procedure', but a 17 st professional prop forward does not have a standard neck!

BARRISTER
So the traction had not worked?

PHIL HAMPSON
No.

BARRISTER
What were they proposing to do next?

PHIL HAMPSON
We were told that they had been liaising with
Stoke Mandeville and that Matt needed to have
an operation to reduce the dislocation. We had
heard of Stoke Mandeville, I suppose most
people have. I didn't know then how bad it is.
I thought it was the place. I said, 'I want him
to go to Stoke Mandeville — and quick!' They
said, 'There are no beds available at Stoke
Mandeville.' I said, 'I am not interested if there
are no beds. Just get him in there.' I couldn't
accept what they were telling me.

BARRISTER
You felt they could have done more?

PHIL HAMPSON
Much more . . . Say, for example, it had been
Jonny Wilkinson or Jason Robinson? They would
have found a bed immediately. They would have
been airlifted straight to Stoke Mandeville and
been operated on within two hours. There
wouldn't have been any of the faffing about that
Matthew had at Northampton.

BARRISTER
I'm sorry, Mr Hampson . . . What do you mean by
faffing about?

249

PHIL HAMPSON
There was no sense of urgency. They didn't seem to know what they were doing! They said there was a surgeon at the hospital who could do the operation, but he was not a spinal specialist. I remember being told either that the surgeon had never done the operation before or that he had only done it a few times, but also that it was relatively straightforward and that there should be no problems. They also said 'But we can't do anything immediately because we have to send away to Nottingham to get the screws.'

BARRISTER
The screws?

PHIL HAMPSON
The surgical screws they needed for the operation. I was getting worried by this stage. I thought: This sounds really dangerous. They don't have a proper spinal unit here. They don't know what they are doing! But I still didn't appreciate the implications of the delay. Matthew's spinal cord is trapped, his nerves are dying off; he is losing more and more feeling. I said to Mr Kerr, 'If this was your son, would you want the operation carried out sooner rather than later?' The question seemed to unsettle him.

BARRISTER
What was his reply?

PHIL HAMPSON
He hesitated and said, 'Well, sooner.' Anne and I

250

became really quite upset at this point. We were worried that the delay could be a real issue. This was the first time we realized that time was an important factor in Matt's treatment, and Anne had had enough: 'I'm going to do a press release,' she said. 'I am going to say that my son has been injured playing for England and you can't even find him a hospital bed.' She phoned her sister to ask her to help produce a press release. It seemed to me that the chief executive and Mr Kerr got quite anxious. They went off and made a lot of phone calls. Suddenly, they said they would be transferring Matt to Stoke Mandeville for his operation and then back to Northampton General afterwards. He was going to be transferred by ambulance and it would not be a fast journey as they needed to take care of his neck. At the end of the meeting with the chief executive and Mr Kerr, the chief executive ushered us out of the hospital via a shortcut.

BARRISTER
A shortcut?

PHIL HAMPSON
A fire escape at the back of the hospital. It did not feel like a shortcut to me — I believe it was because they wanted to avoid us having any contact with Sky TV on our way out of the hospital.

BARRISTER
Did you have any contact? What about the press release?

PHIL HAMPSON

Anne's sister typed it up and faxed it through. I have the original copy here if you'd like to see it . . .

The barrister examines the press release and asks for some copies to be made.

Fax: 01604 702850
For attention: Tim Wayman, RFU
                              (& Anne Hampson)

Northampton Hilton

STRICTLY CONFIDENTIAL — press release

- Firstly, we would like to thank the hospital staff who are doing everything they can to help my son. They have been truly wonderful but the truth of the matter is they have also been frustrated and restricted in what they can do due to lack of resources.
- Yesterday, Matthew was injured during training. He dislocated two vertebrae in his neck which needed immediate treatment.
- He was admitted to Northampton General Hospital where he was placed immediately in an Intensive Care ward. They stabilised his breathing and placed him on traction. However it has been identified that he needs an urgent operation. This has been delayed due to lack of beds.
- Staff at the highest level have been contacting spinal injury units around the country

but have been unsuccessful in finding a vacant bed. We are worried that this delay may have an adverse effect on Matthew's recovery.

- The RFU spinal injuries consultant is based at Stoke Mandeville which is 40 miles from here. Matthew will be transported by ambulance to Stoke Mandeville but will then have to be returned to Northampton because there are no available beds. Such a journey will inevitably add to the risk.
- What are we to think when a young man who represents his country cannot get the hospital bed he needs and deserves? It is a very worrying state of affairs not just for Matthew but for all patients who are in this serious and highly distressing situation.

Please note that this is the only statement that will be provided and we now ask the media to respect the privacy of Matthew's family at this most distressing time. Thank you.

BARRISTER
Why was it faxed to the Hilton Hotel in Northampton?

PHIL HAMPSON
We couldn't get a fax number from the hospital and were told that there was no point in going to Stoke Mandeville until Matt's operation was

underway. The team were staying at the Hilton and Tim Weighman offered us the use of his room for the afternoon. We had a rest and some food, but Anne was quite upset at seeing Matthew's team-mates there.

BARRISTER
When did you issue the press release?

PHIL HAMPSON
We didn't. Matthew was transferred to Stoke Mandeville that afternoon and was operated on by Dr Jamous, the duty consultant, at 6 p.m. He was still having his operation when we arrived at the hospital and it was not until about 8 p.m that we met Dr Jamous. He invited us into his office and made us a drink. He told us that the operation had gone well and that the spinal column had been secured. He said that Matt was going to be admitted to St Andrew ward and would be staying at Stoke Mandeville.

BARRISTER
Did Dr Jamous offer you a prognosis?

PHIL HAMPSON
Not really. I asked a lot of questions. 'When will Matthew be able to talk? Will he walk again? When do they normally start moving after a neck injury?' He said that we would have to wait and see what would happen. 'Every patient is different,' he said. 'Every spinal injury is different. I cannot tell you anything.'

BARRISTER
Which is not what you want to hear?

PHIL HAMPSON
No . . . We then visited Matthew in intensive
care. He was unconscious. I thought he would be
on his own but there were three or four beds in
there . . . a couple of old people I think, dying. It
was very upsetting.

BARRISTER
Where did you spend the night?

PHIL HAMPSON
Matthew's good mate Cabbage — James Buckland
— offered us a room. His mum lives quite close to
the hospital and we stayed with her that night,
and the following night. A lovely lady, we had
never met her before.

BARRISTER
Do you remember your first conversation with
Matthew?

PHIL HAMPSON
No. It was months before he could actually
talk. He was out of it, sedated, for the first
three days but sometimes his eyes would flicker,
as if he understood what you were saying to
him.

BARRISTER
What were you saying to him?

PHIL HAMPSON
Stuff to keep his spirits up, to encourage him.
'Matt, you cannot keep a good man down, you
know that, don't you?' I'd say. 'It is not possible.'

5

Three days of darkness and dreams and a world that makes no sense to me, even when I open my eyes. Is this it? My life now. Is this real? This darkened room? This rectangular patch of ceiling above my bed? Is that really my mother looking exhausted and anxious? Is that truly my father trying to comfort me with words? Is this Filipino nurse with the clipboard, real? Was she not with the SAS when I defused the bomb in France? She was. I'm sure of it. So it's obviously the drugs. I'm obviously hallucinating. How else do I explain this bed? I feel like I'm standing and that my body has been sucked through a hole in the mattress. Where are my legs? I can't feel my legs. Where are my arms? I can't feel my arms. It has to be the drugs. Yeah, that's some powerful shit they've given me! But I'm going to wake up any minute now and everything will be okay.

6

I am lying in the darkness staring at the rectangular patch of ceiling. This is not a dream. Everything is not okay. I cannot move my head or feel a thing below my chin; someone has wedged a jam jar in my throat and run a hose-pipe up my nose. I feel nauseous and weak and incredibly thirsty. A low-pitched clicking sound has replaced my voice. I cannot speak.

My mind is racing with questions. Where am I? How long have I been here? Why can't I feel my arms and my legs? Why can't I speak? Is this it? Am I paralysed? Will I walk again? Will I play rugby again? Where is the doctor? Where are my parents? Who do I ask? How do I ask?

Some of it makes sense to me. I know I am Matt Hampson. I know I am twenty years old. I know I play for Leicester Tigers and the England Under-21s. I know I hurt myself in a collapsed scrum at Franklin's Gardens. I know I am lying flat on my back in the intensive care unit of some hospital. I know that *whoosh* is the sound of the machine that is keeping me alive. I know that sobbing is the sound of a woman with a similar injury in another bed. I know it is night. I know I feel trapped. I know I am scared. Yes, mostly I know I am scared.

7

My mother is sitting by my bed reading some of the letters and cards that have arrived at the hospital.

Dear Matt,

I would like to express how concerned I was to hear of your injury yesterday. At times like this you need to show all the courage and strength that you have demon-strated as a player and the thoughts of all the staff at Premier Rugby are with you and your family at this time. We wish you all the very best for your recovery.

With kind regards,
Howard Thomas
Chief Executive

Dear Matt,

I've been thinking about you every minute of every day and I just know that you are going to be ok. I'm keeping my fingers crossed for you all the time! And if anyone can pull through this Matt, you can. I'm so proud of you and I'll be with you every step of the way.

All my love, kisses and hugs,
Big sister Amy xxx

Matt,

We are thinking of you. We love you so much and pray that you will make a full recovery. Miss you lots,

Grandma Brenda and Grandad Fred

Dear Mr and Mrs Hampson,

On behalf of the England squad I wanted to write to you to say how sorry I was to hear of the news regarding Matt and his injury. As a father of four myself, I can only start to imagine how you must be feeling at this very difficult time.

I know that Matt is receiving excellent medical care at Stoke Mandeville and I am being regularly updated through the team doctor Simon Kemp regarding developments.

As you are aware Martin Corry and the squad are donating, through an auction, their match shirts from the game against Scotland and I hope they raise a lot of money to aid Matt's recovery. I also know that the RFU Sports Injuries Administrator has been in touch with you and he will do all he can to help.

At the time of writing we are preparing to

play Scotland but I can assure you that all of us have Matt and yourselves very much in our thoughts. If there is anything I can do to help during this time, please do not hesitate to contact me.

Yours sincerely,
Andy Robinson OBE
England Head Coach

Dear Mr and Mrs Hampson,
   I am writing on behalf of the PRA members to express our sadness about Matt's injury. I understand that he now has a permanent bed at Stoke Mandeville, and will be given the best treatment possible. It goes without saying that if you or Matt need any support over the coming months, then please do not hesitate to contact us at the PRA, and we will do our utmost to help you all through this difficult time.

Yours sincerely,
Damian Hopley
Chief Executive

To Mr & Mrs Hampson,

Just a little note to let you know how much I'm feeling for Hambo at the moment. I'm truly devastated by what's happened to him and my thoughts will be

with you and him constantly through this.
Just the phone calls and concerns I've
received from people solely because I'm his
friend speak volumes for his popularity and
character. He is a wonderful lad and a
great friend and you guys have my full
support anytime you need it. It will be a
long road but I'm confident he'll receive
everything he needs to get him through it.

With love,
Cab [James Buckland]

To Matt,

I wanted to send you my best wishes as I've
been thinking about you since your accident
and hope you are going on ok.

From Mitch Burton
Bath Rugby and England Under-18s
(We played together in Scotland.)

Bomb Head,

Thought I'd get the gayest card [picture of a
puppy spaniel on the cover] for you, hope
you like. All the lads hope you have a speedy
recovery and battle through this. We know
you will.

Get well soon,
Harry [Ellis]

8

'See you in the morning,' my father says, rising from the bedside chair. 'You looked much better today, son,' my mother chimes, caressing my forehead. She said that last night, and the night before. And like last night and the night before I smile and pretend to be brave. I don't feel brave. I feel scared. I don't want them to leave. How long has it been now? Four days? Five? A week? I'm losing track. So I look better today, but what does that mean? I'm still tied to the ventilator; I still feel like a corpse in the bed. Nobody has explained what has happened to me, or what my prognosis is. Will I walk again? Play again? Live again? These thoughts continue to haunt me. Where are the nurses? I can't see the nurses. I'm frightened of being alone and unable to speak. I'm worried about the ventilator. What happens if there's a problem? I hate the night. I can't sleep. I lie here wishing for morning and my parents' swift return. Because then I'll feel safe.

9

Two nurses are rolling me in the bed to prevent pressure sores. They are talking about the woman who has been crying every night.

'She's a jumper.'

'Really?'

'Yeah, third floor of a multistorey car park. Don't know how she survived.'

'How bad is she?'

'She'll live. C6.'

'Christ! She was lucky.'

'She obviously doesn't agree.'

10

Another card. My mother opens it and holds it in front of my eyes. 'I think this is one you should read for yourself,' she says.

Hi Matty Boy,

I hope you are feeling better and better every day. I am thinking about you all the time constantly, I really really want to come and see you as soon as possible if you want me to. As soon as you want me to visit you, let Amy know and I will come straight away. All my love and lots and lots of hugs and kisses,

Jennie xxxxxxxxxxxxxxxxxxxxxxxxxxxxxx
xxxxxxxxxxxxxxxx

I smile and count the xs . . . Forty-six is pretty impressive!

11

My lips feel like strips of parched leather. My mouth feels like the inside of a bus driver's glove. I am trying to convey how thirsty I feel to my parents but they are struggling to read my lips.

'He wants something, Anne. What's he saying?'

'I don't know, Phil.'

Can I have a drink of water, please?

'What was that, Matthew?'

'Try again, son.'

A drink of water, please?

'No, I can't . . . What do you think, Anne?'

'No, I can't make it out.'

WATER! FUCKING WATER!

'He wants a hammer or . . . a screwdriver.'

'Are you sure, Phil?'

'I'm telling you. He is asking for a screwdriver.'

I want to scream! *What the fuck would I want a screwdriver for?*

266

12

The thirst has become so unbearable that I dreamt about it last night — a dream crazier than the French bomb, the Welsh assassin and the SAS nurse combined. I was stranded on the beach of a desert island somewhere, buried to my neck in sand, and Dallaglio — the tormentor-in-chief — had placed a pint of ice-cold Robinson's Orange Squash beside my head. 'Get well soon, Hambo,' he chortled. 'This one's on Wasps.'

I tried to reach it with my mouth; I tried to lick it with my tongue; I stared at the icy rivulets running down the glass and started to cry.

13

Mum has become increasingly frustrated at not being able to lip-read and rocked up this morning with a sheet containing the alphabet. 'Okay, Matthew,' she says. 'I'm going to call out each letter and you're going to spell some words. I want you to blink once for 'yes' and twice for 'no'. Have you got that?'

Blink.

'Is there anything you want to say?'

Blink.

'Okay, let's try this: A-B-C-D-E-F-G-H-I-J-K-L-M-N-O-P-Q-R-S-T . . . '

Blink.

'First letter T?'

Blink.

'Next letter: A-B-C-D-E-F-G-H . . . '

Blink.

'H! Second letter H.'

Blink.

'Okay, third letter: A-B-C-D-E-F-G-H-I . . . '

Blink.

'I! Third letter I?'

Blink.

'A-B-C-D-E-F-G-H-I-J-K-L-M-N-O-P-Q-R . . . '

Blink.

'R! Fourth letter R?'

Blink.

'T-H-I-R . . . THIRST?'

Blink.

'You're thirsty? You'd like a drink?'

Blink.

'Well, unfortunately the ear, nose and throat specialist won't allow you to have a drink yet, but what I can do is swab your mouth.'

Blink.

She started rubbing the inside of my mouth with a swab. I grabbed it with my teeth and sucked until it was dry.

14

Eleven days have passed since Matt's accident but it's business as usual in the World Point-to-Point and a large crowd has gathered on this Easter Saturday afternoon for the Puckeridge fixture at Horseheath racecourse near Newmarket. In the opening Club Members race, the 2–1 favourite Catch On is travelling beautifully up the hill under jockey Paul Taiano, when it stumbles on take-off at the open ditch. We hear the crack of thorn and birch as the horse crashes through the fence. We hear the gasp from the crowd as the 48-year-old jockey is fired into the ground. We see a temporary screen being erected and the horse being put down; we see the prostrate jockey being rolled on to a stretcher and follow him to the air ambulance as it lifts into the clouds.

PAUL TAIANO
First time in a helicopter and I can't even get a window seat.

FADE TO

Scene 22: INTERIOR — STUDY — EVENING

As Taiano is being airlifted, Anne Hampson is typing an email to friends in the study of her home in Cold Overton.

Dear All,

Have not had access to the internet for 2 days so have been unable to update. Yesterday seemed more positive, he was able to drink small amounts of liquid with a straw, had his hair washed and asked to be propped up in bed. We had a brilliant nurse who was able to lip-read and help us communicate with Matt. He was less frustrated and his temp dropped by one degree. However today he was not good, the temp has risen higher and he seemed very low. We organised a visit for Dawsey and Cornwell (two of his rugby team-mates). The sister felt it would make him feel brighter. I have just called now and the lads are there, visiting. The sister said she is hearing things she doesn't know if she should be hearing but she is listening anyway!!! We have come home for 16 hours (I have been away all week and need a short emotional break) our other children are coming back with us and we have been given the keys to my cousins' friend's house who lives in Harpenden (35 minutes drive). I will be staying all week and the family will join me next weekend. I think Matt will need one or two visitors this week so will ring round. It's going to be a long painful slow job. Our first target is to get him breathing independently.

Love Anne

15

Jennie leans across the bed and kisses me softly on the lips. She has brought me a teddy and a DVD (*The Incredibles*) and looks happy to see me. But not as happy as I am to see her. My first thought: She looks beautiful. My second: Everything will be okay.

16

I have been propped up in bed for the first time.
Oh fuck!
Not sure I like the view.
Oh fuck!
All these wires and tubes and monitors . . .
Oh fuck!
My dormant foot protruding from the sheet . . .
Oh fuck!
I've been staring at it now for twenty minutes . . .
Oh fuck!
Willing it to move with every fibre of my being . . .
Oh fuck!
But not a flicker . . .
Oh fuck!
I can't even wiggle a toe . . .
Oh fuck!
This is bad.

17

Annie Wilkes, as anyone familiar with the psychotic nurse in Stephen King's brilliant novel *Misery* knows, does not care much for profanity. 'It has no nobility,' she complains to her captive, Paul Sheldon, before taking a sledgehammer to his foot. So I knew I was in trouble this morning when her *doppelgänger* here on the St Andrew ward was deployed to address a problem with my feeding drip. The tube running up my nose and down my throat had kinked and blocked in my stomach and had to be withdrawn. My face is the most sensitive part of my body but she grabbed the tube with her big, stubby fingers and started yanking it out of my nose like a rope in a tug of war. The pain was excruciating. My mother and sister started crying. There was blood and nose cartilage splattered all over the sheets. And now, every time she comes near me I feel the terror of Paul Sheldon.

18

Okay, so call me legally blond but I have never given a moment's consideration as to how people in wheelchairs went to the toilet. 'Don't they just grab a *Daily Mail* and spend twenty minutes on the shitter like the rest of us?' So this morning was a rude awakening. It was just after six when the nurse (thankfully not Annie Wilkes) arrived with a disposable Inco sheet and rolled me on to my side. 'Just putting your suppository in,' she said. Then she proceeded to do the same to every patient in the ward. I lay for an hour 'baking' and listening to my neighbours . . .

'Fucking hell! That was a smelly one.'

'Christ! That Indian did not go through me that well.'

. . . but could not see the funny side. Then, after the nurse had returned to clean us up, breakfast was served.

Bon appétit.

19

Every day brings a new and unpleasant twist. Today, it was a visit from one of Dr Jamous's underlings — a rather stern-faced young lady — who arrived at my bed with a clipboard and pin and proceeded to jab me from chin to toe.

'Do you feel that?'

'No.'

'That?'

'No.'

'Do you feel that?'

'No.'

'That?'

'No?'

'Do you feel that?'

'No.'

That?

'No.'

And then, oblivious to the fact that she had reduced me to a blubbering mess, she left without saying a word.

20

Scene 23: INTERIOR — HOSPITAL — DAY

A large bluebottle is feasting on an abandoned slice of pizza in the kitchen of the St Andrew ward at Stoke Mandeville Hospital. The table is littered with a discarded pizza box, an empty Pepsi can and a newspaper.

THE INDEPENDENT
Monday, 6 June 2005

SUPERBUG KILLS 12 AT SPINAL UNIT AS DOCTORS WARN OF NEW THREAT TO NHS.
By Jeremy Laurance, Health Editor

An outbreak of a lethal new bug at a leading specialist hospital has claimed 12 lives and is posing a grave new threat to the NHS, doctors have warned. More than 300 patients have been infected with the bug, a virulent new strain of Clostridium difficile, at Stoke Mandeville hospital in Buckinghamshire, known for its world-famous spinal injuries unit supported by the former disc jockey Sir Jimmy Savile. But all attempts to control the infection, which causes severe diarrhoea that can be life threatening, have failed.

The disclosure raises new concerns about

NHS hygiene following a series of scares over the superbug MRSA and the pressure on hospitals to hit waiting list targets.

Cases of C. difficile have soared from fewer than 1000 in 1990 to 43,672 in 2004 but it has not received the same attention as MRSA. Latest figures show there were 943 deaths in 2003, a 38 per cent rise in two years. A similar number of people died from MRSA in the same year, with 955 people dying from the infection, a 30 per cent increase in two years.

The bug poses a particular threat to hospitals because it produces hardy spores that are resistant to normal methods of cleaning and can persist on hands, clothes, bedding and furniture, transmitting the infection to new patients.

Alcohol gels used by medical staff to clean their hands between patients, in an attempt to combat MRSA, are ineffective against the spores of C. difficile. The Health Protection Agency (HPA) said washing in soap and water was necessary to eliminate the bug and powerful disinfectants were needed instead of ordinary detergents to clean the wards.

The outbreak at Stoke Mandeville, which started in 2003, is caused by a more virulent strain of the bacterium closely related to a type found in the US and Canada, which is more infectious and harder to destroy. Stoke Mandeville is the only hospital in Britain where large numbers of cases of the new strain have been recorded. The hospital treats patients with severe spinal problems who may remain there for months, putting them at a high risk of hospital infections.

Doctors at the hospital blamed managers' 'obsession' with hitting government waiting list targets for the failure to eradicate the bug, and claimed HPA advice had been ignored. In a statement, Buckinghamshire Hospitals NHS Trust said 225,000 people had been seen at the hospital in the last 18 months and everything possible was being done to contain the outbreak. The average age of the patients who died was 85, although it is understood some younger patients have been affected. The number of infections peaked, then fell and then peaked a second time.

Dr Andrew Kirk, director of Infection Prevention and Control, said: 'Infection control is one of the top priorities for this trust. We are adopting the most up-to-date technology to ensure that we minimise any risk of patients acquiring infection while in hospital. We do however need to be realistic about the prevalence of these bacteria in our community and ensure that patients who acquire it are effectively and quickly treated to prevent any further spread.'

A spokesman for the HPA said the pressures on the hospital had hindered its capacity to deal with the outbreak. 'We have met with them quite a lot of times and we have gone into a lot of detail about the measures they should take,' she said. 'We wanted them to keep all the infected patients in one ward but that meant they could be left with empty beds.

They didn't want to turn patients away and they have had difficulty obtaining sufficient staff to implement all the measures immediately.'

FADE TO

Scene 24: INTERIOR — COURTROOM — DAY

Anne Hampson has been called to the tribunal. She is accompanied by her husband, Phil.

BARRISTER
Mrs Hampson, could you please describe to the tribunal the meeting with Dr Jamous on the evening on 16 March 2005?

ANNE HAMPSON
We saw him in his office just after the operation. He was wearing his surgeon's outfit. 'I will make you a drink,' he said and he made us a cup of tea. I have always liked Ali Jamous and had a good relationship with him. I was relieved Matt was in Stoke Mandeville. They had operated and released the dislocation. I just felt: Thank goodness he is here.

BARRISTER
What exactly did Dr Jamous say?

ANNE HAMPSON
He explained what he had done to Matt. He said that they had had to screw the vertebrae together. He also said that he knew how upset we had been

and he did not understand why Matt had not been brought straight to Stoke Mandeville Hospital. He said that to make room for Matt, they had moved somebody from ITU to somewhere else. He said that they would have done that anyway if Matt had been brought to Stoke Mandeville earlier. We were shocked and in distress. I remember Phil asking him lots of questions.

BARRISTER
What kind of questions?

ANNE HAMPSON
Phil wanted to know whether he would walk again. I don't think he could deal with Phil; I think he found him difficult. He just said, 'Look, you know, some people have had terrible things happen to them and they have made good recoveries. And there are other people who have had small accidents and they have not made any recovery.' He said that spinal injuries were quite complicated and there were lots of different stages. The first stage was to stabilize the injury following the accident and to focus on Matt's breathing. The breathing was a surprise to me. You don't think about people with spinal injuries not being able to breathe, or having to use a machine. And after the operation he went into some sort of shock.

BARRISTER
Could you explain that, please, Mrs Hampson?

ANNE HAMPSON

Dr Jamous said that because Matthew had been left for so long, he had some swelling in the spinal cord which had risen. He said that the injury was at the 4/5 level, but because of compression and the time taken to release the dislocation, the injury had gone higher up to C2. He was quite bad, Matthew. The swelling went right up to his brain and they were worried because it sent his heart into shock and all sorts of things. He went into temperatures for months and we had to pack him in ice and things like that. It was all very surreal . . . the enormity of what had happened . . . You just can't absorb it really.

BARRISTER

How long did it take to absorb, Mrs Hampson?

ANNE HAMPSON

(Stares pensively for a moment) There are different levels of absorption really. I can't describe it. There is the absorption that he has had a serious accident and then this feeling of: What does the accident mean? Because you have never been through anything like this before. And each stage is more horrific than the last. You knew that when he woke up he would want to know what had happened to him. You know? And then, when he woke up, he could not speak. So you are just feeling for your son, who is lying there and he can't ask you anything. He is trying to speak but you can't understand what he is saying. And you don't really want to tell him anything anyway.

BARRISTER
I can just imagine what that was like, Mrs Hampson.

ANNE HAMPSON
With all due respect you cannot — not unless you have been there . . . You are trying to be brave all the time and not to cry because he has no idea how bad things are and your face is all he can see. All he has is his eyes and his ears. What's he going to think if he sees me in bits? The only way I could help him was by being strong and brave. I just wanted him, however awful it was, to feel as good as he could feel. And he would not have felt that unless I was being positive.

BARRISTER
What about when you were away from the hospital? Mr Buckland will say in evidence that he saw you break down?

ANNE HAMPSON
That was the following morning. We were staying with Cabbage's . . . Sorry, Mr Buckland's mum, Carole, and I was watching him at breakfast loading ten Weetabix into his bowl and it reminded me of Matthew. They are very similar in a way and I suppose that triggered it. It wasn't the first, or the last time, I've cried since Matthew's accident, but the most important thing was that he didn't see it. And to make sure that everybody who came to visit him was the same.

BARRISTER
Was that difficult?

ANNE HAMPSON
Well, I think initially, they didn't know what to
expect and were all scared to death but I'd say,
'Look, if Matt is going to lead as normal a life as
he can, he needs everyone to be as normal as
they can be.' You don't want him to feel like a
freak. He wants people to be normal and treat him
as Matthew. All right, he does not have the physical attributes but he still has the brain. And he is
still the way he has always been. But it was horrible at Stoke Mandeville. I feel as traumatized
after being there as I was with Matt having his
accident.

BARRISTER
I'm sorry, Mrs Hampson, but haven't you just told
the tribunal that you were relieved your son had
been offered a bed at the hospital? 'Thank goodness he is here', I think were your exact words?

ANNE HAMPSON
That's true, and I did fight to get him there, only
to have a life of hell.

BARRISTER
When did this 'life of hell' begin?

ANNE HAMPSON
Intensive care was all right. They were very nice.
Then we went on the ward and . . . it was filthy.
The fridges were filthy, the toilets were filthy . . . I

284

just could not bear my son being there. So, I kept a diary. I wrote a list of what I saw there and used to make notes all the time.

BARRISTER
What did you do with the notes?

ANNE HAMPSON
I brought them to Dr Jamous. He put his coffee machine on. He has this little coffee Tassimo or whatever. He always liked to make you a strong espresso coffee. I said to him, 'Right. This is what is happening to my son. He has not had a shower for ten days. My son had a shower twice a day when he played rugby. More sometimes. I cannot bear to see my son in there. He has not had a shower for ten days because nobody cares.' I asked him, 'How would you feel if that was your son?'

BARRISTER
What was his reply?

ANNE HAMPSON
He said, 'If that was my son I would want to cry.' I said, 'Yes, you would.' So I went through my list and told him. I said, 'You have got no systems, no organization. If you had a list on the wall of who has been showered and when, then they could cross them off and move along.' I went through the list of the things that were wrong and ways they could be improved and he said, 'I'd like to give you a job. Would you come and work for me?' I said, 'No. I am a head teacher. I know

nothing about medicine but I know about systems and organization. I know about team spirit — and you have not got it here.' So we had a long conversation.

BARRISTER
And did it make any difference?

ANNE HAMPSON
They made some changes as a result of it. And then Matt got C. diff.

BARRISTER
The bacterial infection Clostridium difficile?

ANNE HAMPSON
Yes, and I went ballistic — because that is purely down to filth. A lot of it is on the floor, you see, and because a lot of them are in wheelchairs, the bugs are carried on the wheels. I said, 'How can you have cleaners who just go over to the canteen, put another apron on and then serve food?' So we wouldn't let him eat the food. We started cooking and bringing him his meals.

BARRISTER
What about the impact of all this on your life, Mrs Hampson? It has been said that you coped better than your husband?

ANNE HAMPSON
No, I have just coped differently. I think people have their strategies for coping. Phil wanted to talk to everybody whose child had a similar injury. He

liked talking to people at the hospital about it, whereas I could not bear all that. I would rather read about it, find out about it, and make my own decision. So, it is just different. You have different strategies. You just cope.

BARRISTER
What was the low point, Mrs Hampson? At what stage were you at your lowest ebb?

ANNE HAMPSON
I've thought about that actually and it is hard because there were so many. It is hard because there were so many horrible times . . . the phone call . . . getting to the hospital . . . the whole implication of what a spinal injury is.

BARRISTER
Mr Jackson, President of Leicester Tigers, has said in evidence that there were also problems with the RFU.

ANNE HAMPSON
Yes. I kept a list of those as well.

21

The National Spinal Injuries Centre is the oldest and one of the largest spinal injuries centres in the world.

'NURSE!'

It was founded by neurologist Professor Sir Ludwig Guttmatt at Stoke Mandeville Hospital in 1944 to treat servicemen who had sustained spinal cord injuries in the Second World War.

'NURSE!'

I wasn't around sixty-one years ago but I've watched a lot of war movies and can imagine what it was like.

'NURSE!'

The dead and the dying piled high on stretchers, the bruised and battered bodies, the frantic cries for help . . .

'NURSE!'

. . . exactly as it is at Stoke Mandeville today.

'NURSE!'

Clostridium difficile is the new aggressor . . .

'NURSE!'

We've been under siege for weeks . . .

'NURSE!'

That's a lot of poo and a ton of Inco sheets . . .

'NURSE!'

That's every cripple in the hospital, screaming for a wipe . . .

'NURSE!'

That's the seventh time today my colon has exploded . . .

'NURSE!'

That's my poor, distraught father trying to read my lips . . .

'NURSE . . . I THINK HE WANTS THE NURSE!'

That's progress, of sorts.

22

Diarrhoea — as anyone familiar with a severe dose of the trots will testify — waits for no man . . .

'NURSE!'

Which is a bit of a problem when you can't do much trotting.

'NURSE!'

Or when you're lying in the dark at two in the morning trying to call a nurse but you haven't got a voice.

'NURSE!'

Thankfully, the guy in the opposite bed could tell I was in trouble from my agitated clicking and spent the night championing my cause.

'NURSE! COME ON! HE NEEDS HELP!'

I glanced across this morning and did my best to mime a 'thanks'. 'I think he's a jockey,' my father observed.

23

Your name is Paul Taiano. You are forty-eight years old, a father to two teenage children and live with your (second) wife, Alice, in a beautiful fifteenth-century country pile in Hertfordshire. A jockey? Yes, that was always the dream, but your father, a bookmaker, had seen a lot of beaten dockets washed up around the yards and steered you towards a career in accountancy. You join Nyman Libson Paul as a trainee in 1978, qualify three years later and are promoted to partner in 1986 but the thrill of racing never leaves you. And after thirty-two years as an amateur, on this fresh Easter Saturday afternoon in March 2005, the thrill has never felt greater. Catch On, a potentially brilliant young gelding trained by Josie Sheppard from Royston, has won its last three races and, as you gallop up the hill towards the open ditch at Horseheath, you are favourite to win again. The horse is cruising. You pick the stride and ask him for a big one and just as he's about to take off . . .

Craaaaaaaacccccck!

. . . his hind leg snaps and he crashes through the fence, firing you into the ground. Instinctively, you know you will never walk again. You also know that if it had happened at any other point on the track, you would probably get away with it.

Craaaaaaaacccccck!

That's what bad luck sounds like.

Craaaaaaaaccccccck!

That's what hurts as you lie on the ground. You think of your wife and your son and your daughter watching in the crowd. You think of your job and whether you will work again. You think of other bad falls you have had through the years and some of the camels you have survived. But your abiding thought is the unfairness of it all. You spend thirty-two years of your racing life waiting for Pegasus . . .

Craaaaaaaaccccccck!

. . . And he's the one that brings you down.

24

The stench on the ward is withering. Poor Jacqui arrived this morning with tears in her eyes and said she could get it five miles from Aylesbury. The positive for me is that I can't smell anything but that doesn't outweigh the negatives: the assault on my dignity, my acute sense of embarrassment. Sorry, Jacqui.

25

Just when I thought things couldn't get much worse, Leicester were beaten 14–39 by Wasps in the final of the Zurich Premiership this afternoon and Dallaglio was man of the match! Bravo. The shit hits the fan.

26

Scene 25: INTERIOR — HOSPITAL — DAY

Dr Ali Jamous is sitting in his office at Stoke Mandeville with a coffee and a copy of the Observer. The date is Monday, 30 May 2005.

SPINE DOCTORS RAISE HOPE OF ELECTRIC CURE
By Robert McKee

Scientists have found a startling way to heal serious wounds, including broken spinal cords: stimulating them with electric currents.

The technique has been used as the basis for an operation which, in newly completed clinical trials, produced dramatic improvements in patients paralysed by spinal injuries.

After inserting battery packs beside their broken spinal cords, many had feelings restored to their legs and arms after a few weeks' treatment. Feeling was also restored to their lower limbs.

'We have only just started working with this technique but it is going to have a major impact,' said Professor Colin McCaig, head of Aberdeen University's school of medical sciences. 'In a few years, everyone could have an electric device for speeding up wound-healing in their first aid box, a sort of

295

electronic witch hazel.'

The basic technology that underpins the battery packs, known as oscillating field stimulators, has been developed by McCaig, who has grown human nerve cells in laboratory dishes. By placing them in a carefully controlled electrical field he found they could direct their growth in a particular direction.

'We have known for centuries that nerve and other cells respond to electrical stimulation,' McCaig told the *Observer*. 'However, in the 19th century, charlatans claimed they could do great things for patients by sitting them in the middle of electric fields. It just made their hair stand on end. As a result, electrical fields fell into disrepute.

By carefully introducing electrical fields around damaged tissues, McCaig and his team found they could improve the time taken for skin and cornea wounds to heal. The first experiments were carried out on cell cultures. McCaig then began working with Professor Borgens, from the Centre for Paralysis Research at Purdue University in Indiana, on a device that could be implanted in humans.

'We realised that if we put the ends of the broken spinal cord together, we might be able to entice nerve cells to grow towards each other by using an electric current,' said Borgens.

There was a problem, however. Some nerve cells — the ones that carry signals from the brain — would need to grow down the spine, and some, which carry signals to the brain, would need to grow up the spine.

'You need a signal from your brain to tell your hand to move. Equally you need sensory signals from the body to the brain to tell you exactly where your hand is so you can move it to a new position,' said Borgens.

However, detailed research by McCaig then demonstrated that by oscillating the electrical field so that its direction switched every 30 minutes, nerve cells could be induced to move in both directions, up and down the spine.

Borgens' team then built a stimulator based on this principle and this was inserted in a small group of quadriplegic and paraplegic patients. The surgery was carried out by Professor Scott Shapiro of Indiana University.

'We are trying to see if there would be any unforeseen side effects. There weren't. However, we got a major surprise in the way patients responded. In one case, a patient who had lost all sensation in his body had it restored completely. Others — mainly the quadriplegics — noted significant improvements in their ability to move their limbs.'

A second, more detailed set of tests has now been launched. At present, only those with fresh injuries appear to respond to the technique. 'We have a long way to go: nevertheless, it is encouraging,' said Borgens.

27

Matt Cornwell is giving me a blow by blow of what went wrong at Twickenham and the gossip from the Tigers changing room. I'm listening and nodding and enjoying the banter. I'm grinning and smiling and trying to be brave. I don't feel brave. I'm thinking of our last morning together at Franklin's Gardens when he watched from the sideline, injured. I'm wondering: *Why couldn't I have been injured? Why me?*

28

More visits: Cabbage and Dave Young and Alex Dodge and Tom Ryder and Harry Ellis and Paul Cowling and Tom Cowling and Dusty Hare. They eat my grapes and tell me I look great, but I think my grandmother is probably closer to the mark. 'Oh Matt, what happened?' she cries. 'You used to be such a lovely-looking lad.'

29

Harry Ellis brought me a new Peter Kay DVD for my burgeoning collection. 'I think you'll enjoy this, Hambo,' he said, frantically flashing his eyebrows. Hadn't a clue what he was playing at until my mother suggested we watch 'something to cheer us up' this evening and found *Debbie Does Dallas* inside. Thanks, Harry, it's the thought that counts.

30

I'm in bed watching TV at eight-thirty in the evening. Liz and Nigel Green — the parents of my friend and boyhood rival Rob Green — have just left after spending most of the day here. People are good. You expect it from your family, but God knows how I would feel now without the friendship of Matt Cornwell, the love of my sweet Jennie and the support of Jacqui Pochin, Julie Cornwell, Liz Green and Adam Wheatly.

Adam has been a real surprise. The first time I ever set eyes on him was the final of an 800 m at a sports day in Oakham, when we were both fifteen. I was playing for Syston at the time and watched from the sideline, amazed as he sprinted clear of the pack and ran the last 100 m backwards. I thought: Where did they get this guy from? What a cocky, arrogant bastard! So you can imagine how I felt, two weeks later, when he walked out of the local disco with my sister on his arm. It took me three years to warm to him — he had more front than Brighton — but he clearly loved my sister and we slowly started to gel. He was my number 1 fan at England games and loved flaunting my team-issue kit. 'You're a lucky bastard,' he'd say. We used to train together at a Leicester gym, spend long afternoons in Starbucks and had some great nights out in Birmingham when he started university. But these last nine weeks have seen the best of him. He is supposed to be studying for exams, but drives down every night from Birmingham to sit by my bed and watch telly with me. He has also washed me and brushed me and trained to do my bowels.

He has just arrived for another late shift carrying a Domino's pizza and apologizes as he opens the box. 'Sorry, mate, haven't eaten today.'

I smile and motion for a bite.

'You're not supposed to eat solids yet,' he protests.

I motion again.

'I can't! What happens if you choke?'

I am not taking no for an answer.

'Okay, okay but if anything goes wrong, your mum is going to kill me!'

He breaks off a corner and slips it into my mouth. I bite and swallow the warm, melted cheese and slide my tongue across my lips. *Delicious*. He smiles and shakes his head and feeds me another morsel and soon I have eaten a whole slice. This may be my last supper; these may be my final words, so I will address them to Adam because there is something I think you should know.

I love you, man.

31

Jennie came running at me with a pair of tweezers last night. 'This is disgusting,' she said, attacking a hair in my nose.

'AGGGHHHH!'

Then, after I drifted off to sleep, she got bored and painted my toenails with a bright pink varnish. I'll have to beg her to remove it before the Tigers boys come in or I'll get slaughtered. Do I mind? Not really.

I love you, girl.

32

People express love in different ways. Take my grandfather, Bill Wilkinson. Almost two months have passed since my accident and every week without fail he sits down at his home computer and makes me a card ('Created just for you by me') adorned with photos of my childhood. This morning's was typical:

Hi Matt,
We have had a fairly busy week feeding a number of animals at 'Corner Barns' [our home in Cold Overton], so that your folks could visit you together over the weekend. I'm glad that you were able to watch the Bolton game — like I did on your TV. I was disappointed that they lost after such an attacking first half. The brood of ducks are cute, however 2 have died so they are down to 8. The mother duck is very protective of them and goes for your hand if you put it near them. This morning when I let them out they scurried across the patio and started down the steps, but the last one rolled over onto its back and couldn't get upright again; mother duck came back and poked at it but it couldn't roll over, so the mother ran off as if she was saying 'Sod you'! So I was able to

pick it up and put it upright — and it scurried off to catch the others. I hope that you are slowly beginning to feel more like your old self. With love, Grandad Bill x

33

Scene 26: INTERIOR — COURTROOM — DAY

Dr Ali Jamous has been called to the tribunal.

BARRISTER
Dr Jamous, could you tell us a little about your
background, please. You were born in Iran, is that
correct?

Dr ALI JAMOUS
No, that is not correct. I was born in Aleppo in
Syria . . . And there is a big difference between
being born in Aleppo in Syria and being born in
Iran.

BARRISTER
I'm sorry, Dr Jamous. Thank you for clarifying
that. How long have you worked in England,
please?

Dr ALI JAMOUS
I came to England in 1977. I have worked here for
more than thirty years.

BARRISTER
What was your official title at Stoke Mandeville
Hospital in March 2005 when Mr Hampson sus-
tained his injury?

Dr ALI JAMOUS
I was the duty consultant spinal surgeon at Stoke Mandeville as well as clinical divisional chair.

BARRISTER
Thank you, Dr Jamous. Now, could you please explain to the tribunal when you first heard of Mr Hampson?

Dr ALI JAMOUS
When? Oh, when he was admitted to Northampton General Hospital. From my recollection, there was no ITU bed available at Stoke Mandeville to accept Mr Hampson. I recall being contacted by Mr Kerr at home late that evening seeking guidance in relation to Mr Hampson's treatment. He advised me of the steps he was taking and that he had not been able to reduce the dislocation with increasing weights and that he had no experience in this type of surgery to undertake an open reduction. I advised against doing any manipulation and not to leave the patient on traction with high poundage overnight. We agreed to leave him on 15 lbs and that I would try to find a way of transferring him to Stoke Mandeville the following day as Northampton had not been able to find any other establishment capable of dealing with Mr Hampson.

BARRISTER
And he was admitted the following day?

Dr ALI JAMOUS
The following day, there was still no ITU bed at

Stoke. In an effort to assist, we arranged for Mr Hampson to come over to undergo surgery with the aim of returning to Northampton ITU. During the procedure, I believe that the consultant anaesthetist was able to repatriate another ITU patient to make room for Mr Hampson.

BARRISTER
Now excuse my ignorance, Dr Jamous — I have a layman's appreciation of medicine and spinal injury — but when Mr Hampson arrived in Stoke Mandeville on the 16th, which was the . . .

Dr ALI JAMOUS
. . . Wednesday evening. He came from Northampton and went straight into theatre.

BARRISTER
Straight into theatre, thank you, Dr Jamous. Now can you explain to the tribunal, please, what was wrong with him?

Dr ALI JAMOUS
What was wrong with him? He had dislocated two vertebrae in his neck! The vertebrae are the units which make the spinal column. The spinal column supports the head and encloses the spinal cord. So if you look in any anatomy book . . .

BARRISTER
I'm sorry, Dr Jamous . . . Just one moment, please.

The barrister signals to the clerk and a diagram of the spinal column is projected on to a screen.

Dr ALI JAMOUS
So, as you can see, the spinal column is made
of thirty-three vertebrae, seven in the neck
which we call cervical vertebrae. We give them
the prefix letter C. So you have a CI, a C2, a
C3, a C4, a C5, a C6 and a C7. You have
twelve dorsal or thoracic vertebrae. They have
the prefix T or D. Then you have the lumbar
vertebrae, with the prefix of the letter L — LI
to L5. Then you have the sacral vertebrae which
are also five, but these are fused together to
make the back wall of the pelvis. Then you
have the four coccygeal vertebrae which are
. . . well, a source of ongoing debate depending
on whether you're an Evolution man or a Creation man. Is it the remnants of a tail we had a
million years ago? Nobody really understands
the value of a coccyx in a human other than it
is bloody painful when you fall on it! All clear
so far?

BARRISTER
Thank you, Dr Jamous.

Dr ALI JAMOUS
So, the individual block is a vertebra, right? Then,
you stack them on top of each other to form the
spinal column. Of course, they are not just sitting
up in mid-air, you know? They are buttressed by
ligaments and muscles and so forth. So, when a
vertebra falls off the edge, or comes out of its
rightful place due to an abnormal movement in an
abnormal direction, this is called a dislocation, like
when your shoulder comes out of its socket. Mr

Hampson's injury happened while playing in a rugby game, this is what we call a 'low-velocity' injury. A car accident is a 'high-velocity' injury.

BARRISTER
What is the difference between a low-velocity injury and a high-velocity injury in terms of the spinal column, please, Dr Jamous?

Dr ALI JAMOUS
Well, it's interesting. In a low-velocity accident, things happen in slow motion and that tends to damage ligaments more than bones. The block comes out of its place but the bone remains intact and you might think: Oh great, he did not break any bones. But that's actually a disadvantage.

BARRISTER
Why is it a disadvantage?

Dr ALI JAMOUS
Because of this very important structure called the spinal cord sitting in the middle. Think about it. You have these two pieces of bone, and when one is pushed out but does not break, it puts a considerable amount of pressure on the spinal cord in the middle. But if it bursts and breaks open, the cord has more room. Sometimes the damage to the cord is far less in a high-velocity accident where the bone has burst open than a low-velocity accident where there is no break in the bone. So this is what happened to Mr Hampson; one vertebra, the fourth cervical vertebra or C4, went out of

its place and over on C5 and caught the spinal cord in the middle.

BARRISTER
How did you correct that, Dr Jamous?

Dr ALI JAMOUS
The first thing we did was to relocate it back into its rightful place. It was mainly a ligaments injury so we need to give it the means to heal. And the way that we give it the means to heal is by going in between the two vertebrae to cut away the disc and replace it with a sliver of bone (grafted from the hip) and then hold it together with a plate and some screws so that it all knits together.

BARRISTER
How long does it take to perform the operation, Dr Jamous?

Dr ALI JAMOUS
It is a laborious, lengthy operation because you need to operate on the back of the neck first to relocate the dislocation. Then hold it temporarily with something, like a big knot, and then turn him over to get access to the front of the spine to put the plate in place. I remember quite clearly that he arrived at about five-ish and he was in theatre until nine-thirty, ten o'clock.

BARRISTER
But your work is not yet finished, is it Dr Jamous? Mr Hampson's two distraught parents are waiting outside.

311

Dr ALI JAMOUS
Yes.

BARRISTER
You begin by inviting them to your office and offering them a drink?

Dr ALI JAMOUS
(*Smiles*) We make all our people welcome.

BARRISTER
Mr Hampson's father wants to know if his son will walk again but you tell him you don't know. Is that always the case with spinal injuries, Dr Jamous? Or is it that you know but you're not saying?

Dr ALI JAMOUS
No, no. I am only a doctor. I always say to my patients, 'I am not a clairvoyant. I do not have a crystal ball.' In general terms, in spinal injuries, your long-term outcome has been written the minute you hit the ground.

BARRISTER
Is it really?

Dr ALI JAMOUS
But nobody knows what that is. It could be that you are destined to remain paralysed for the rest of your life. It could be that you recover. I work on that basis. I don't know what is going to happen. I don't think anybody knows. That is why, I think, if you say to a patient, 'You *will*

312

walk' then you are lying. Or if you say, 'You are *not* going to walk', again you are . . . Well, not lying, lying is a strong word . . . Actually you don't know. I keep telling this story of a patient of mine, aged fourteen, who fell from a mountain bike and fractured a T4 — now you understand what a T4 is?

BARRISTER
The fourth thoracic vertebra.

Dr ALI JAMOUS
Yes, and he had complete paralysis. He came to Stoke Mandeville. We looked at him — his name was James — and we said, 'James. You have got two options. You can lie in bed for six weeks and your fracture will knit or alternately we can do an operation. But, James, remember the operation is just to fix the fracture.' And I gave him the spiel about 'Well, I don't know what is going to happen to you.' The whole six weeks that young lad was completely paralysed, but a while later, I'm doing my walk around and he shows me that he can move his big toe. I congratulated him and brought him down to earth. 'Well, that's great, James, if it is the beginning of something more substantive. Because, otherwise, what can you do if you can just move your big toe?'

BARRISTER
Was it the beginning of something more substantive?

Dr ALI JAMOUS

Well, if you pass James on the street today you would not know that he had had a spinal injury. Now, I could have been justified to have told James on day one or on week one or on week four, 'You are going to be paralysed for the rest of your life.' But I didn't. Because I didn't know. So it is a mistake of the medical profession to give a prognosis so early. And it has nothing to do with what the spine looks like or how smashed it is — absolutely nothing.

BARRISTER

Can you explain that, please, Dr Jamous?

Dr ALI JAMOUS

Absolutely nothing. I have shown MRI scans of people to the medical fraternity and they've said, 'That looks good. Normal.' But the guy is completely paralysed. And I could show you scans where you can hardly see the spinal cord because it looks so smashed and yet those guys are walkers. There are no correlations between what we can see on the X-rays and reality. That's why I adopted that attitude. I say, 'I have not got a crystal ball. I don't know what is going to happen to you.'

BARRISTER

Which is not what your patients or their families want to hear?

Dr ALI JAMOUS

Of course not — but that is the truth. You see, it

is devastating. People hang on to every word you tell them. And if you tell them, 'Oh, don't worry, he will be fine', it would be terrible when it starts to dawn on them that it is not going to happen. 'Why did he not tell us the truth straightaway?' And if you tell them, 'Oh, he is going to be paralysed for the rest of his life', you are just killing any hopes in them. I tell them the basic facts. I tell them 'I want you to hope.' Because humans live by hope and I try hard not to take people's hopes away even if I, deep inside, might be convinced that it is unlikely to happen.

BARRISTER
And did you feel, deep inside, that it was unlikely Mr Hampson would make a recovery?

Dr ALI JAMOUS
No, no, I didn't. In fact at the time I was more concerned that he regain the ability to breathe. At C4–5, you should be able to breathe by yourself. Unfortunately, this did not happen. He must remain ventilator-dependent. So, in other words, although Mr Hampson's injury and level should have been a C4–5, he is, for all intent and purposes, a C2.

BARRISTER
Which, if I am not mistaken, Dr Jamous, is the same level of disability as the late actor Christopher Reeve?

Dr ALI JAMOUS
That is right. Christopher Reeve had a fracture at

C2. So unfortunately he is behaving as a C2. Or he ended up by being a C2.

BARRISTER
Why did that happen, Dr Jamous? You must know. There must be some reason?

Dr ALI JAMOUS
The 'why' is the extent of the damage — the spinal cord has been well and truly squeezed between the two vertebrae and when you squeeze a structure which is alive . . . And there are no carbon copies in humans, we are all slightly different. This one will have an extra blood vessel, that one will have a smaller artery. It's a lottery.

BARRISTER
I'm sorry, Dr Jamous, what do you mean by lottery?

Dr ALI JAMOUS
I've always said that if you believe in Evolution we evolved badly. And if you believe in Creation, the spinal cord must have been the Saturday-night job before he rested on Sunday. Because it is abysmal. He got it right with the brain. The brain, and its blood supply, is the perfect design . . . but that is understandable because the brain is your hub, your computer controller. So whenever anything happens to you, everything in your body will shut down to make sure that enough blood and oxygen goes to your brain. Because the design has been geared to this. Now in order for your brain to communicate with the rest of your body, you have

to go via the spinal cord. Unfortunately, when it comes to the blood supply of the spinal cord, the design is abysmal. It relies on two little branches from the top, coming from two main arteries, going into the brain. Those two branches are like a water supply that starts as a good stream and then dwindles into tiddly little things. It is not sufficient to work all the way down so it starts to rely on little branches, coming into it, to feed it. And that is where the lottery is.

BARRISTER
Because some people have more of these little branches than others?

Dr ALI JAMOUS
Exactly. So the guy who has got six or seven laughs all the way to the bank, because if he damages one or two, he still has enough to bring the blood in. Whereas the guy who has only got one . . . Well, he's had it. Do you remember what I said about the MRI scan that looks perfect but the guy is completely paralysed? Well, now you know. He has damaged the one little branch that he had.

BARRISTER
And this is what happened to Mr Hampson?

Dr ALI JAMOUS
Well, obviously his spinal cord was squeezed between the two vertebrae and quite a bit of damage occurred. His father, even today, says, 'I wonder what would have happened if he had his problems resolved earlier.' The answer is, 'I don't

317

know.' I mean, from a logical point of view, you know, if your leg is in a vice, the quicker you get it out of the vice the better. But that does not necessarily mean the damage won't be the same. He has asked me that question on numerous occasions.

BARRISTER
Whether things might have been different if you had operated earlier?

Dr ALI JAMOUS
Yes. It is not the million-dollar question; not even the trillion-dollar question — we will never know.

BARRISTER
Is that difficult, Dr Jamous, confronting angry parents? Or is the ability to disconnect part of the job?

Dr ALI JAMOUS
You don't disconnect completely but you do need to remain slightly above it because, you know, this would be a pretty miserable life if I became emotionally attached to my patients.

BARRISTER
And how do you remain above it? How do you stay sane when you are surrounded by so much misery and pain?

Dr ALI JAMOUS
Two ways. You say, 'I am here to help you. I don't feel responsible because I have not caused your

paralysis.' When you adopt that approach you have protected yourself to a certain degree but anybody who says, 'It doesn't affect me one iota' — that's rubbish. Of course it affects you. Hopefully that is what distinguishes us from other species. We have emotions. I went to the Falkland Islands recently to do an operation on a patient and paid a visit to the Argentinian cemetery — a godforsaken land, wind howling over the hill and across the soldiers' graves. And I felt emotional. I thought: Why are you here? This is why we are humans.

BARRISTER
So when Mr Hampson enters your surgery at five o'clock on the evening of 16 March, you are not looking at him as overtime?

Dr ALI JAMOUS
No, no, no. One of the reasons I like this job is
. . . I came from a neurosurgical background. I trained in neurosurgery in Oxford before I came to Stoke Mandeville. Good times. Well, you know how it is when you are young: 'Look at me. I am a neurosurgeon.' And for sure it was interesting, but once you have done an operation 200 times it is like chlorine for God's sake! Bloody boring! And that is not what medicine is about. I still do my surgery. I haven't lost my craft, but one of the things I like most about my job is the contact with my patients. With all due respect, I may forget your name tomorrow but I do not forget things about my patients. So when a patient comes to see me in outpatients, I do not need to

look at their records. I know what happened to them. I know what is in their records. You have asked me about Mr Hampson. Mr Hampson was injured on a Tuesday and came to me on a Wednesday. I can still see his mother sitting in ITU, telling me she was disgusted with how her son had been treated and that she was going to the press. I said, 'Well, please do if you feel you want to, but will it make any difference?' I remember it extremely well. Mr Hampson is one of many patients I treat. I don't need to consult his records. I know exactly. And that makes a difference to me and to them.

BARRISTER
Is empathy the word?

Dr ALI JAMOUS
Yes, it is empathy but it is also . . . we sometimes forget that we are treating people, you know? I had a go at a doctor not so long ago. I said, 'Would you like to be treated this way?' This is what we should always ask ourselves, 'Would you like to be treated this way?' There are, among our fraternity, some people who really believe in their status or in their importance.

BARRISTER
This is the God complex?

Dr ALI JAMOUS
Yes. But when you feel so important, remember you are no more than a hand in a bucket of water — take it out and when the ripples settle, nobody

will even know it was there.

BARRISTER
Mrs Hampson will tell the tribunal that she came to you with a list of complaints about hygiene at the hospital. Do you recall that, Dr Jamous?

Dr ALI JAMOUS
I do, I do, and she had my sympathy. I don't need people to complain to me — I know exactly which area is doing a good job and which area, sometimes, leaves a lot to be desired. Ninety-nine per cent of the time the staff at the hospital do a good job but there is always that one time when we will let ourselves down. You keep asking why . . . Well, let me try to answer that. There have been a lot of changes in the NHS in terms of discipline and quality of service in the thirty-plus years since I came to England. Some people will say, 'Well, the good old days weren't very good.' Well, maybe, but they were better than they are now in the areas that I worked in. The standards were much, much higher. People were relating more. The attitude now seems to be: 'I come to work, do my job and go home — if you're not happy with that, that is your problem.' So it is difficult when you are faced with a mother who is trying to deal with this tragedy and things are not right.

BARRISTER
And also a father?

Dr ALI JAMOUS

Yes. And again, that is one of the more difficult aspects of the business. It's not just the person lying in the bed that you have to deal with — it's the family and the dynamics of relationships breaking down and . . . they have all my sympathy.

BARRISTER

Did you find Phil Hampson difficult to deal with?

Dr ALI JAMOUS

Some people might find him difficult, but I can see how he saw a dream falling to bits in front of him. You know? He had high hopes his son was going to be an England international and then one fluke accident and that dream comes to an end. He struggled, and I have not met him for a long time but I am sure he is still struggling. He cannot come to terms with what has happened. His wife is also struggling but in a different way. She coped with it slightly differently — but is she happy? Of course not. Is she not struggling? Of course not.

34

I have not spoken a word for two months now since my (rather colourful) speech at Franklin's Gardens. This morning, they fitted a new speaking valve to the pipe running from my ventilator and I'm up and swearing again. Okay, so I sound like I've had a sex change and it's taking me five minutes to string even a short sentence together but I don't think I've lost my sense of humour. My first words? 'Where are my boots?'

35

Hi Matt,
We did a good run back on Sunday, without
a stop it only took us 3.5 hours! I expect that
you know the front picture, on this card is
from the balcony of your Mum's room, and
it must be one of the nicest views in Leics.
The ducks seem to have a set pattern of
what they do and where they go each day.
When let out of the kennel they first head for
the pond, then they start to visit different
parts of the grounds. In the early evening
they have another dip and then rest at the
side of the pond before retiring to the kennel
for the night. Regards and best wishes,
Grandad Bill x

36

If there is one blessing about being dumb for so long, it's the refuge it has provided from the questions I've thought about constantly but didn't want to ask: Will I walk again? Will I play again? Is this it for the rest of my life? But now that I can talk again there is no place to hide. And I want to hide. I don't want to hear the answers to those questions. I *know* I am paralysed. I *know* this could be it. And when Jamous visited my bed this morning, I had no desire to ask my prognosis.

Some things are better left unsaid.

37

Hi Matt,
I've had a very busy week this week doing lots of little jobs in readiness for the plumber who will be fitting a new bathroom suite, and a tiler who will be re-tiling the room afterwards. He just might ring tomorrow to say that he will start on Monday, but if he hasn't finished this week's job, he will ring next Saturday! So I'm sorry if I have dropped behind with the cards. Love & best wishes from Grandad Bill xx

38

Another day, another freak show. Today's was called 'Quasimodo is Introduced to His Wheelchair':

ACT 1: After almost three months on the flat of his back, Quasimodo is roused with a shot of adrenaline.

ACT 2: The audience is cautioned: 'Stand back, folks!', as his huge, lifeless carcass is winched from the bed.

ACT 3: Quasimodo is suspended in mid-air, squealing for his head to be held.

ACT 4: The squealing becomes louder and more frenzied. 'I feel dizzy. I'm going to be sick. Put me back in the bed.'

ACT 5: Quasimodo is lowered and strapped into the wheelchair to a tumultuous round of applause.

ACT 6: The ringmaster explains that there will be a repeat performance tomorrow and every day until Quasimodo has been tamed.

39

Hi Matt,
Still not heard from the plumber, so it looks as if he might ring next Saturday. (We hope so.) The Wanderers slipped up again on Saturday after being two goals up — that's a typical BWFC trick which they practise regularly! More news later in the week. Love and best wishes, Grandad Bill xx

40

More visits: Cabbage and Alex Dodge and Dave Young. Cabbage is feeding me a Magnum when there's a call on my mobile. He picks it up and places it on my shoulder. It's Mum, calling from the café downstairs. 'I've just got word that Johno and Jonah Lomu are on the way,' she says. 'They'll be here in fifteen minutes.'

'Fucking hell! We'd better go,' Davey says, jumping out of his chair.

'No, stay,' I plead. 'Don't leave me on my own with them.'

Before we can blink, the two rugby icons have strolled into the ward, followed by Leon Lloyd and Pat Howard. They've been preparing for a special game at Twickenham on Saturday to mark Johno's retirement.

'All right, Hambo?' He smiles, planting his huge frame on my bed.

'Yeah, good, thanks, Johno,' I squeak. 'Have a grape.'

Lomu is more reserved: 'All right, Bro.' He nods.

'Yeah, nice to meet you, Jonah,' I reply. 'Thanks for coming down.'

'No worries, mate.'

I ask about the game and notice Lomu eyeing my ventilator. A year ago, he too was wired to a machine and on dialysis three times a week for a serious kidney disorder. He's had a transplant and, since returning to training in January, has set his heart on playing for the All Blacks in the next World Cup. It felt surreal to have him standing by my bed. 'Hang in there, Bro.' He smiles before leaving.

41

Hi Matt,
I've had a busy day today — the plumber
came to install the piping to the electric
shower which I bought six weeks ago and I
had done quite a lot of preparation work so
that it made his job easier — and therefore
quicker so that his bill was cheaper! I am
now awaiting a call from an electrician to say
how soon he can come and finish the job. I
just broke off this note to answer the door
and it was the electrician to say if I was
ready for him he'd do it today. He did a
good job and I'm very pleased with the
shower. Grandma Babs and I had a nice
weekend — dinner at Susie's, then she
motored us to Manchester to the show 'My
Fair Lady' and after the show we returned to
Susie's and stayed the night. So, that's all for
now. Love and best wishes. Grandad Bill x

42

Took my first tour of Stoke Mandeville in my chair this morning and couldn't believe how many disabled people there are.

'Look at that poor cripple over there, Adam.'

'Look at him!'

'Look at her!'

Call it denial or a result of being legally blond but I've been imbued with the spirit of Lomu since they winched me from the bed and haven't thought of myself as disabled. *This wheelchair is only temporary. In a couple of months I won't need it. Bring me a set of callipers and I'll be right as rain soon.*

We took the lift downstairs to Jimmy's café and decided to explore the gym with its tilt tables and weights and gear. *I'll be down here soon working out again.* And then we stopped in front of a mirror. It was the first time I had seen my reflection since the accident and it took a moment to register. This guy with the wasted body and the pasty skin and the thinning hair; this bloke with the tiny shoulder blades and the legs shrivelled like twigs; this cripple with the bag of piss strapped to his leg and the pipe coming out of his neck . . . was me! And the spirit drained straight out of me.

43

Every day brings a new irritation. Yesterday, it was the steaming temperature of the ward and the constant itch from the sweat on my face.

'Wipe my eyes, please, Adam.'

'Wipe my nose.'

'Again, please.'

'Again.'

Today, it was that annoying bastard, Jimmy Savile. Okay, I accept that he has raised millions for charity and worked miracles for this place (he has an office at Stoke Mandeville and the café off reception is named in his honour) but he's just full of his own self-importance. The first time he came into the ward I was almost in awe of him: 'Oh, it's Jimmy Savile!'

'How are you?' he enquired. 'Ten out of ten?'

'Yeah, not bad thanks, Jimmy. I've had C. diff. and lost a lot of weight but I'm . . . '

And then I realized that he wasn't actually listening. He didn't appear that interested in how I was feeling, and every time he comes into the ward it's the same old lines . . .

'Now then, now then . . . '

Sorry, not today, Jimmy.

'Good morning. Good morning.'

Erm, it's three in the afternoon.

'How are you? Ten out of ten?'

No, I'm feeling shit.

'You have always got women around you, you have.'

Yeah, that's my mother and my sister, Amy.

'And better looking than me.'

Well, try washing the string vest and changing the tracksuit, mate!

44

'I'm taking you out,' Jeff says. 'We'll go down to the Woolpack.'

Jeff, my vent nurse, is one of the good guys at the hospital. The Woolpack, a pub, is one mile from Stoke Mandeville's door. Expeditions have travelled to Everest with less equipment. I glance at all the bags with the batteries and cables and probes and think: Is this what it's going to be like every time I go out? I'm shaking like a shitting dog as he wheels me outside to an old Transit van and straps me in. He has secured my neck with a plastic brace but my head still feels attached with a piece of string and the lack of control is a real worry. It's a beautifully warm Thursday afternoon, rest day at Tigers, and a few of the lads — Cabbage, Cornish, Dodgy, Davey Young, Ollie Smith, Harry Ellis, Brett Deacon, Jim Hamilton, Tom Ryder — arrive on a visit and follow us down the road. Cornish brings me a pint of Stella with a straw and it feels like old times as we settle around a table in the garden . . . Well, almost. The lads are being overly friendly and too nice to me. And I'm trying much too hard to show them nothing has changed.

45

My sister, Amy, has pushed me into the small sitting room just off the ward. She has picked up a copy of *Hello!*; I'm staring out the window across the roof tops. It's another endlessly dull Stoke Mandeville afternoon, until the alarm on my ventilator trips. She jumps out of her chair and scans the battery. 'It looks okay,' she says. 'I don't know why the air is not coming through.' She's rattled. I'm terrified. There is no breath in my lungs. I am three minutes away from turning into a vegetable. She runs outside and grabs a nurse who spots that a small pipe at the back of the ventilator has become detached. I'm breathing again and furious. 'FOR FUCK'S SAKE, AMY, I WILL NEVER TRUST YOU AGAIN! I WILL NEVER TRUST YOU AGAIN!'

46

Midnight; the sobbing on the ward is mine. I gaze into the darkness, listening to the ventilator, with no one to turn to and no place to hide. The black thoughts have returned; same shit, different night . . .

Why me? Why the fuck has this happened to me? Why am I being punished like this? What did I do that was so wrong? My life is over. There is no way back from here. I will never walk again. I will never play rugby again. I will never make love to Jennie. She will never marry me. We will never have children. I will spend the rest of my days shackled to this lifeless shell. Why me? Why the fuck did it . . .

I feel a presence at my side. I turn my head and there's a guy sitting by my bed in a wheelchair. 'Go on, just let it out,' he says.

47

Scene 27: INTERIOR — COURTROOM — DAY

Indeep Sidhu has been called to the tribunal.

BARRISTER
Mr Sidhu, you are what's known as an 'old legion'
at Stoke Mandeville Hospital. Is that correct?

INDEEP SIDHU
That is correct.

BARRISTER
Forgive me, Mr Sidhu, but you don't look very
old.

INDEEP SIDHU
(*Smiles*) No, I'm thirty-two.

BARRISTER
How does that qualify as old?

INDEEP SIDHU
It does when you've been in a wheelchair since
the age of twelve. An old legion is someone
who has been injured a long time — ten
years is usually when you join the club so to
speak.

BARRISTER
So Mr Hampson will become an old legion in 2015?

INDEEP SIDHU
Yes, when he hits the ten-year mark.

BARRISTER
Now, you were born in Kenya, is that correct?

INDEEP SIDHU
Yes, in Nairobi.

BARRISTER
But Sidhu is not an African name.

INDEEP SIDHU
No, my grandad grew up in Punjab but decided as a young man to spread his wings a bit. He boarded a sailboat in Bombay with some friends and they sailed for forty days to Kenya to find work. He did odd jobs at first, set up his own carpentry works and then bought into a successful car business. My dad was his only son and they had three daughters. Same story with my mum: her father came over in a similar way from India and set up in Nairobi doing carpentry and upholstery. My parents met and married in the seventies and I was the firstborn. I have three younger sisters.

BARRISTER
Did you go to school in Nairobi?

INDEEP SIDHU
Yes, boarding school. Probably the best years of
my life because they encouraged a lot of sport and
sport was my first love. I was never really moti-
vated by studying but I used to play a lot of rugby
and cricket up until the day of my accident on 24
April 1988.

BARRISTER
What happened, Mr Sidhu?

INDEEP SIDHU
It was a Sunday morning. I was home on a break
from school. My grandad was chairing a function
for the business community of Nairobi that afternoon and we were all very excited. Dad decided
he would take me and my sisters swimming for
the morning. We arrived at the clubhouse and Dad
sat down for a drink with some friends. I got
changed and ran to the side of the pool. There
wasn't much happening, just a couple of kids
playing in the shallow end, so I thought I would
do what I usually did: dive in. The next thing I
know I wake up under the water and I cannot
move. I was drowning and I couldn't move. I dis-
tinctly remember what my last thought was: I am
going to die today.

BARRISTER
You had hit your head on the bottom?

INDEEP SIDHU
Yes. There was no lifeguard on duty. I was down
for about two minutes before an old family friend,

an English guy, saw me and pulled me out of the pool. Someone shouted. My dad ran out and saw it was me. My sisters tell me, to this day, that he just picked me up in his arms, carried me to the car and whizzed me down to the hospital — which is probably the most inappropriate thing he could have done. The next thing I know I'm being wheeled out of theatre and into intensive care.

BARRISTER
How long did you spend in hospital?

INDEEP SIDHU
Eight weeks. I did not understand what was going on. I had tons of visitors and they would see me spasm and think: He's going to be okay. They were prodding me, trying to move my toes and telling me to do things. They wanted to take me outside and allow my feet to touch the grass — as if that was going to change things. I was from a very religious Sikh family and prayers were said for me. You could not tell them, 'He's not going to walk again' — because they just didn't want to hear it. My dad got this specialized French physio in to help me out, but nothing worked.

BARRISTER
What was the level of your injury?

INDEEP SIDHU
I was C5, C6. I could breathe and had some slight movement in my arms. There were talks about

341

bringing me over to Stoke Mandeville for rehabilitation. And then, after a few months at
home, my mum saw a little mark on my
bottom. No one had told us anything about
pressure sores. She put a bit of Elastoplast over
it, but over the next week or so it kept getting
bigger and bigger until there was this gaping
black hole in my bum. So that accelerated
everything and I was brought over to London
for three weeks and then spent nine months at
Stoke Mandeville.

BARRISTER
What contact did you have with your family
during this time?

INDEEP SIDHU
My mum came with me. My dad and sisters
stayed behind and would visit periodically. It
put a lot of stress on their relationship. My
father hit the bottle and had a couple of affairs.
He had a flourishing business that went down
the toilet. Eventually, they separated and Mum
decided we would live in England. I did not
speak to my father for seven years.

BARRISTER
Why not?

INDEEP SIDHU
I don't know . . . I just woke up one day when I
was fifteen or sixteen and analysed my relationship with him. I thought: He has never been there
for me. And I think he resented the fact that Mum

342

had taken charge and he had been pushed aside.

BARRISTER
How did she manage financially?

INDEEP SIDHU
Dad bought a house for us and used to send
money. Her family helped a lot and I was on disability living allowance. Compared to the life we
had in Kenya, we weren't well off, but we never
went without. I am very close to my mum. She
has always kept me grounded, but I had to learn
to grow up and be a man on my own. My goal in
life was to be a businessman. I went to university
and got a degree in business strategy and management, and decided to call my dad. His liver was
shot to pieces. He trivialized my degree and said
something really crude. It was the last conversation I had with him before he died.

BARRISTER
What did he say?

INDEEP SIDHU
I said, 'Dad. I passed my degree. I thought I
should let you know.' He said, 'What did you pass
your degree in — masturbating?' And I just
couldn't handle it.

BARRISTER
Thank you for that, Mr Sidhu. Now could you tell
the tribunal about your first meeting with Mr
Hampson, please?

INDEEP SIDHU

I was in the kitchen near to his ward. It was a boiling hot day. There were some gloves in the fridge with ice in them. His mother was there — a fantastically strong woman, you don't want to mess with Anne — and I think Jacqui Pochin was also there. I had an initial conversation with them and was introduced to Matt. He wasn't speaking at that point so it was just a quick hello. A few weeks later I was driving through Aylesbury and I saw Phil. He was looking for a bungalow or something local to move into and we had a chat. And I could see in his eyes that he was looking for help.

BARRISTER

What did you see, Mr Sidhu?

INDEEP SIDHU

Pain. He reminded me of my dad. He would tell me stories about Matthew's rugby career and of his expectations that he would get better. I didn't have the heart to say, 'Phil, he may not get better. This may be it. And you had better accept it because if you don't it will eat you up. Because it ate my dad up.' Phil was my biggest worry. It was obvious how much he loved his son. I wasn't worried about Matt. I was sure I could help Matt, but I wasn't sure I could help Phil.

BARRISTER

How were you so sure, Mr Sidhu?

INDEEP SIDHU
Because I knew exactly how Matt was feeling, but I didn't know what it was like to be Phil.

BARRISTER
How was Matt feeling?

INDEEP SIDHU
Well, if you passed through the ward during the day you would say he was doing fine. He was always surrounded by people, always had a smile on his face. I'd watch him from a distance and think: This guy is loved. But the night is when you feel it, the night is when you start hurting and need to let it out.

BARRISTER
And did he?

INDEEP SIDHU
Yes, the usual stuff: his life, the future. I said, 'Matt, I am not going to pretend I could ever understand what has happened to you but I can give you some perspective. Okay, you may not be able to move your arms or your legs but you have got a flaming brain! And there is so much that you can do with that. Go back to school. Educate yourself. That is the most powerful tool you have got.'

BARRISTER
Did he reply?

INDEEP SIDHU

He said, 'My whole life was rugby. I never studied. There was nothing else.' I said, 'Well, this is the start of a new journey for you now.' He began to cry. I said, 'Mate, just let it out, but remember this is not the end. This is just the beginning. So get out there and kick life in the arse.'

PART 4

GROUND ZERO

1

They say the Lord helps those who help themselves. Is that the secret? Is that how Paul Taiano has made such constant progress these last four months? Two weeks after his accident, he was dictating letters to his secretary, dealing with his post and receiving clients at his bed. Later, when some movement returned to his arms, he was hooked up to a laptop and worked from a quiet room downstairs. Some might say he was lucky his injury (C6) wasn't worse, but luck is not a word you would use if you had watched him eat his dinner this evening. I say eat but it was actually more like a wrestling match between his mind and his hands. Two hours it lasted; two hours of the fork struggling to find his mouth; two hours of his knife falling into his lap; two hours of the nurse offering him an out . . .

'Paul, do you need a hand?'

'No, thanks.'

'Would you like me to cut that for you?'

'No, thanks.'

'Will I pour you a drink?'

'No, thanks.'

It wasn't about the food or his appetite. It didn't matter that his veg was cold or his meat was congealed or that he wasn't really that hungry. It was the principle. He was not going to stop until the plate had been cleared.

I have never met anyone so driven or strong-willed and I asked him about it this evening. 'Whatever you get in life you tend to have to work for yourself,' he said. 'No one gives you anything. I am not from a rich family. Any success I have ever had comes from an ability to work hard and do a good job. It would be very easy to give up in this place and say, 'Right I can't do anything any more.' I am not going to accept that.'

A lesson.

2

Out of the bed and into the chair and out of the ward and into the lift and down to reception and out across the cheap maroon carpet to the big sliding doors. Adam is pushing. We choose the usual spot to the right of the entrance and sit (well, at least I have a seat) in the sun for an hour.

'What is it about Stoke Mandeville that sets it apart?' I ask.

'Don't know,' he says.

'That car park.' I smile.

'How's that?'

'It has more disabled parking spots than anywhere in England.'

'Yeah.'

Two old guys from a different ward have come outside to smoke. They look like zombies or death barely warmed and suck on the nicotine like it was the only thing keeping them alive. What's rotting them? I wonder. The trauma? The bad food? The C. diff.? The MRSA? This is one godawful place . . . But enough of that. I must think positive thoughts. I close my eyes and feel the sun kiss my face.

This is good.

3

'You've got to set yourself a goal for when you leave here,' Indy says. 'Think of somewhere you've never been and would really like to go.'

'New York,' I reply. 'I've always wanted to visit New York.'

4

Out of the bed and into the chair and out of the ward and into the lift and down to reception and out across the cheap maroon carpet to the big sliding doors. Ellie, our black Labrador, is waiting in the car park. She sees me and comes bounding and howling to my chair for the first time since my accident. Instinctively, I reach for her head; instinctively, she looks to my hand. The moment hits like a kick in the crotch and turns a good day to bad.

5

Scene 28: INTERIOR — STUDY — EVENING

Anne Hampson is sitting in the study of her home at Cold Overton with a copy of an article from the *Observer*. She opens her laptop and begins typing an email:

From: *Anne Hampson*
To: *Shapiro, Scott A*
Subject: *Dr. Jamous (National Spinal Injuries unit Stoke Mandeville, England)*
Sent: *Wednesday, July 13 2005*

Dear Dr. Shapiro

We have been in contact with Professor McCaig at the University of Aberdeen in Scotland with reference to the work which is being carried out by yourselves in relation to the electric implant research. My son Matt Hampson aged 20 was training for the England National rugby team (under 21s) when he sustained a dislocation to his neck at the C4-C5 level. This has left him paralysed from the neck down. He has been classified as incomplete but currently, at 14 weeks, he has gained some sensation but has only regained movement in his neck and shoulders. We

354

are humbled by his bravery at a time in his life when he was poised to become a star. Dr. Jamous, his consultant, has read with interest the article in The Observer which outlines the work of Professor McCaig and his team and your group at Indiana University. He has agreed in principle that he would be prepared to undertake the implant procedure with Matthew and further trial the work at the National Spinal Injuries Centre at Stoke Mandeville. We noted that the article stated that the procedure was aimed at 'Fresh Injuries' and we felt that time was an important issue. We are therefore trying to enable things to move forward with Matthew's treatment. We hope you and your colleagues are agreeable to work with us. It is a devastating time for our family and friends and we would like to feel in our hearts that we have given our son every chance possible. I look forward to hearing from you at your soonest convenience.

Anne Hampson.

FADE TO

Scene 29: INTERIOR — STUDY — MORNING

Anne Hampson reading Dr Shapiro's reply.

From: Scott Shapiro
To: Anne Hampson
Subject: Dr. Jamous (National Spinal Injuries unit Stoke
Mandeville England)
Sent: Thursday, July 14 2005

Anne,

Presently, the device is experimental and only approved for implantation within 18 days of injury. We do have a promising treatment for chronic SCI but it will not be available for humans for at least 1 year.

Scott Shapiro.

6

August. Five months since my accident; five months of unrelenting darkness and despair; five months of being prodded by that bastard doctor with that bastard pin . . .

'Can you feel that?'

'No.'

'That?'

'No?'

'That?'

'No.'

'That?'

'No.'

'That?'

'No! No! No! No! No!'

. . . and then you turn a corner.

7

The doctor is crunching the numbers from my latest phrenic nerve test. 'There's an improvement on the right side of your diaphragm,' he says. 'We're going to start you on a programme to try and wean you off the vent.' I can't believe it. Dad can't believe it. Mum can't believe it. Adam can't believe it. Amy can't believe it. Jennie can't believe it. We flood the wards with tears. Yes! Yes! Yes! Yes! Yes!

8

I am five years old; we live in Langham; Dad has his hand on the saddle of my BMX and he's pushing me down Church Street Road.

'Keep pedalling Matt,' he urges.

(I'm feeling scared.)

'Don't worry, I won't let you go,' he says.

(He takes his hand away.)

'YOU'RE DOING IT! YOU'RE DOING IT!'

(I swerve into a thorn bush.)

'Never mind, let's try again.'

That's how the first day of weaning felt this morning.

9

This morning Jeff, the vent nurse, disconnects me from the ventilator and attaches a small reservoir of oxygen to the pipe running into my neck. 'Just wink' (I can't talk without the ventilator) 'if you are struggling and I'll increase the flow,' he says. I open my mouth and make a conscious effort to breathe. 'Try gulping,' Jeff says. Nothing happens. I try again but feel I'm drowning and start to panic. I stare at Jeff with terror in my eyes and he reattaches the ventilator. I'm rattled. It feels much worse than hitting the thorn bush. 'That's normal,' he says. 'We'll try again later.'

10

Later. Jeff is back. Mum is watching. 'You're a strong boy, Matt,' she says. 'I know you can get off this ventilator.' The pipe is removed. The reservoir is attached. I try to focus . . .

Come on! Kick-start those lungs!

But after two minutes I raise the white flag.

Mum is thrilled. 'That's brilliant, much better than this morning,' she says. The last time she spoke to me that way was after my first dump in a potty.

11

Jennie is giving me a manicure. I'm gazing at her lovely face as she clips and files and feel a tingle in my finger. My pulse quickens; my mind is in a spin: Fuck! Was that a nerve impulse? Did I just *feel* something?

An assistant of Dr Jamous is floating through the ward. I explain the tingle and this strange sensation (feeling?) lately in my chest whenever I spasm. She makes a note and appears quite interested. My parents react like I've been told I'll walk again. But now I'm worried. *Did I really feel something? Is my mind playing tricks with me? Maybe I should have kept it to myself.*

12

24 September. Two hours have passed since we left Stoke Mandeville; my father is driving; my mother is cradling my head in the back. We have reached the village of Cold Overton and a red-brick dormer called 'Corner Barns'. 'Welcome home, son,' Mum says. She is crying. Adam, Amy and Tom are waiting in the driveway. Ellie barks with excitement as I am eased down a ramp. The sight of my old silver Polo sparks a flashback: I've got my kit bag on my shoulder, my mobile in my hand and I'm running out the door to drive to Northampton.

Will I ever run again? Will I ever drive again?

Home is sweet but not as I remember it — the front door is too narrow for my wheelchair and I must enter via the patio doors at the back. It's a scrape (literally) to get from the sitting room to the kitchen and I can't reach my bedroom upstairs. 'It will be better when you have your own place,' Dad says. 'I'm starting on converting the barn next week.'

I gaze out the window haunted by old memories as Mum prepares dinner: the goal posts in the garden . . . the ball on the grass. I feel different. Everything feels different.

We feast on a sumptuous meal and return before dark to Stoke Mandeville. My parents are exhausted. The day has been bittersweet. They wait until I am settled in bed and tell me they will be back in the morning with croissants for breakfast.

'It was great to have you home,' Dad says.

'Next time you can stay the night,' Mum chimes.

'Thanks, Mum, that would be great,' I lie.

I'm not ready to stay the night. I'm not ready to leave this place. I feel relieved to be back in my safety zone.

13

Scene 30: INTERIOR — COURTROOM — DAY

The clerk at the tribunal of inquiry is arranging a folder of cuttings, letters and emails he has received from Anne Hampson.

EXHIBIT A: A report of Matt Hampson's injury in the *Daily Mail* on 16 March 2005

ENGLAND PROSPECT HAS NECK SURGERY
By Peter Jackson

Leicester player Matt Hampson, one of England's best young prop forwards, underwent emergency surgery last night after suffering a serious neck injury. The 20-year-old was taken to intensive care at Northampton General Hospital after damaging his neck during scrum practice with the England Under 21 squad.

Hampson, who has been on the fringes of Leicester's Premiership team, was treated on the pitch by the side's medical team before being taken to hospital. An RFU statement said: 'The medical teams have consulted Matt's parents and it was agreed that an operation to realign his neck using traction will take place.'

England Under 21 manager Pete Drewett

said last night: 'Our immediate concerns are with Matt and his family. He is getting the best treatment available and we aim to make a further announcement following his operation.'

EXHIBIT B: A letter from Malcolm Phillips, President of the RFU, to Matt Hampson on 17 March 2005

Dear Matt,

We were all devastated to hear of your accident. I have been in the offices at Twickenham for the last two days. Everyone there is affected by your news. On behalf of us all at the RFU I am sending you our best wishes. We are all thinking of you and your family.
   This sounds very inadequate in the circumstances but if there is anything I can do for you or your family please do not hesitate to let me know.

Yours sincerely,
Malcolm Phillips

EXHIBIT C: A letter from Chris Spice, Performance Director at the RFU, to Anne Hampson on 20 July 2005

Dear Anne,

I am writing to follow up on our meeting on Monday which I hope you feel was positive.

There have certainly been some communication issues which I have taken up with the staff here. We now have action plans to ensure that regular meetings of the support group take place and that relevant information is passed to you much more quickly.

Nathan Martin will be in touch regarding the specific actions from our meeting. But please feel free to contact him if you need clarification on any matter and cannot get hold of Dave Phillips.

I offer you, Matt and your family my personal support and I will be making sure I am kept up to date with issues as they arise.

With best wishes,

Chris Spice

EXHIBIT D: A letter from Nathan Martin, Head of Performance Services at the RFU, to Anne Hampson on 20 July 2005

Dear Anne,

I do hope our meeting this week went some way to reassuring you that the Rugby Football Union is trying to support Matt and your family as best it can in the current circumstances. It appears communication has not been as effective as it could have been and I would like to take this opportunity to reiterate that if there is anything which you wish to discuss with me directly please do not hesitate to call.

As we agreed I have outlined the action points below and these will be reviewed by the Support Group at our next meeting.

1. Please continue to send all expenses to John Allen at Leicester Tigers and the RFU will ensure the club receives reimbursement.

2. The investigation into Matt's accident is now underway and the factual report will be completed by the end of August. Shortly after this a copy of the report will be made available to the family. Dr Colin Fuller will be contacting you regarding an interview with Matt.

3. The RFU agreed to provide the required funds for a day carer for Matt whilst he is at Stoke Mandeville from the RFU medical rehabilitation budget. We agreed that this additional care would be reviewed in six months' time in conjunction with advice from the lead consultant.

4. The Support Group's next meeting is on the 10th August and regular meetings will be arranged from this date onwards to review progress and support from all parties.

5. We discussed the insurance conditions associated with Matt's injury and confirmed that he is covered under two

schemes. Firstly, the compulsory Player Accident Policy under which Matt would receive £500,000 and secondly, the Professional Players Policy which would make a further contribution of £625,000. This total amount (£1.125m) would be payable to Matt by the RFU insurers assuming his injury is a permanent total disability.

I shall be in touch shortly to check on Matt's progress and, providing you are in agreement, would like to arrange to see you to ensure everything we discussed has been implemented.

Best wishes,
Nathan Martin
Head of Performance Services

EXHIBIT E: An email from Nathan Martin, Head of Performance Services at the RFU, to Anne Hampson on 18 August 2005

Dear Anne,

Thanks for your time earlier it was good to catch up, albeit briefly. The update on Matt is very encouraging and I hope he gets more positive news on a regular basis from now on.

I would like to pop up and see you both next Tuesday (2pm), if convenient. I'm assuming you will be at Stoke Mandeville, but if not I could make trips to see you both. Perhaps you could let me know in due course if this is ok.

Best wishes
Nathan Martin

EXHIBIT F: Anne Hampson's reply on 18 August 2005

Dear Nathan,

Thanks for the email. I will be at SM on Tues and will look forward to meeting with you. Matt has had lots of strange sensations in his chest, stomach and arms today and we have seen the doctor. She feels his central nervous system is kicking in which is just fantastic news. At last we feel that something is happening and his condition is changing. Matt is quite tentative and dismissive! It must be strange after so long feeling sensations in your body. He is also sleeping more than normal which I feel is a good sign. We met with Pete Drewett yesterday and had a good chat. I know Matt enjoyed seeing him. The visits are so important.

See you next week.
Best wishes,
Anne

**EXHIBIT G: A letter from Leigh Day &
Co to Nathan Martin, Head of Performance
Services at the RFU, on 28 September 2005**

Dear Mr Martin,

<u>Re: Matt Hampson</u>
<u>Accident: 15 March 2005</u>

We have been instructed to act on behalf of
Matt Hampson in connection with the above.
    We would be extremely grateful if you
could assist us by confirming and clarifying
the following:

- Please provide a copy of any Contract of
  Employment/Services existing between the
  RFU and Matt Hampson.
- Please provide a copy of any policy (personal accident, private health or otherwise)
  that Matt is entitled to the benefit of,
  under the terms of that Contract or otherwise.
- Please confirm the identity of the individual or expert instructed by the RFU to
  investigate the events leading up to this
  accident and the timescale for the provi-
  sion of the report.
- Please identify the witnesses that your
  expert/investigator intends to contact prior
  to finalising his report.
- Please confirm that our client will be provided with a full copy of the report and a
  copy of all the evidence referred to therein.

- We assume that the RFU would be agreeable to a meeting to discuss the content of the report, any conclusions and recommendations with our client/his representatives. We would be grateful for your assistance in that regard. We confirm that any arrangements should be made via ourselves.

- We understand that the RFU has been able to provide assistance with the accommodation and other associated costs that have been and continue to be incurred by our client's family in attending to him at Stoke Mandeville. We would be grateful if you would confirm that this assistance will be ongoing until such time as our client is returned (either from Stoke Mandeville or any other medical institution that is not within the immediate vicinity of our client's home address in Oakham) into the care of accommodation at Oakham LE15. Please also confirm that this assistance is provided by the RFU on an entirely gratuitous basis and no claim for refund of any monies paid in relation to accommodation assistance will be made either from our client and/or members of his family/the direct beneficiaries of the financial assistance at any point in the future.

- We understand that the RFU has agreed to meet the cost of a carer. Obviously the question of sufficient care is one of the paramount concerns and we would welcome confirmation as to the basis upon which the RFU proposes to provide this assistance.

We look forward to hearing from you in due course and would thank you in anticipation of your prompt full response.

Yours faithfully

LEIGH DAY & CO

EXHIBIT H: An email from Nathan Martin, Head of Performance Services at the RFU, to Anne Hampson on 11 October 2005

Anne,

Thanks for your expenses form (up to end of Sept) which I received yesterday. I think there may be some confusion over the fee for the carers. You seem to have included two people for the period (Amy Hampson and Adam Wheatly) when we discussed providing a fee for Amy only to cover her university accommodation. I'm sure this is just an over-sight on your part but I wanted to bring this to your attention as I shall be amending the fee accordingly.

Looking forward to hearing from you in due course.

Best wishes

Nathan Martin

EXHIBIT I: Anne Hampson's reply on 12 October 2005

Dear Nathan,

Thank you for your responses with regard to the conference group. I am sorry but I have been ill and unable to reply any sooner. I think the whole family has reached rock bottom following conversations with Matt's consultant last week. We are finding it difficult to communicate with our own family members never mind other people at the current time. It is difficult for others to appreciate the grief we are all feeling. The longer time elapses the less hope we have that Matt will even breathe independently. The last thing any of our family would wish to do would be to exploit a situation, particularly in terms of money which seems so shallow and meaningless at a time like this.

The final nail in the coffin came when I received the email with reference to the expenses. We mistakenly thought we had clarified the situation that Amy and Adam would support Matt as carers. Amy would have been unable emotionally to have lived on her own, working what amounts to a 14 hour day seeing to Matt's needs which are constant — weaning him off the ventilator every hour, running back to the house to prepare meals. Taking Matt outside, to give him some quality of life (which requires two trained people because he is still classed as critical).

Adam showering Matt after hydro-therapy; to allow him a shower with a spray head rather than a hose-pipe because there are no nursing resources to allow for this etc., etc. Nobody knows how dreadful it is. I am proud of the praise that Amy and Adam have received from the staff of Stoke Mandeville during this time.

We therefore feel upset that you have disputed the claim and disappointed that you could not have rung to discuss any misunderstandings. You ensured us that we must claim for all expenditure costs that we might have incurred. Adam played a vital role during this time. We are confident that the care which Amy and Adam provided helped Matt move forward in his recovery. We do appreciate the many efforts made by the RFU to help Matt at this point. We are finding the stress after seven months unbearable. We are only just surviving at the moment.

We are awaiting the long winter months ahead which we now have to consider and it is particularly stressful not knowing where we will spend Christmas and how long we will have to endure the trek to Aylesbury.

Best Wishes

Anne Hampson

EXHIBIT J: A letter from Nathan Martin, Head of Performance Services at the RFU, to Anne Hampson on 14 October 2005

Dear Anne,

Thank you for your email of 12th October 2005.

I fully appreciate that this is a tremendously difficult time for you and your family.

The RFU has tried to provide appropriate support wherever possible. In particular, the RFU has agreed to fund a carer for Matt during his stay at Stoke Mandeville. I had anticipated that this would be in the region of 2 to 3 hours per day. I understand it is now going to be 40 hours per week based on a 3 day week. The funding will end on the 20th January 2006 six months after our meeting at Leicester Tigers or at the date of Matt's discharge from Stoke Mandeville, whichever is earliest.

Whilst I am no expert in these matters I understand that there may be the option of funding from either the local authority or similar body, following Matt's discharge from hospital and I would not want to take any steps which prejudice Matt's opportunity from getting maximum benefit from such funding. However, this is an issue upon which you will no doubt be advised by your solicitors and/or those at Stoke Mandeville.

In order to clarify the RFU's ongoing commitment I summarise below the monthly expenses we are prepared to meet up to 20th January 2006 (or earlier discharge from hospital);

1. Rent for bungalow — £820 for October then reducing to £750 per month as you are moving to an alternative property
2. Council tax — £147 per month
3. Gas bill — £45 per month
4. Petrol — £160 per month
5. Additional food supplements for Matt — £200 per month
6. Carer (Glen McGuire) — 40 hours per week as described above. Fees will be paid directly to ICCU.

Please note that the RFU will be unable to continue to pay for the costs of accommodation beyond 20 January 2006 (or discharge from hospital). You should bear this in mind when negotiating any tenancy arrangement for the alternative property once you leave the bungalow. If Matt is discharged earlier than the 20th January 2006 and this means you are able to leave the rented property earlier if there is any problem with terminating the tenancy the RFU will still cover that item of cost up to 20th January 2006.

As Glen McGuire has now started caring for Matt it is appropriate for the RFU to cease making payments for Amy Hampson. I have looked through the expense claims for the past few months and the RFU has funded 15 weeks worth of care at £100 per week. I have reduced the most recent expense form by the appropriate amount so it reflects this. Please continue to submit your monthly expenses to me in the normal manner. I have spoken with John Allen at Leicester Tigers who suggested, as a trustee of Matt's trust fund, that should there be any additional funding you require that it may be appropriate to source this from the fund.

In view of the complex issues surrounding funding in these circumstances, I suggest it would be sensible for your legal advisors to contact the RFU's solicitors, Beachcroft Wansbroughs, 100 Fetter Lane, EC4A 1 BN, contact Philip Treacy if you have any further enquiries on this letter.

I do not wish to appear in any way unsympathetic and the RFU will continue to provide guidance and support where it can, but as the ongoing funding is far from straightforward, I consider the above may be the most sensible way forward.

Yours sincerely,

Nathan Martin

EXHIBIT K: Anne Hampson's reply on 19 October 2005

Dear Nathan,

Thank you for your letter outlining the RFU

proposals to withdraw support for Matt and have forwarded them to Leicester Tigers, PRA and Sue Bence, the Solicitor who has been instructed to protect Matt's interests in matters arising from his injury. It was felt by all parties that we should digest the contents for a day or two before offering a response.

Following your phone call last Thursday you outlined that your letter to follow would be a proposal and you would welcome further discussions. However, the letter suggested that any queries should be addressed to your legal people and not yourself. I feel very sad that this type of communication is lining the pockets of solicitors but is not providing a solution to helping support Matt. We should be sitting around a table, to come to a common agreeable solution.

We feel it is reasonable to use the trust fund to support the costs incurred by the family. (For your information John Allen is not a Trustee of this fund.) We still believe however, that the RFU have a duty to support Matt with a carer until such time that he leaves hospital. Having promised to help and support the family and eventually provide a carer which Matt desperately needs due to the high level of care he requires (And for the first time since the accident we have felt properly supported) you then write on the Friday to say this support is to be withdrawn. I wonder if

379

people really understand the seriousness of Matt's condition!

Having spoken to all other parties they all find your proposal totally unacceptable and you have actually created stress rather than alleviate it. I never dreamed that the RFU would ever be a heartless institution. I will now have the additional burden of arranging meetings with all concerned.

Yours sincerely,

Anne Hampson.

EXHIBIT L: A fax from Leigh Day & Co (solicitors) to Beachcroft Wansbroughs (solicitors) on 18 October 2005

Dear Sirs,

Our Client: Matthew Hampson
Your Client: RFU
Accident Date: 15 March 2005

We assume you have seen the enclosed letter, sent by your clients to Mrs Hampson.

In the light of the content, which confirms termination of financial support for Matt with effect from the 20th January 2006, we trust that the matters raised and requested by our letter of the 30th September will be addressed by return.

In particular we would ask that you provide copies of the relevant policies and contract as a matter of urgency.

Yours faithfully,

LEIGH DAY & CO

EXHIBIT M: A letter from Nathan Martin, Head of Performance Services at the RFU, to Anne Hampson on 24 October 2005

Dear Anne,

Thank you for your letter of the 19th October 2005.

I am extremely sorry if my letter has caused offence as this was certainly not the intention. I have asked the lawyers to respond quickly to the points raised by Leigh Day & Co and this should be done early next week.

I, and the RFU, very much appreciate the seriousness of Matt's injury and condition and would like to continue the positive dialogue we had until recently in order that we can be as supportive as possible.

I shall give you a call later this week with a view to reinstating the key communication channel between us.

Yours Sincerely

Nathan Martin

EXHIBIT N: An email from Nathan Martin, Head of Performance Services at the RFU, to Anne Hampson on 1 November 2005

Anne,

It was good to talk on Friday, thank you for putting some time aside. Apologies for emailing but as you are back at work this week it's probably the easiest method of communicating and you can pick this up as and when you have time.

I can confirm that the medical information requested from Mr Jamous has still not been received. I am pleased to confirm, however, that the report is complete and the investigating panel are keen to get this to you as soon as possible. I have spoken to them this morning and they have already processed the report and copies of which have been sent to Sue Bence of Leigh Day & Co. I know you mentioned that you were keen for the medical info (supplied by Mr Jamous) to be incorporated but it looks as if events have overtaken themselves slightly. No doubt Sue will be contacting you shortly but if there is anything I can help with please do not hesitate to contact me.

Best wishes

Nathan

EXHIBIT O: An email from Sue Bence of Leigh Day & Co to Anne Hampson on 7 November 2005

Dear Anne,

I have received the RFU investigation report and dvd of the training session this morning. I am not in the office for most of today so I will contact you tomorrow regarding this. The letter from the solicitors also confirms that a copy has been sent directly to you.

Kind Regards,

Sue Bence.

EXHIBIT P: An email from Chris Spice, Performance Director at the RFU, to Anne Hampson on 7 November 2005

Anne hi,

Just to let you know that Nathan Martin is on paternity leave as of today and that Peter Drewett (England Under-21 manager) who sits on the support group will be standing in for Nathan for the next two weeks.

On a personal note I visited Matt with Peter last Thursday night and although he was tired he was in good spirits and it was a pleasure to meet Jackie at the same time.

With best wishes,

Chris Spice

EXHIBIT Q: An email from Anne Hampson to Nathan Martin, Head of Performance Services at the RFU, on 9 November 2005

Dear Nathan,

Congratulations on the birth of your first child. Welcome to the world of emotional turmoil!! I know it is a difficult time for yourself but we are feeling more and more frustrated with the very poor communications which we are experiencing. We have not received a copy of the investigation report as promised. We have been told a number of conflicting reasons including that a copy has been sent to the family and the solicitor (by yourself when you telephoned on Friday 28th October) and that two copies have been sent to the solicitor, one of which is intended for the family (by Dave Phillips on Tues 8th November). Neither of these actions have happened. Sue Bence is now in receipt of one copy of the report + a dvd in a broken case with a scribbled reference to Matt's accident. This was posted to the Manchester office which I believe is a breach of confidentiality. I thought the RFU were endeavouring to improve communications but cannot even ensure that we receive a copy of a very important report. I sent an email to Chris Spice yesterday with reference to a number of issues which need to be resolved quickly and I have not as yet had any response. Is anybody responsible during your absence??? I think the RFU needs to take seriously its responsibility for one of their players and realise that people need to be treated with sensitivity.

Anne Hampson

EXHIBIT R: A fax from Leigh Day & Co (solicitors) to Beachcroft Wansbroughs (solicitors) on 9 November 2005

Dear Sirs,

Our Client: Matthew Hampson
Your Client: RFU
Accident Date: 15 March 2005

Your letter of the 2 November arrived at our office on the 7th.

Please refrain from writing to what was our Manchester office.

The only correspondence you have ever received concerning Matthew Hampson is from the address at the foot of this letter.

Would you please immediately revise your records accordingly and ensure that all future correspondence is appropriately directed.

Having spoken to Mrs Hampson today we understand that the RFU have not in fact, sent copies of the report and DVD of the training session directly to her. We await hearing from you further in relation to the policies.

Yours faithfully

Leigh Day & Co

EXHIBIT S: An email from Chris Spice, Performance Director of the RFU, to Anne Hampson on 9 November 2005

Anne,

I am sorry but I have not received an email from you yesterday so I am unable to respond to that note. I have just now checked with our legal department regarding the sending of the report. Nathan was correct in saying that two copies were sent to our lawyers on 28th October for forwarding to your solicitors. Having just checked with them it seems there was some misunderstanding between the legal teams and only one copy was forwarded to Sue Bence. This has now been rectified and our legal department is contacting our lawyers to inform them to forward the second copy as per Nathan's original request. I am also asking the legal teams to check why anything went to Manchester.

In terms of the broken case, this is unfortunate but I am informed it was in good order when it left our offices.

Anne, we fully understand the need to act sensitively but Nathan has done everything that he was asked to do in this case and reported it to you appropriately. I apologise for the inconvenience caused as we had expected both copies to arrive as discussed with you. I have now spoken to all the respective parties in order to ensure we do not have any similar occurrences.

Please let me have a copy of the email you sent yesterday and I shall deal with it when I am back in the office tomorrow.

Kind regards,

Chris Spice

EXHIBIT T: An email from Nathan Martin, Head of Performance Services at the RFU, to Anne Hampson on 21 November 2005

Anne,

Just a quick email as I am now back in the office (as of this morning) having been away on paternity leave for 2 weeks and I shall speak to Chris Spice and Peter Drewett for an update on events during my absence and come back to you once I have done so.

Best wishes, speak soon.

Nathan.

EXHIBIT U: An email from Anne Hampson to Nathan Martin, Head of Performance Services at the RFU, on 22 November 2005

Dear Nathan,

Leicester Tigers arranged the meeting with yourselves to alleviate the stress we have been under recently dealing with yourselves. The clear lines of communication have certainly not been evident. The cold tone of your email and recent letters reflects the RFU's attitude towards our family. Dialogue should be through conversation not emails! Chris Spice refused to answer my email during the time you were absent even though I forwarded it as he had requested. Maybe a phone call would not have been amiss to clarify any concerns we had. Matt had a major setback during that week and had to undergo brain scans as he had lapsed into an unconscious state. Support at this time would have been welcome. Maybe such a response would have been too personal and human for the RFU. My husband currently has his mother, father & son in different hospitals.

We were saddened and frankly shocked by the treatment and lack of warmth. At our last conversation three weeks ago you said that mistakes have been made and lessons have been learned so I was disappointed to have another terse email from yourself. I have forwarded a copy of this letter to Andy Robinson who spent an afternoon with us and showed great compassion and empathy. As a head-teacher, the many colleagues and parents I have dealt with over the years would not describe me as a 'neurotic' person in any shape or form merely a mother incensed by the treatment I have received. I take great exception to this being reported at an RFU meeting.

If you want to move forward and improve communications maybe a few truths need to be admitted. It was reported by Chris Spice at last Friday's meeting that you had carefully explained the detail of your letter outlining the withdrawal of funding from Jan 20th before posting it to the family. Alas again this is far from the truth. We deserve more respect than this. It made us realise how little you appreciate the severity of Matt's injury when my husband took another Stoke Mandeville patient to Twickenham in Matt's place. The parking and access was extremely difficult. The seating was totally inappropriate with little cover for a patient who cannot control his body temperature. Do you not feel that Matt was worthy of a special day having represented his country on numerous occasions. Would a place in an enclosed box cost the RFU too much money?

We know in 135 years nobody has ever received such a serious injury at an elite level. We feel your board are currently in denial. Matt should be treated with the respect he deserves as an England player. You owe it to Matt and the rest of the rugby community to show you do care for one of your boys. We do not want confrontation, we simply want you to help and support our son and make him feel valued by all of you at the RFU.

Anne Hampson

EXHIBIT V: An email from Chris Spice, Performance Director of the RFU, to Anne Hampson on 25 November 2005

Cc: Andy Robinson; Damian Hopley; Roy Jackson; Sue Bence: Alex Anderson; Dusty Hare; Peter Drewett: John Allen: Phil Winstanley: David Phillips; Nathan Martin

Dear Anne,

I was very concerned at the contents of your email below to Nathan. Like you, I much prefer to speak to people than communicate via email but it does help to keep a written record of what has been discussed, and when so many people are copied in on correspondence it does make replying to all concerned much quicker. I hope you don't mind in this case.

I need to state first of all that the RFU is fully committed to supporting Matt now and in the future. This is evident through the efforts of the support group and I thought it appropriate to reaffirm this to you today. As you are aware we are in uncharted waters and we are all learning by the process whilst at the same time providing as much support to Matt, you, and your family as we can. Supporting Matt remains at the forefront of everything we are doing.

I was therefore saddened by the contents of your email to Nathan who was quite upset by the charges you have levelled against the RFU and Nathan personally. We are all trying to stay focused on what is best for Matt, however your response has meant that Nathan has asked to be removed from the support group. I find this very disappointing as Nathan has managed Matt's support programme in a sensitive but highly professional manner. He has spent an incredible amount of time on this, not only with the creation and management of the support group but also in championing support for Matt within the corridors of the RFU. I asked several other people to read through his email to you and none of them found the contents 'terse', 'cold' or having a 'lack of warmth'. I am sorry you feel this way. Nathan was trying to clarify what had and had not been agreed and explain areas where we could be of further help — for example, an up-front payment of your expenses so you are not waiting on us to process your invoice each month.

I also need to clarify a number of issues you mentioned in your email.

You referred to Leicester Tigers as having arranged our recent meeting when it actually came about at the suggestion of Damian Hopley to myself.

In terms of your reference to me ignoring your emails nothing could be further from the truth. I have never received a copy of any of the emails to which you refer. Each time I was alerted to a problem (generally an email forwarded to me by someone else) we dealt with it as swiftly as possible, often in the same day, and we communicated our action to you immediately. To date, I have still not received any direct email correspondence from you, on any issues, which makes me think there might be a technical problem somewhere.

I do think it's best that we remove Nathan from Matt's support group for the moment and I will need to consider who to appoint in
his place. If you could bear with me until I have found an appropriate person, that would be appreciated. In the meantime it would be most helpful if you could please email me with the acknowledgement of this email so that I can see if there are any technical problems at my end.

Anne, can I assure you that we do appreciate the severity of Matt's injury and that we are all working hard to make things happen as quickly as possible for you. In some instances we can move quickly, in others it takes more time and I am mindful that the responses you get are not always what you want to hear. We try and deliver these messages as sensitively as possible but in written communication this is sometimes very difficult.

If you would like to discuss any of these issues please let me know the most appropriate time that I'll be able to call you.

Kind regards,

Chris Spice.

Dear Chris,

This email appeared in my contacts list and therefore the address corresponds with the address where emails have been sent. There must then be a problem at the RFU? Hopefully you will have received this reply. We are only asking for what should be a part of any good organisation which is good communication. Resolution is always the best policy with people learning from each other to move forward with issues and problems. I would prefer to be talking to people in preference to writing this email.

It is disappointing that Nathan feels he would prefer to turn his back on the situation. We appreciate that he has done some good work along the way. However mistakes have been made and need to be rectified. Maybe you could seek feedback from us on why we found the emails cold. If he would like to telephone or maybe pay us a visit we would be glad to have discussions. If any of you were in our situation you would realise how upsetting this comment was which was used frequently in his correspondence 'unless of course Matt is released from hospital before the 20th January'. We are struggling to get a decision from the consultant whether Matt will be able to have Christmas day at home so it would seem highly unlikely that he will be home for some time yet. Most people who have an understanding of our situation find comments like this upsetting. If the email is a façade for legal dialogue then please send these as letters through the post.

The second component of any good organisation is valuing people and putting them at the heart of your vision. If you want to work with us I think you will have to start communicating through talk. So many misunderstandings could have been avoided if somebody could have picked up the phone. The reason we feel so well supported by the Tigers and the PRA is because they chat regularly and have a very good understanding of problems as they arise. As you comment you are in new territory. The situation will not go away for any of us! We need to find common ground and work collaboratively. We are looking forward to meeting your chairman on Sunday, maybe then more of your people will realise what a brave and courageous son we have who deserves every support from the RFU.

Thank you.

Yours sincerely

Anne Hampson

EXHIBIT X: An email from Anne Hampson to Martyn Thomas, Chairman of the RFU Management Board, on 28 November 2005

Dear Martyn,

Many thanks for your visit yesterday. I know Matt enjoyed the chat and we all felt our discussions were both positive and constructive. I will meet with Peter Wheeler and discuss how we can move forward together with the RFU to further support Matt. I will put some thoughts down on paper over the next few days. I think a meeting at Tigers may be the most appropriate at the end of December if you are available.

Kind regards,

Anne Hampson

EXHIBIT Y: An email from Anne Hampson to Roy Jackson, President of Leicester Tigers, on 28 November 28 2005

Dear Roy,

We had a very productive meeting with Martyn Thomas yesterday. He wants me to work on a proposal of how we feel the RFU can support Matt and the family. He said he was happy to come to Tigers to meet with Peter Wheeler, myself and other interested parties. I need therefore to chat and draft some notes of what we feel is reasonable. He has already guaranteed that Matt's carer will remain for six months from the 20th Jan.

Will speak to you soon.

Best wishes

Anne

EXHIBIT Z: An email from Martyn Thomas, Chairman of the RFU Management Board, to Anne Hampson on 30 November 2005

Dear Anne,

Thanks for your email. You have a delightful and courageous son. It was a privilege to meet Matt on Sunday. Hopefully Matt got home for his birthday. I wanted to ring last night to wish Matt all the best, but I know how much you have to plan and do to facilitate a home visit so I did not want to trouble you. Nevertheless my thoughts were with Matt on a special birthday. To confirm our talk on Sunday, the Rugby Football Union will maintain the cost of Matt's personal carer, Glen, on the same terms as at present for a period of 6 months from the 1st January 2006 or until Matt is discharged from Stoke Mandeville Hospital, whichever is the earlier.

I will be pleased to attend a meeting at Tigers

as you wish. It would be helpful if you could let me know a suggested date as soon as possible. Although Matt is and must be the focus of all our thoughts, I would take the opportunity to say how much I admired the quiet dignity and fortitude shown by you and Phil.

Best wishes,

Martyn

14

20 October. This morning, after 208 days of captivity, Paul Taiano left Stoke Mandeville. I asked if he had any immediate plans. 'I'm in work on Monday and have three meetings arranged,' he replied.

Ask a silly question . . .

15

Perhaps you played this game in school?

Twenty seconds.

The boring maths class when you decided to switch off, fill your lungs and hold your breath.

Thirty seconds.

Were you bothered that pi is a mathematical constant whose value is the ratio of any circle's circumference to its diameter in Euclidean space?

Forty seconds.

Did it matter that this is the same value as the ratio of a circle's area to the space of its radius?

One minute five seconds.

Did you care that it is approximately equal to 3.14159265 in the usual decimal notation?

One minute twenty seconds.

No, you didn't give a toss.

One minute thirty seconds.

The only decimals that mattered were on the clock above the blackboard.

One minute forty seconds.

The only notation that mattered was the 1′ 52 you set during science.

One minute fifty seconds.

Could you beat it? Could you handle the screaming in your lungs?

YESSSSSSSSS!

And here I am, a decade later, still playing the same game.

16

These are the targets Jamous set in July to wean me off the ventilator:

LEVEL 1: Two minutes three times a day.
LEVEL 2: Two minutes every hour.
LEVEL 3: Five minutes every hour.
LEVEL 4: Ten minutes every hour.
LEVEL 5: Twenty minutes every hour.
LEVEL 6: Thirty minutes every hour.
LEVEL 7: One hour on, one hour off.
LEVEL 8: Through the day.
LEVEL 9: Through the night.

It's November. I have stalled at level 4.

17

Initially, the process appealed to me. I was used to setting targets at Tigers and enjoyed the challenge of weights or intervals in the gym. I thought: I'm an athlete; I've got discipline; I can do this. But it's not the same. Every second feels like a minute when that pipe is off my neck. I've tried to ignore the clock and pushed myself to the absolute limit but it's like trying to walk on water. I want to quit. I've had enough. But how do I tell my father? He phoned this afternoon and started squeezing me again. 'How's the weaning going?' he says. It's never 'Hi, Matt' or 'How are you?' any more, it's 'How's the weaning going?' And the first thing he will do when he visits this weekend is examine my chart. 'Oh! Still stuck at level 4 I see!' He is absolutely desperate to get me off this ventilator; I am absolutely desperate not to let him down.

18

Saturday, 12 November, a day of many firsts: my first visit to Welford Road since the accident; the first time I have watched Tigers from a corporate box; the first time I've been treated to a standing ovation; my first time to meet Tony Spreadbury since the day he saved my life. The reception from everyone at the club was extraordinary.

Gloucester opened the scoring with a penalty after three minutes and then Michael Holford, my friend and I guess now former team-mate, replied for Tigers with a typical props try. As he was running back for the restart, he saluted me on the balcony. I was deeply moved. It was a scrappy old game and we just about did enough to win. The match referee came to see me when it was over: 'How are you, Matt?' He smiled. 'How's it going?'

'Yeah, fine, thanks, Spreaders,' I replied, lamely.

I should have said more; I wanted to thank him, but found myself choking for the umpteenth time. It was a long and emotional day.

As I left the ground with my parents for the drive back to Stoke Mandeville I was approached by Owen Rushton, a nine-year-old Tigers fan, who looked at me like he had just seen Johno. 'Hi, Matt.' He beamed.

'How do you know Matt?' my father enquired.

'Because he's a Tigers player,' he replied.

It made my day.

19

From the Tigers lads, a canvas portrait of Al Pacino in *Scarface*; from the Cornwell family, a canvas from *Pulp Fiction*; from the Cowling twins, an Armani watch; from Indy, a giant portrait of New York; from Sue Dowse, a silver tankard; from Jennie, a card:

To Pumpkin,
Happy Birthday.
Love you lots & lots & lots & lots & lots
Jennie xxxxxxxxxxxx

It's 29 November. I am twenty-one today.

20

Twelve days to Christmas, one question turning over and over in my head: Do I keep torturing myself trying to reach level 5 or start living with what I've got? I booked an appointment with Jamous this morning and announced my decision. 'I cannot breathe by myself,' I said. 'I've done everything you've said to try and wean off the vent but it's killing me.'

'I understand, Matt,' he replied. 'And if you decide you want to try it again, I will support you.'

'I'm sorry, Dr Jamous. I didn't want to let anyone down.'

'Don't be silly,' he said. 'You gave it a good shot. We can start thinking about moving you downstairs now and getting you ready for discharge.'

'Okay, thanks.'

And I felt a weight lift from my shoulders.

21

Scene 31: INTERIOR — COURTROOM — DAY

Amy Hampson has been called to the tribunal. She is accompanied by her fiancé, Adam Wheatly, and her younger brother, Tom.

BARRISTER
Miss Hampson, you're a teacher by profession. Is that correct?

AMY HAMPSON
That is correct.

BARRISTER
How old were you on the morning of 15 March 2005?

AMY HAMPSON
I was twenty-two.

BARRISTER
What effect did that day have on your family?

AMY HAMPSON
It changed our whole lives completely. We went from a fairly normal lifestyle — watching Matt play rugby, meeting up at the pub — to spending every weekend in hospital. No one could imagine the stress of what it felt like

. . . driving down there, trying to find some-where to stay. It was getting ridiculous until Mum and Dad got the bungalow. We stayed in that for weeks on end. It had a tremendous effect on everybody and makes you look at life differently.

BARRISTER
How differently? What do you mean by that?

AMY HAMPSON
I don't know just . . . sometimes when you are being petty or selfish which we all are at times or . . . I remember when I got my first job thinking: God! I have to teach a class. This is going to be awful. But it's all pretty trivial com-pared with what my brother has to deal with. It makes you think that life is too short and you have to just get on with it.

BARRISTER
How would you describe your relationship with your brother before his accident?

AMY HAMPSON
Typical brother and sister I suppose — we used to fight like cats and dogs when we were younger — and our characters are quite different. I take after my mum — we are both teachers — but Matt is . . .

BARRISTER
He takes after his father?

AMY HAMPSON
Not physically. They have probably got a similar
sense of humour but that would be it. Matt
has his own character; loud and boisterous at
times but essentially quite shy; big and tough
and strong but one of the most kind-hearted
people I know. He was always very protective
of me but I think it was only when he
started playing for England that we became
really close.

BARRISTER
Could you explain that, please?

AMY HAMPSON
Rugby has always been part of our lives. I was
never that fussed about watching it but was
dragged along for years. In 2003, I went to Australia for a few months with Adam and we got a call
from Mum just before we were due to come home
saying Matt had been picked for the Under-19
World Cup in France. We flew straight back to
London and got a connection to Paris. It was
amazing.

BARRISTER
Yes, I'm sure but how did it change your relationship?

AMY HAMPSON
It marked a turning point I suppose between
Matt and Adam. We had been going out for
almost four years at that point, but they had
never really got along. Then Adam moved into

our house and they started spending more and more time together.

BARRISTER
Miss Hampson, are you familiar with this photograph?

The clerk hands her a photograph of her brother signing an autograph.

AMY HAMPSON
Yes, the Italy game, four days before Matt's accident. I took a lot of photographs that night. It was weird seeing these little kids asking for his signature.

BARRISTER
Is photography a hobby?

AMY HAMPSON
No. I was at Bristol University and we had a photography project as part of our degree. I decided to base mine on Matt's rugby career and took photographs at the France and Italy games at Northampton. It was the last time I saw him before his accident.

BARRISTER
How did you hear about it?

AMY HAMPSON
I was in Bristol. It was weird. I had a meeting with the art teacher about my project and what it was about and I came out and there was a missed call

from my mother on my phone. I called her back and she told me that he had been taken to Northampton hospital. I had an exam the following morning and didn't see him until the day after his operation at Stoke Mandeville. I remember driving down there, a cold, drizzly day. I was trying to stay positive: Matt has always pulled out of everything. Of course he is going to be okay. Mum and Dad were waiting in the car park. They looked completely exhausted.

BARRISTER
Your brother was in intensive care?

AMY HAMPSON
Yes.

BARRISTER
What were your first impressions?

AMY HAMPSON
His body was completely swollen, just enormous and he was sedated. I was told he might be able to hear my voice, I said, 'Matt, hi, it's Amy,' and his eyes flickered. There were so many questions that you wanted to ask but he was out of it.

BARRISTER
Did you stay or go home?

AMY HAMPSON
We stayed at Carole's house — Cabbage's mum. We went back the following day and he was awake but he could not talk. We were trying to

411

reassure him that he was going to be okay. He was mouthing things but we could not read his lips. Dad would get very worked up and cross with himself. It was very frustrating.

BARRISTER
How long was it before he spoke for the first time?

AMY HAMPSON
Two . . . two and a half months . . . I was back at university and got a call saying Matt was on the phone. It was amazing because I had been having this one-way conversation with him by phone for months — I'd talk and he would listen. Suddenly there's this squeak on the other end: 'Hello, Amy, I am gay . . . I have a gay voice.' And he did actually sound quite camp for a while. I went over that weekend. It was so nice to be able to talk to him, although I think he found it quite awkward.

BARRISTER
Why was it awkward?

AMY HAMPSON
Because now that he had his voice back, he could talk about everything.

BARRISTER
And did he?

AMY HAMPSON
Not really. He told us about some of the dreams he had had and flashbacks of what he could remember, but he was restricted by the ventilator.

He would say something and his voice would go and he would have to repeat it. We would be there until 12.30 a.m. most nights because it took him so long . . . Not that we wanted to leave him. We did not ever want to leave him.

BARRISTER
How much time did you spend with him?

AMY HAMPSON
Adam and I spent the whole of the summer holidays with him. We had no knowledge about spinal injuries or anything when we first went but we just watched the nurses, especially Adam who picks up things very quickly. He watched what they did and we learned how to do a suction and how to bag him if there was an emergency. Adam would wash him and dress him and do his bowels. It was very draining and very hard. I'll never forget the first time I saw him in a wheelchair . . . it was actually harder than seeing him in bed.

BARRISTER
Why was it harder?

AMY HAMPSON
It made it more real. They brought him this awful disgusting wheelchair — this great big tank of a thing that looked like something off Scrapheap Challenge. There were quite a few people there, a few of the Tigers lads, and I think that made it hard for him. They brought this big hoist around, put him in a sling and hoisted him up. He was

panicking, shouting, 'Hold my head! Hold my head!' He could not even hold his own head! And to see him being lifted, this big dead weight . . . That is when the reality hit.

BARRISTER
You found it distressing.

AMY HAMPSON
It was awful. I felt sick. And to see the look on his friends' faces! God, it was not nice to see him in that chair. We lifted his legs and rested them on a pillow for five minutes. Then he said he felt sick and wanted to get straight back to bed. 'Hold my head. Hold my head.' From there on, it was a case of lifting him into the chair and back again. He would do fifteen minutes, and then twenty minutes and after a while we were able to push him around. He was glad to get out of the ward and see other people. And he was finally able to talk to Paul about his accident. Paul was so lovely . . .

BARRISTER
I'm sorry, Miss Hampson, Paul is?

AMY HAMPSON
Paul Taiano. They became very close. Paul's injury is lower down and it was amazing to see him progress. He would say, 'I can move my little finger today. I have moved it.' And we would say to Matt, 'You'll probably start doing things soon.' But another week would pass and Matt was still showing nothing. Those were the most difficult

414

times, those first three to four months. And then he had this phrenic nerve test and they said there had been an improvement in one side.

BARRISTER
Were you there that day?

AMY HAMPSON
Yes, I think we all were. He came back and said, 'There is a chance that I might breathe again,' and he burst out crying. We all had a bit of a cry. This was such good news. 'Right, let's get you weaning. Let's get this diaphragm working. Let's practise it.' It started with the nurses coming in every hour and then it almost felt like the nurses had given up. They said, 'If you guys want to do it with him, then you can.' So we took it in our own hands.

BARRISTER
You started weaning him?

AMY HAMPSON
Yes. Every hour it would be a case of 'Right, Matt, are you ready to start?' We would give him a bit of oxygen and then take him off. We used to write down when he did it, for how long and how many litres of oxygen we had given him. It carried on for months. He got a chest infection and we had to stop and start again. He was finding it so hard and it was obvious that it wasn't coming naturally to him. It was really tiring — he would do it, fall asleep and then wake up in time for the next

one. It got to the stage where it was making him miserable. And after that there was Jennie . . .

BARRISTER
You are referring to Miss Marceau?

AMY HAMPSON
Yes. I had never met her before. I didn't know he was seeing anybody until his bag was sent back from the hotel in Northampton and we picked up his mobile phone and there were all these text messages from this Jennie girl asking: 'Where are you? Are you okay? What has happened?' She wanted to come and see him. She came to visit him about ten days after his accident when he was still in intensive care. I met her and was trying to reassure her. 'Do you think he will be okay?' she asked. 'I really like him.' I said, 'Yeah, he will be fine.' We were both reassuring each other really. She spent a lot of time at the hospital. I was glad she was there. She kept him upbeat — she would pinch people's grapes in the other beds and make him laugh or lie on the bed and watch DVDs and talk to him. At the time, it was great but everybody, especially my parents, had it in the back of their mind: 'How long is this going to last?'

22

Every moment she discovered in Quasimodo some additional deformity. Her eye wandered from his crooked legs to the hump on his back, from the hump on his back to his one eye. She could not understand how a beast so awkwardly fashioned could be in existence. But withal there was so much sadness and gentleness about him that she began to be reconciled to it.

— Victor Hugo,
The Hunchback of Notre-Dame

23

It has been almost a year since my incarceration. I have one regret. It happened late one Friday evening, about five weeks after my accident, when Jennie and I were alone. I still couldn't speak at that point but Jennie can talk for England and regaled me for hours with stories of her life and our calamitous first date. 'You get one chance to sleep with me and you blow it by snoring.' She smiled. 'What am I going to do with you, pumpkin head?' We gazed at each other in silence. 'I love you,' I mouthed. She smiled and caressed my face with her hand but looked shaken. It was as if I had just pointed a gun at her head . . . which, in a sense, I had.

24

Three nights passed; three nights and three more 'I love you's'; three nights when those words must have wreaked havoc on her mind. And then, she yielded. It was late. We had just watched a movie and she was lying by my side. I gazed at her tenderly and said it again. 'I love you too,' she replied. The covenant was signed. We were together now, for ever: Quasimodo and Esmerelda.

25

The late Christopher Reeve once said, 'The body and mind, in trying to survive, can be totally selfish. You say, 'Screw the rest of the world, take care of me. Me first.' ' How true. In the eleven months since my accident, I have perfected the art of the bright, cheery smile and learned to calculate and manipulate. Do I smile because I'm enjoying myself here? No, I smile because I am totally dependent. Do I shout at the doctors or nurses? No, I shout at my mother and my sister because I know they won't hurt me. Am I aware my parents are hanging on by their fingertips? Yes, I am. Has it stopped me making demands of them? No. Did I truly love Jennie or was that too about survival? I wasn't sure.

26

The bit I can't quite fathom is that first visit to Stoke Mandeville. Think about it: you're a bright, beautiful young girl and the boyfriend you have just started dating has had a terrible accident. You send him a card and decide to visit. They escort you to a darkened room in intensive care and the object of your desire has tubes coming out of every orifice and a piss bag strapped to his bed. He looks battered and bruised and swollen; there's a machine keeping him alive. Some of the other patients in the room will be lucky to survive the night. And you stay, you keep coming back.

27

James Haskell and Tom Rees have driven up from London. We haven't met since that morning at Franklin's Gardens and now life has moved on. They've got some big games with Wasps and England ahead, they've got World Cups to play and interviews to give and boot contracts to sign. I've got Jennie. She is sitting by my side. That means everything on a day like this when my friends have come to visit.

Take a good look, boys. Isn't she lovely? And she's mine. I have still got a beautiful girlfriend. I have not lost everything. I am still a man.

28

I have just taken delivery of a new electric wheelchair. Jennie is sitting on my lap and we are bombing around the ward. She makes me laugh. She has become much more to me than a trophy. Every week I find myself enjoying her more; every week I find myself needing her more; every week I find myself wanting and loving her more. But how do I express that love? How do I show her affection? I can't take her in my arms or run my fingers through her hair. I can't give her a hug when she is upset. I can't move so I have to ask whenever we kiss. We will never make love. Every week I find myself feeling more and more inadequate. And every week I get a sense she is having second thoughts.

29

She is lying by my side with her arm around me; I can't feel her or touch her or smell her; we are separated by a Grand Canyon I may never cross. 'I want you to close your eyes and feel my energy,' she says. 'I'm going to hold your hand and pinch your fingers.' I close my eyes and concentrate . . .

'Do you feel that?'

'No.'

'What about this?'

'No.'

'This?'

'No.'

'This?'

'No.'

'This?'

'No.'

I feel her salt tears on my face. I have run out of fingers. 'Oh, Matt, you are going to get better, aren't you?' she implores.

'Of course I am.'

'Tell me you are going to get better.'

'I am going to get better, Jennie.'

'Say it again.'

'I am going to get better, Jennie.'

And now the tears on my face are mine.

30

Scene 32: INTERIOR — COURTROOM — DAY

Jennifer Marceau has been called to the tribunal.

BARRISTER
Miss Marceau, could you tell the tribunal a little
about your background, please? Marceau
. . . What a lovely name.
French, obviously?

JENNIFER MARCEAU
Yes, my great-grandfather was French. My mum is
Yugoslavian. My parents were teachers. I was born
in Reading but grew up in Abingdon and then,
when I was thirteen, we moved to Leicester.

BARRISTER
And is it Jenna, Jennie or Jennifer?

JENNIFER MARCEAU
I'm Jenna on my birth cert, my friends call me
Jennie and Jennifer is my stage name.

BARRISTER
You're an actress?

JENNIFER MARCEAU
Yes, mostly theatre but I've done a couple of independent movies since moving to Los Angeles.

BARRISTER
How long have you lived in Los Angeles?

JENNIFER MARCEAU
Just over a year now. I'm looking for new representation at the moment. I'm trying to do more screen.

BARRISTER
Miss Marceau, you are slightly older than Mr Hampson. Is that correct?

JENNIFER MARCEAU
Yes, two years older.

BARRISTER
And on the night you first met you were in college. Is that correct?

JENNIFER MARCEAU
Yes. I was studying law at De Montfort University. I was not sure about him in the beginning — it definitely wasn't love at first sight. He was quite drunk and he snored and I wasn't going to call him again. And I didn't think he would call me but he started sending me these strange little texts: 'What are you doing?' I just thought: 'Oh. That's a bit weird.' Then he called and we went out again and I really started to like him.

BARRISTER
What did you like about him?

JENNIFER MARCEAU
On our first date . . . well, our first real date, he took me for a drink on the Queen's Road. He was really shy — I liked that — and really sweet. 'Can I kiss you?' he says. I couldn't believe it.

BARRISTER
That he would ask permission?

JENNIFER MARCEAU
Yeah. I just felt really comfortable with him. We'd speak on the phone for hours every day when he wasn't in Leicester. Then, when he was, we used to hang out.

BARRISTER
You first met on the night of Saturday, 19 February 2005.
Is that correct?

JENNIFER MARCEAU
That sounds about right.

BARRISTER
Four weeks before his accident.

JENNIFER MARCEAU
Yes.

BARRISTER
And during those four weeks he played several times for England so you would have dated what . . . three . . . four times?

427

JENNIFER MARCEAU
Yes.

BARRISTER
How do you fall in love with someone you hardly know?

JENNIFER MARCEAU
Well, for him it was like . . . he hadn't been with girls before. And for me . . . I'm slightly older than him and had had a few relationships and . . . I don't know, I can't explain it. Sometimes you meet someone and they are everything you have been looking for. I couldn't stop thinking about him. I hadn't had that before.

BARRISTER
How did you hear about his accident?

JENNIFER MARCEAU
I had a feeling something weird had happened. We would always text, like every second of the day, so I sent him a message and a few hours went by and there was no reply. I thought: That is so weird. Maybe he has lost his phone or something. And then a friend — a guy who liked rugby — called me at home and told me Matt had had an accident. I thought he had hurt his arm or shoulder or something. I said, 'Okay, at least he has an excuse for not texting me back.' But then he said, 'It was a bad accident. He's had a neck injury.' I still didn't think anything of it. I was like, 'Okay, whatever.' I knew he was one of those people in that circle thingy . . .

428

BARRISTER
You mean the scrum?

JENNIFER MARCEAU
Yes, but I still didn't think it was serious. I thought: His phone is probably in his locker. He will text me as soon as he comes out of the injury room. I called him a million times and sent a million texts: 'What is going on?' But there was still no reply. Then I called his sister — I can't remember how I got her number — but she was really nice. 'He's had an accident,' she said. She sounded really upset. I was still a bit confused until she told me he was unconscious. I didn't eat. I didn't sleep. I must have cried for over a week. And then Matt took me down to see him.

BARRISTER
Mr Cornwell?

JENNIFER MARCEAU
Yes. I was really happy to see him, really happy. He wasn't moving. I thought they had given him something to keep him still and then, I guess, gradually I found out more about what had happened.

BARRISTER
So when you saw Mr Hampson first, you didn't fully appreciate the gravity of his injury?

JENNIFER MARCEAU
People didn't really tell me much. I researched it

429

on the internet — the C and T vertebrae; complete and incomplete spinal cord lesions and injuries. I kept asking the nurses when he was going to get better. 'We don't know. We don't know.' Then I was like, 'Well, is he ever going to move again?' They never gave me a proper answer. I couldn't come to terms with it.

She starts to cry and reaches for a handkerchief. The clerk hands her a glass of water.

JENNIFER MARCEAU
I'm sorry.

BARRISTER
That's okay, Miss Marceau. Take your time.

JENNIFER MARCEAU
I kept looking for cures on the internet. I would hold his hand when he was asleep and try to channel my energy into him. The more time we spent together the more attached we got. I stopped going to college so I could spend more time at the hospital. I wanted him to get better but nothing was happening. He wasn't improving. I thought: Why has this happened to me? I have gone through all these bad relationships and I finally find someone I can see myself being with and this happens to him.

BARRISTER
In hindsight, Miss Marceau, would it have been easier if you ended the relationship sooner?

JENNIFER MARCEAU
Yes.

BARRISTER
How did you end the relationship?

JENNIFER MARCEAU
He started asking whether I could be with him for
ever. We started talking about it all the time.

BARRISTER
When?

JENNIFER MARCEAU
It was just before I moved to London, about nine
or ten months after his accident. I didn't know at
that point. I was like, 'Well, I am okay for now
but I can't be like this for ever. I want you to get
better.' But he kept pushing me: 'I need an
answer. I need to know whether you can be with
me for ever.'

BARRISTER
He wanted you to make a commitment?

JENNIFER MARCEAU
Yes. I said, 'Look, I want to be with you now but I
can't say about the future.' I didn't want to
commit and hurt him further down the line. I
already felt so bad about him. I didn't feel sorry
for him, not in that way, I just felt that we were
both losing out on something special. But as soon
as he started asking if I could stay with him for
ever it was a no-win situation. 'I can't answer

that,' I said. He took it badly. 'Then it's better if we don't speak,' he said. I kept calling him but he wouldn't speak to me. I was really angry about it.

BARRISTER
Why were you angry?

JENNIFER MARCEAU
He didn't understand that it was hurting me as much as him. Or even more . . . Well, maybe not more, but he didn't understand that it was just as hard for me. Because it wasn't like I was saying, 'Oh, I'm going to find someone else; I don't want to be with you because you can't walk.' And I really wanted to stay friends with him but he didn't want to talk to me. I got really depressed for a while and drank too much alcohol. I was on anti-depressants. I just felt really alone.

BARRISTER
What about your family . . . your friends?

JENNIFER MARCEAU
They were okay but there was nothing they could say to make me feel better. Because however sup-portive your family are, it's not going to make a difference as to whether or not the person you love is . . .

She breaks down again and takes a moment to com-pose herself.

JENNIFER MARCEAU
The pain was too bad. Nothing they could say could help. I couldn't stay in Leicester any more — everything just reminded me of Matt. I felt worthless. I didn't know what to do. I thought: I completely gave up my life to be with him and he doesn't even want to talk to me now.

BARRISTER
Could you see it from his point of view, Miss Marceau?

JENNIFER MARCEAU
Yes, of course, but I guess I just felt that he . . .

BARRISTER
. . . couldn't see it from your point of view?

JENNIFER MARCEAU
No. I've tried to date and stuff since and had one or two short relationships but I don't think I'll find someone like him again.

BARRISTER
Have you had any contact with him since?

JENNIFER MARCEAU
Yes. He sent me a message on Facebook recently. I was really happy to hear from him, really glad, because I always felt so awful at the way that it ended.

BARRISTER
What did the message say?

JENNIFER MARCEAU
'How are you doing? I still think about you.'

31

She had altogether ceased to see or to hear Quasimodo. The poor ringer seemed to have departed from the church. One night, however, as she lay wakeful, thinking of her handsome captain, she heard a sigh near to her cell. She rose up affrighted, and saw by the moonlight, a shapeless mass lying before her door. It was Quasimodo sleeping there upon the stones.

— Victor Hugo,
The Hunchback of Notre-Dame

PART 5

OMNIA CAUSA FIUNT

1

Why me?
  These were the words . . .
  Why me?
  The words haunting me . . .
  Why me?
  The words making me cry . . .
  Why me?
  The words fucking destroying me . . .
  Why me?
  Jennie was gone . . .
  Why me?
  I was consumed by self-pity . . .
  Why me?
  The same question . . .
  Why me?
  Night after night . . .
  Why me?
  Week after week . . .
  Why me?
  . . . when the answer was literally surrounding
me.

2

On the evening of 12 November 2005, as I was being driven back to Stoke Mandeville after an emotional return to Welford Road, Natalie Mackay, a 35-year-old mother of four, was heading in the same direction. She just didn't know it yet. It was a typical Saturday night in Yateley, Hampshire. She had spent it at a local pub with a group of friends and then someone had mentioned a party. Bruce assured her he was fit to drive so she handed him her car keys. The last thing she remembers before they hit the tree and the roof was cut from the car was fastening her seatbelt. Her face and arms were speared with glass, she was covered in blood and could not feel her legs.

'What is your name?' the paramedic asked.

'My name is Natalie,' she replied. 'I can't breathe very well. Please don't let me die.'

3

Megumi Wilson could say nothing at the scene of her accident, said nothing during her prolonged stay at Stoke Mandeville and is unlikely to speak again before she dies. When you entered her room on the St Andrew ward the explanation was a framed notice on the wall.

MEGUMI COMMUNICATES BY BLINKING:
ONE BLINK = YES
TWO BLINKS = NO.

The last time she moved a muscle other than her eyes was at 11 p.m. on 29 May 2005. It was the spring bank holiday weekend and she was out for a drink with friends in her native Monmouth, Wales. Her home in the Kymin was a twenty-minute walk from the town centre, but as she reached the Wye Bridge traffic lights, and attempted to cross the road, she was hit by the driver of a speeding Ford Mondeo. John Dummett, a 34-year-old heroin addict, fled the scene of his crime and was jailed for fourteen months. Megumi, age twenty, has locked-in syndrome and is doing life.

4

Alison Brown was almost twenty-seven on the day she began her journey to Stoke Mandeville in August 2005. She had not had a period for eighteen months since the birth of her daughter, Maddie, and had checked in to Maidstone General Hospital for a scan on her pituitary gland. A day later, she was called back and shown a picture of the tumour on her spine. 'It may not be cancerous but we need to take a look,' her doctor announced. She was operated on a week later at King's College in London. The tumour trapping her nerves was shaped like a honeycomb and bled into her spinal cord when they attempted a biopsy. Two surgeons battled for five hours to keep her alive. She spent the next four months in intensive care and was transferred to Stoke Mandeville in January 2006. The good news was that her tumour was benign. The bad news was that she was now tetraplegic.

5

There were more, lots more:

Steve Brown (25) paraplegic: fell from a
first-floor balcony in Germany.
Marvin Douglas (26), paraplegic: crashed
his car after skidding on black ice.
Nick Graham (23), tetraplegic: dived from
a pier in St Tropez and hit his head on a
sandbank.
Matt Grimes (40), tetraplegic: a friend
jumped on his back.
Mike Smith (61, former lead singer of the
Dave Clark Five), tetraplegic: fell trying
to climb the gate of his villa in Spain
after locking himself out.
James Taylor (24), tetraplegic: *Baywatch*
dive into the sea on the first day of a
holiday in Portugal.
Daryl White (25), paraplegic: fell from a
9-ft ladder painting a friend's house.
Matt Hampson (20), ventilator-dependent
tetraplegic: from a collapsed scrum at
Franklin's Gardens, Northampton.

Why me?
Why not me?

6

Scene 33: INTERIOR — COURTROOM — DAY

Natalie Mackay has been called to the tribunal.

BARRISTER
Mrs Mackay. You are sitting in the wreckage of a car that has just hit a tree; a paramedic is asking you for your name; you are covered in blood, struggling to breathe and can't feel your legs. Can you tell the tribunal, please, what happens next?

NATALIE MACKAY
I remember the sound of the generator and being told they were taking the roof off and then the next thing after that was waking up in an emergency room at Frimley Park Hospital and arguing with this lady who was trying to take my clothes off. I said, 'Why are you cutting my clothes off? They are new.' I was out of it and did not know where I was. My parents turned up. I told my dad what I remembered. He said, 'Well, there is nothing wrong with Bruce — the guy who was driving — he is fine.' But I was so high on morphine that those first few days were just a blur of waking up and going to sleep.

BARRISTER
At what stage did you realize you were paralysed?

NATALIE MACKAY
They told me I had broken my hip and that they were going to put a screw in it. I remember being taken down to theatre but they didn't put me to sleep. I could not feel anything but it still didn't click until I was moved to a general ward and this lady, a physio, said she was going to move my legs. 'Okay, that's fine,' I said. 'But just out of interest how many people recover from this injury?' And she said, 'None. None recover.' I said, 'Sorry?' She goes, 'Oh, you won't walk again.' I could not believe it. I thought I was going to be sick. I phoned my dad and he came down to see the doctor. 'We can't tell you whether she will walk again,' the doctor said. 'We can't say what the prognosis is.'

BARRISTER
At what stage were you transferred to Stoke Mandeville?

NATALIE MACKAY
Two weeks after my accident. When you arrive there, you go into a room and they assess you. I remember the doctor saying, 'You are going to be here for at least three to five months.' I was miles away from home and did not have any family around me. A lot of the staff don't speak proper English — they do their jobs well but they are not very understanding. I was alone a lot of the time. You do a lot of thinking.

BARRISTER
Are you a rugby fan, Mrs Mackay?

NATALIE MACKAY

No, footie girl, me. Chelsea all the way.

BARRISTER

So you had never heard of Mr Hampson before you met him in Stoke Mandeville?

NATALIE MACKAY

No, I did not know about Matt. It wasn't until Sky came to interview him one Sunday that it registered with me.

BARRISTER

Do you remember when that was?

NATALIE MACKAY

I think it might have been the anniversary of his accident.

He said, 'Come and sit in the restaurant with us. They are going to film me but I want you to be there.' I went down and there was this camera crew. I thought: Oh my God. We were just sitting around having a chat and then my dad phoned up and said, 'I have just seen you on the news.' I could not believe it. But he is my friend because of who he is, not because of that.

BARRISTER

How did he become your friend?

NATALIE MACKAY

I was the only lady at that time on the ward. My bed was at the end opposite Matt's room. I could hear him and see people going in there but I never

446

actually got to see them because I was flat on my back for months. I did not have any family around me and I cried a lot. His carer came over and spoke to me. He said, 'Matt says you need to drink more.' I said, 'I don't feel like drinking. I don't feel like talking to anyone.' He said it again, 'You need to drink more.'

BARRISTER
So you didn't actually speak to Mr Hampson?

NATALIE MACKAY
No, just passing hellos and then one day I said 'Hiya' and he came to talk to me. He said, 'We call you Barbara.' I said, 'Why do you call me Barbara?' He said, 'You looked like a Barbara.' So, they gave me this nickname. Whenever my phone would ring, his carer would pick it up and go, 'Hello, Barb's phone.' They were always taking the piss. It was hilarious and left me with a choice to make — I could either stay depressed, stay crying or I could try to make the best out of a bad situation.

BARRISTER
So you had reached a crossroads so to speak?

NATALIE MACKAY
Yes, the same crossroads that everybody reaches. You can go one way or the other. You can either have a chip on your shoulder for the rest of your life or you can get on with it the best that you can. Matt is a lot worse than me. I thought: Well if he can do it, why can't I? And that is what did

447

it for me. From then on, we were inseparable. He was my best friend in there. We did everything together. It was me, him and Ali. Without them I would not have got through it.

BARRISTER
I'm sorry, Mrs Mackay, Ali is . . . ?

NATALIE MACKAY
Alison Brown. She came in about a month later than me, after Christmas. She was on a ventilator, like Matt, and couldn't talk for weeks. Then one day, I was chatting with Matt and we heard this thick London accent: 'Oi, are you not going to talk to me then?' It was little Ali in the corner. I said, 'Blimey, you have got your voice back.' Matt used to take the mickey out of her accent all the time. She used to come and sit by my bed. That is how our friendship developed.

BARRISTER
Why your bed?

NATALIE MACKAY
I had pressure sores. They should have rolled me more often during the two weeks I spent at Frimley Park and they were bad, very bad when I got to Stoke Mandeville. Matt and Ali used to come and sit by my bed. We would tell stories and eat sweets and chocolates. One night, we had a curry in the ward and played this game where you had to write the name of a star, stick it on your forehead and guess who it is. I know it sounds pathetic but that's a good night in hospital when

you can't go out. We were the terrible trio. We did some very bad things.

BARRISTER
What kind of things, Mrs Mackay?

NATALIE MACKAY
One night, Matt took off and went into Aylesbury with some friends. He was always doing this — taking off and not telling them when he was coming back. And because it used to take two of them to put him into bed they used to get really humpy about it. Anyway, he comes back and everyone is asleep. I had been up watching DVDs and could hear his chair coming down the corridor, weaving from side to side. He was drunk. 'I want to kiss you, Nat,' he says. I said, 'Shut up and go to bed.' 'No,' he says. 'I want to come over and kiss you.' 'All right,' I said. 'Whatever.' And he crashed into just about everything that he could. He woke everybody up and got told off. I remember seeing him getting into bed and he was asleep in the hoist, completely out cold. It was hilarious. And then he took me — this is funny — on my first town visit.

BARRISTER
And town is Aylesbury?

NATALIE MACKAY
Yes, Aylesbury. He said, 'Come on, I want to get some DVDs.' I said, 'I can't go into town.' He said, 'Of course you can, I will take you.' His sister's boyfriend, Adam, helped me in and out of

449

the car. He is lovely. And Amy. She is lovely, too.
So we get to HMV and his chair stops in the doorway — the barrier has tripped the motor in his
chair — so now Adam has to push him in this
big, heavy chair around Aylesbury. So, it was just
things like that. He never made me feel left out.
He used to come and see me every day, no matter
what he was doing. 'You all right?' What are you
up to?' He is funny. I do miss him.

BARRISTER
What about Miss Wilson?

NATALIE MACKAY
Oh, Megumi! Yeah. Matt introduced me to
Megumi, actually. She could only talk with her
eyes. She is such a lovely girl. That is when
you realize there are people worse off than you.
At first I thought: God, I can't walk, I can't
drive, I can't do this, I can't do that. But then I
look at Matt and think: Well he does it. He
made me realize that, you know, it is not that
bad really. Although it is a change in your life,
it is just things that you have to change. But
your life does not stop just because you are in
a wheelchair. You can still have fun, go out
and do things that you want to do. He took
me out to the pub that first night of my shopping trip. 'Go on,' he said. 'We will get you
drunk.'

BARRISTER
And did he?

NATALIE MACKAY
(Smiles) Well, let's just say I felt a little tipsy . . .

BARRISTER
Do you have children, Mrs Mackay?

NATALIE MACKAY
Yes, a boy and three girls. My eldest, Daniel, is eighteen. Then there is Hannah who is sixteen, Samantha who is fifteen and Georgie who is eleven.

BARRISTER
How has your injury impacted on them?

NATALIE MACKAY
It has been hard for them to adjust as well, very hard. We have been through all the 'For God's sake, why did it have to be my mum?' They were all separated when I was in hospital. It was a tough time because for those six months we were not a family. They used to come and see me in hospital, but it was hard for them. They all love Matt anyway — he helped my daughter with her homework once. It was tough for them, but we are getting there now.

BARRISTER
What about those who don't get there? Did you see many people like that in Stoke Mandeville?

NATALIE MACKAY
There were a couple of them. There was one lad, a young lad, who was paralysed in a car accident,

451

who would not get out of bed. He could not find the motivation to go to physio or do anything; he was rude to the nurses, rude to everyone, just did not want to get up. I used to say to Matt, 'Why are people like that?' He said, 'Well, you know, they just can't accept what has happened to them.' So you do get people like that but I always tried to avoid them because they drag you down. And once you are on that slippery slope, there is no way out of it. I wanted to be around people who would motivate me and make me happy.

BARRISTER
Did you ever see Mr Hampson down?

NATALIE MACKAY
Sometimes, not often. I don't know how he did it. I honestly don't know. If anything he was the one cheering us up. 'Oh, God. You are not crying again are you? Come on, Nat, pick yourself up.' You know, things like that. For a long time I was lying flat on my back, and after about six weeks they said I might be able to sit up. It sounds silly but it is a big thing sitting up. I was really pinning my hopes on it, and then they said I could not. My fracture was not mended properly. I was so upset. He went, 'Ah, I wish I could hug you.' I said, 'I wish I could hug you as well.'

7

In an interview with Christopher Goodwin in the *Sunday Times* last year, the award-winning Irish actor Michael Fassbender made some very interesting observations about his role as Bobby Sands, the IRA hunger striker, in *Hunger*. Fassbender, thirty-two years old and pencil-thin, had to lose 42 lbs so he could convincingly play Sands in the last days of his fatal 1981 hunger strike in the Maze prison. To lose weight, Fassbender locked himself in a cottage near Venice Beach in LA for a month and cut his food intake to less than 1000 calories a day by eating just berries and nuts in the morning and a can of sardines at night. The weight loss, Goodwin notes, had two profound effects on his psyche. 'I was so focused it was unbelievable,' Fassbender says. 'I felt I had the answers to so many things. What was also interesting was that my libido left me. Who was that writer who said he was glad he reached his seventies and his libido left? It's like the shackles being taken off.'

My libido had probably left me the moment I hit the ground, but it wasn't until the end of my relationship with Jennie that the shackles were taken off. We were not going to marry; I was not going to have sex with her or any other woman and, after almost a year of gazing inwards, I started to look beyond the limit of my navel, and the first person to register was Natalie Mackay.

453

She cried a lot during that first month at Stoke Mandeville and hardly had any visitors. It really made me appreciate how fortunate I was. Natalie was witty, intelligent and fun to be around and she taught me an invaluable lesson: there is nothing like dealing with somebody else's problems to take your mind off your own.

Alison Brown looked like a child on the day she arrived at Stoke Mandeville but was tougher than any player I had met on the rugby field. She had almost died three times following the biopsy on her spine; she was miles from home and missed her daughter, Maddie, terribly, but you would never hear her complain or cry. She was more reserved than Natalie but had the same wicked sense of humour, and some of the nights we shared were as raucous and profane as any I had spent with the Tigers boys. And, like Natalie, she taught me perspective: I had been crippled knowing the risks and doing something I loved; she had been crippled by a bleed from a benign tumour. Now that's bad luck.

8

The first time I set eyes on Matt Grimes was in the gym at Stoke Mandeville. I was hanging from a tilt table, as motionless as a frozen side of beef; he was being hauled on to his feet and moving like a puppet from *Thunderbirds*. At first I thought he was an old legion and had been in rehab for years, but he had actually broken his neck five months after I had.

Matt was a forty-year-old sound engineer from Richmond, Surrey, and one of the brightest people I have ever met. On the day he arrived in Stoke Mandeville he was placed in a two 'bedder' next to a guy we called 'Rocket Ron' because of the way he shot around in his wheelchair, crashing into foot trolleys and knocking people over. Ron had a really bad snoring habit and watched TV with the volume full on, and within three days Matt wanted to throttle him. He told his friend James Boyle, a fellow sound engineer, and a few days later James returned to the hospital brandishing a channel changer with a bar graph scanner on the back and a booklet with every make of television. They found the make and model of Rocket Ron's TV, scanned the bar graph and from that moment on Matt was in control. Ron loved *EastEnders* but it wasn't much fun when the channel kept changing or the volume was reduced to nil. At one point, he phoned his son

455

and demanded a new TV set. Matt bit his lip and asked what was wrong.

'My fucking telly's on the blink,' Ron fumed. 'It seems to have a mind of its own.'

'Oh, sorry to hear that,' Matt replied. 'If you like I can ask my mate James to have a look — he's a bit of a boffin.'

'Thanks, Matt, you're very kind.'

But Ron had the final laugh. Months later, as Matt was checking out of Stoke Mandeville and stepping gingerly on crutches into the great outdoors, Ron came flying around the corner in his chair and sent him sprawling to the ground. 'I am really sorry, Matt,' he gushed, horrified. As Matt collected himself and staggered to his feet, he thought about giving Ron a piece of his mind but smiled and shrugged his shoulders. He knew, deep down, that justice had been served.

Matt spent most of his time in Stoke Mandeville on St David and St George wards with a motley crew of odd, bright and hilariously funny men that included James Taylor from London, Marvin Douglas from Bedford and the inimitable Daryl White. There's a brilliant, dark comedy to be made about life in a spinal unit and when it eventually hits the screen, White, a 25-year-old painter from Nottingham, will be the star.

One night, after weeks of debate between them about sex and sexual function, he took delivery of a batch of 'Frankie Vaughan' (rhyming slang for porn) discs and decided to set a test. 'Okay, we're going to watch these at the same time on our portable DVDs and we'll see who can raise a

456

flag,' he says. 'But keep you hands outside the sheets! I don't want any cheating.'

Ten minutes passed. 'Anything happening?' Daryl asked, glancing furtively at Matt.

'Nothing,' he replied.

Twenty minutes passed.

'How about you, Marv?'

'Fuck all.'

Thirty minutes passed. The ward was humming with furious coitus but the poor lads were still as limp as the day they were born. Daryl had had enough. 'Fuck it, lads,' he announced, dejectedly. 'It looks like I'm facing a lifetime of contraception.'

Another night they decided to cook a meal together and headed for the kitchen with the ingredients for a giant spaghetti bolognese. Matt wasn't walking at the time and sat around the table with the less able-bodied of the group — James, Martin, Gordon — while Daryl and Marvin went to work at the stove. It was as the onions were being chopped that he first noticed the smell. He looked at Gordon and there was shit running off his wheelchair and on to the kitchen floor.

'Gordon, you've shat yourself.'

'Oh fuck off, Matt.'

'No, Gordon, you've shat yourself. I'll go and get the nurse.'

The nurse arrived . . .

'Oh my God!'

. . . and wheeled Gordon away to clean him up.

Thirty minutes later he had just returned to

457

the table when it happened again.

'Gordon, you've shat yourself.'

'Fuck off, Matt.'

'No, you have. You've done it again.'

Daryl had a ladle in his hands and couldn't quite believe it. 'Fuck me,' he says. 'It's like a scene from *Titanic* when the band is still playing and the ship is going down. He's shitting all over the floor and I'm standing here stirring the spaghetti bolognese.'

And you had to laugh, because if you didn't . . .

* * *

Of the many humiliations forced upon the group, nothing induced more laughter/tears than the horror of your bowels giving way as you tried to lift yourself from a wheelchair to a spinal plinth. We called it 'the Walk of Shame' or 'Wheel of Misfortune'. Because I am a complete tetraplegic (i.e. I have no movement in my arms or hands), it was a ritual I was thankfully spared but witnessed on many occasions in the gym. Because of the lack of sensation below the waist, the first indication something was wrong was a smell coming from the victim's trousers. That left two options: (1) he told himself it was 'just a fart' or (2) he slipped his hand into his trousers and conducted the dreaded finger test. The problem with option 2 was that if he had indeed soiled himself, there was now shit all over his fingers as well as his pants. This was known as 'the Schoolboy Error'. Most incomplete tetraplegics whose hand or hands worked made the schoolboy error. But the embarrassment was only beginning. Whenever a transfer was being attempted, and a bowel gave way, the nutters in the ward would descend on the scene like vultures, taking pictures with their camera phones and chanting 'Shitty' as the poor victim took the walk of shame or wheel of misfortune back to the ward.

★ ★ ★

Life might have been more comfortable but would definitely have been duller without Matt and Daryl and the rest of the Crazy Gang. I remember the hospital DJ calling round one afternoon and asking if there were any requests. 'Yes, please,' Daryl replied. 'Can you play 'These Boots Are Made for Walkin' ' followed by 'Going Underground' by the Jam.'

The DJ smiled and turned on his heels. 'You're a sick bunch.'

9

Scene 34: INTERIOR — COURTROOM — DAY

Matt Grimes has been called to the tribunal.

BARRISTER
Mr Grimes, can you tell the tribunal, please, about the day that changed your life?

MATT GRIMES
It was a Saturday evening, 8 October 2005. I'd been to a game of rugby at London Welsh with a friend, David, and gone for a couple of beers in the pub. His girlfriend had just qualified to ride in the Horse of the Year Show and she invited us to her place for dinner. We left the pub and were walking near Richmond Green and he stopped to do something with his phone. I kept walking. He ran to catch up and jumped on my back like I was a horse and he was a jockey and I staggered forward and hit my head on the ground.

BARRISTER
What time was it? How much alcohol had you consumed?

MATT GRIMES
It was seven . . . eight o'clock. I had had about two pints; he had a bit more, but not much. He

460

was prone to doing stupid things, I should have known better.

BARRISTER
How long did it take to register that your injury was serious?

MATT GRIMES
I was aware something bad was wrong but never thought it was a broken neck. It felt like I was stuck in the ground like a javelin — my head was on the floor but my feet were pointing to the sky. I kept saying, 'Are my feet on the ground? Are my feet on the ground?' I actually thought I had a head injury. I was taken to Kingston Hospital and put in a non-dangerous part of casualty. The ambulance people said, 'Oh, he's fallen over drunk.' They actually said in their report 'He was piggy-backing his friend.' It was no piggy back.

BARRISTER
Didn't they realize you had a problem? What exactly did you say to them?

MATT GRIMES
I kept on saying, 'I can't feel my legs, I can't feel my legs.' They picked me off the floor and put me on a stretcher — they didn't log roll me or secure my neck. It wasn't until five in the morning that the penny actually dropped with them that I had a problem. Then there was a panic and I was suddenly being dripped-up with God knows what.

BARRISTER
So up until that point, Mr Grimes, up until five in the morning, what did they think was wrong with you?

MATT GRIMES
I don't know. At one stage this nurse picked my arm up and it fell back on to the bed. I said, 'CAREFUL!' and a minute later someone came in and said, 'Why were you rude to the nurse?' I thought: Shit, this is a nightmare. The way I am being mishandled, I am not going to come through this. It was shocking. And then a doctor came in. 'I've got some bad news,' he said, 'you've broken your neck.' And I thought: Oh shit.

BARRISTER
How long were you in Kingston?

MATT GRIMES
I was in Kingston for a day and then I was taken to King's [College Hospital] to have my operation. The front column of my C5 vertebra was shattered. They removed a column, put a cage around the cord, took two discs out and then put a titanium fixation over three vertebrae. I was so drugged up my lungs wouldn't inflate for three or four days. Three days later, they took me to Stoke Mandeville. That's when it really hit home: 'Will I walk again?'

BARRISTER
You're a sound engineer, Mr Grimes, is that correct?

MATT GRIMES
Yes, I worked on feature films
. . . Iris . . . Bean . . . Troy . . . Alien vs Preda-
tor . . . I was busy. It was good.

BARRISTER
What exactly did the job entail?

MATT GRIMES
Basically it entailed everything to do with the con-
struction of a sound track: it could be sound
effects, it could be dialogue editing, it could be
re-recording actors. I actually stopped doing the
features to go to Rome for the HBO project. I was
working in Rome when I got injured.

BARRISTER
But you were injured in London, were you not?

MATT GRIMES
I spent nine months in Rome and had come back
to London in March to re-voice the actors before
they mixed it in America.

BARRISTER
So you had just returned to London when Mr
Hampson was injured?

MATT GRIMES
Yes, I remember seeing the report on the BBC
website and thinking: God, this bloke is twenty
and paralysed. What must it be like? I kept checking the Leicester Tigers website to find out how
he was getting on. And a few months later I am

sitting opposite him in a wheelchair. It was the weirdest thing.

BARRISTER
You say you fractured the C5 vertebra?

MATT GRIMES
Yes.

BARRISTER
The same vertebra as Mr Hampson?

MATT GRIMES
Yes, same level.

BARRISTER
But not the same injury?

MATT GRIMES
No, his was a dislocation. It's all about the cord damage. I saw my scan the other day, and if you saw what my cord looks like you wouldn't believe I'm walking. I wouldn't say I was lucky after what I've have to endure, but it is lucky — because I'm a fraction off being like Matt, with twenty-four-hour care.

BARRISTER
Could you tell the tribunal about your first meeting with him please, Mr Grimes?

MATT GRIMES
Well, I am not very proud to admit this but I actually avoided him at first.

464

BARRISTER
You avoided him? Why?

MATT GRIMES
I had said hello to him a couple of times but
when he first started speaking he used to 'swallow' on his vent and I couldn't understand him.
You would think, being a sound engineer, I should
have been able to work it out, but I shied away
from him. I didn't know what a regular bloke he
was or how he was coping with his injury. All I
saw was this bloke who was on a vent.

BARRISTER
At what stage did you start looking at him differently?

MATT GRIMES
It was obvious after a couple of months that there
was a chance I would walk again, and in a place
like Stoke Mandeville that's always going to create
a certain resentment. You go for physio and stand
up, and you are surrounded by people who are
never going to stand up. They are looking at you,
thinking: Why him and not me? It's a natural reaction and one I totally understand, but Matt never
thought that, not once.

BARRISTER
How can you be so sure, Mr Grimes?

MATT GRIMES
You would see him at physio every day and they
would just hang him on a tilt table — that was it!

I remember looking at him and wondering: What must this bloke be thinking? He comes in every day hooked to a ventilator, and they just hang him on this bloody wall. I was like Bambi the first time I stood up and, when I started using crutches, he was the first person to come up to me. 'Matt! You are on sticks! That is absolutely awesome.' I thought: Wow. I didn't know what to say.

BARRISTER
He was pleased for you?

MATT GRIMES
Yeah, genuinely pleased.

BARRISTER
How old were you at the time of your accident, Mr Grimes?

MATT GRIMES
I was forty.

BARRISTER
Were you married? In a relationship?

MATT GRIMES
I was going out with someone before I left for Rome but didn't come home enough and that was the end of it — a blessing when I was injured. It's much easier to deal with on your own. You would see the girlfriends sitting at the end of the bed, thinking: I'm too young to be a carer. I've got my whole life in front of me. I want to have kids. And as much as you love someone, sometimes I think

you have to be selfish. So I was relieved I had been blown out.

BARRISTER
Have you been able to work again?

MATT GRIMES
I can't do my old job — I need both hands to work in harmony on the consoles and my right hand is pretty much dead. I suffer terrible spasms at night that wake me up and I am always tired. Also, something people don't realize when you're a walking tetraplegic is just how tiring thinking about walking is. I have to concentrate on every step, otherwise I'm going to go over, and I fall regularly.

BARRISTER
Forgive me, Mr Grimes, but you don't look like a man with a serious disability.

MATT GRIMES
(Smiles) Daryl used to say that.

BARRISTER
Daryl?

MATT GRIMES
Daryl White, one of the guys at Stoke Mandeville. He used to call me 'Andy' from Little Britain or 'Part-time cripple' or 'Posh boy' because a friend once brought me a bag of satsumas that had leaves on. He had never seen anything like it. I'd have Duchy of Cornwall biscuits and he'd have

McVitie's. I'd want to shop in Marks & Spencer's and he'd want to shop in Tesco. One day, after I had convinced him to come with me, he phoned his missus. 'Kelly, we're never going to Tesco again. Have you seen the grub in Marks & Spencer's?' A great lad, Daryl, great fun . . . I'm sorry, I've digressed. What was the question again?

BARRISTER
It was an observation on how well you have progressed.

MATT GRIMES
I worked hard at it — was doing six hours of physio a week, every week for two years at my own expense. Matt would see me in the gym and say, 'You've got to get a life away from rehab', which, coming from him, was pretty amazing. He was right, all I was doing was rehab, but I thought I owed it to people in wheelchairs as well. You know? I had a chance, they didn't, so I really grafted away. But it hasn't been easy; looks can be deceptive.

BARRISTER
What do you mean, Mr Grimes?

MATT GRIMES
One Saturday evening I arranged to go to dinner with a friend. We were walking back to his place when I started to feel unwell. This soon turned into panic as I realized if I didn't find a toilet immediately I would soil myself. I could see a pub I knew well about fifty metres in the distance and

started telling myself I could make it. As I got closer my friend looked at me: 'You all right?' 'No, I think I'm going to shit myself,' I replied through gritted teeth. My internal dialogue then kicked in . . .

BARRISTER
The thoughts running through your head?

MATT GRIMES
Yeah. I thought: Come on, Matt, you can make it to the pub, look it's right there . . . But what if it's packed and I can't get through the crowd and I shit myself in the pub? What if there's a queue for the toilet and I shit myself in the queue? What if I bump into someone I know and they want a protracted conversation? I'll then have to go back through the pub stinking. Five metres short of the door it was all over . . . a wet patch rumbled and bubbled in my trousers. I stopped to finish the job and carried on home in stony silence. On reaching the front door I asked my friend for a bin liner. He said, 'What do you want a bin liner for?' 'Don't worry,' I replied, 'I'm not going to suffocate myself. I want you to put it on my feet so I don't destroy your house.'

BARRISTER
So you were staying with this friend?

MATT GRIMES
Yes . . . Sorry, I said home but no, I was staying with my friend. Anyway, after much manoeuvring I managed to get in the shower after placing

everything I had been wearing including trainers in the bin bag. I washed myself down several times, put on some clean clothes and slowly went outside on to the green and dropped the bag containing my clothes in the bin. It was a miserable feeling. I thought: Is this how it will always be? I went back inside and my friend was watching TV. 'Give me your clothes,' he said, 'and I'll put them in the wash.' I told him I would never wear them again and had binned them. And I just sat there in silence feeling very sorry for myself.

BARRISTER
I understand, Mr Grimes. My goodness that is tough.

MATT GRIMES
The worse was yet to come . . . After about half an hour, I went to check my phone but couldn't find it. Then I patted my pocket for my wallet and keys and realized that they were still in my shitty trousers in a bin on the green. I went out and to my horror there was a couple sitting on a bench right by the bin, snogging. Oh God, I thought, more humiliation. I waited for a few minutes in the doorway and decided I would go over. I ignored the dirty looks from the couple, sifted gingerly through the bag and thankfully my things were still there. So that's what I mean when I say looks can be deceptive.

BARRISTER
Indeed, Mr Grimes.

MATT GRIMES
And it doesn't matter how many times this happens — you never get over the humiliation. Every time I go out I have to think: Is there going to be a toilet? How far am I going to have to walk to the toilet? Is it going to be upstairs? You are knackered by the time you get there, and then you have to get home and everyone's pissed. Not that I am saying it is awful because it's not. There have been some good things come out of it, really good things.

BARRISTER
What's a good thing?

MATT GRIMES
Well, you think: God, I am quite proud at the way I've come through. And meeting Matt, seeing the way he's coped. I've been to his home several times and seen what he goes through every day just to get up in the morning. It's phenomenal. I have never heard him complain, and if he does have a whinge about something, it's with wonderful humour. I got a text from him the other day saying that Naomi, one of his carers, had managed to put his Timberlands on the wrong feet. He said, 'How the fuck did you do that? It's hard enough getting them on the right way round, let alone the wrong way round.' He's brilliant, just brilliant.

BARRISTER
Do any other 'good things' spring to mind?

471

MATT GRIMES
I suppose it has made me think about what is
important in life. This is probably going to sound
poncey, but it really is only love that matters. You
know? Family sitting around a table, eating; friends
sitting around a table, eating. Simple things, that's
what really hit home to me. I have a brother and
two sisters. We grew up, got mortgages, got married, got divorced and had feuds. My dad recently
had a stroke and was very ill but we all came
together through my injury and his illness and
there have been some really nice moments, really
interesting moments.

BARRISTER
What kind of moments?

MATT GRIMES
My dad's humour . . . the way he looked to me
for inspiration . . . I remember talking to him just
after he had the stroke. I said, 'Dad, this ain't
going to be nice, you are going to shit in the bed,
but it is what it is. So don't be upset and don't be
angry because that only makes it worse.' And I
think it changed his view. I said, 'And if it's a
woman just enjoy having your arse wiped.' He just
laughed, you know?

BARRISTER
When did you leave Stoke Mandeville, Mr Grimes?

MATT GRIMES
I left in February 2006. We went to this bar in
Aylesbury and Matt started giving me all these

472

bloody rugby drinks. 'Shermonguys' or something he called it — absolutely repulsive. He seemed to enjoy watching me get pissed on crutches. I heard later that he came back hammered and didn't get up for three days. That was typical of him. What a bloke. You know?

10

Fourteen months after my accident, in May 2006, there was a match at Welford Road for me between the England Under-21s and a Tigers select XV. Most of my friends and former team-mates were there; it was the first time I had been out with them for a drink. And did we drink! It started after the game with an open tab at the ground and then we went back to the team hotel at the Hilton. Pete Drewett, the England manager, ordered some bottles of red wine and we sat round a table, talking about old (young?) times. There were no inhibitions. It felt good, normal, and I got absolutely battered. It was three in the morning when we left the hotel. Dean squeezed me into the back of the Kangoo (the roof was too low and I had to recline my chair) and we had just reached the junction at Fosse Park when my vent pipe became detached from my neck. Dean stopped the van and jumped into the back to sort it out. I didn't panic or say a word. I was so pissed I wasn't bothered. But sometimes I was very bothered.

★ ★ ★

On the night of my brother, Tom's, eighteenth birthday, we teamed up with some of his mates and went into Oakham for a drink. We started at a pub called the Grainstore and were steaming

474

by the time we hit the Merry Monk. This place had no wheelchair access, so the boys organized some ramps to get me through the back door. I was really annoyed and let rip at one of the staff.

'You fuckers! I cannot believe you have not got any wheelchair access. I'll get my dad to come down. He will build you a ramp.'

'Well, it costs a lot of money,' the guy replied.

'I don't give a fuck how much it costs.'

We came out after a couple of pints and I went bombing down the street to the kebab shop where this guy just glanced at me and made some innocuous comment about my chair.

'What are you looking at, you twat?' I snarled. 'I'll fucking run you over.'

The poor bloke didn't know what to say.

'Adam, knock him out for me! Go on. He's been a wanker!'

Not my finest hour.

* * *

I drank too much in those first two years after my accident; some of it to remember, most of it to forget, but I never lost sight of the pact I had made with my father at Stoke Mandeville one night. It was about a month after the split with Jennie. He had come straight from work on his own and maybe it was the reality of my condition hitting home or a fight he had had with Mum but he was oozing pain from every pore. We sat in silence for what seemed an eternity, trying to find some positive that might emerge from my injury. And trying. And trying. It was desperate.

There was nothing; just the *whoosh* of the ventilator taunting us. Then I said, 'I think it will make me a better person in the long run, Dad.' I didn't mean it and I'm not sure I believed it but I'd have said anything to ease his pain and it seemed to give him a lift.

A month later, I gave my first interview since the accident to the *Sunday Times* but the stand-out quote was my father's: 'One thing Matthew said to me which I couldn't believe was, 'I'll be a better person for this in the long run, Dad.' I thought it was an amazing thing for a twenty-year-old to say. I don't think I could have said it.' And that was it. I would strive to be a better person. I had promised Dad.

The reaction to the interview — a 4000-word piece spread over two pages in the sports section — was extraordinary. A YEAR AGO, MATT HAMPSON WAS A YOUNG ENGLAND STAR. NOW HE LIES PARALYSED IN HOSPITAL. THIS IS THE INSPIRING STORY OF ONE OF RUGBY'S FALLEN HEROES, the headline screamed. I had never thought of myself as inspiring, I had never set out to be a hero. I had the same injury as people who had caught their trouser leg on a fence or tripped on carpet. But I had a platform, they didn't; I had headlines and people writing to me. It started me thinking . . . *Omnia Causa Fiunt.*

What if there was a reason for this?

A few weeks later Shaun Edwards, the Wasps coach and Wigan legend, came to visit. 'You are an inspiration,' he said. 'I can learn from you. You've got great mental discipline and great mental strength.' He reached into his pocket and placed a medal on my bed. 'I want you to have this.' It was solid gold, his prize for winning the Zurich Premiership with Wasps the season before. I was gobsmacked.

11

Scene 35: INTERIOR — HOSPITAL — DAY

Matt Hampson is dictating a letter from his hospital bed in Stoke Mandeville to Professor Geoff Raisman FRS, the world-class British neuroscientist at the Institute of Neurology in London.

3 May 2006

Dear Sir,

I was inspired by reading your article in the Sunday Times magazine on the 9th April; having suffered a serious spinal cord injury myself (C4/5, incomplete) on 15th March 2005 it gives me some hope for the future. I was an International rugby player training with the England U-21 squad when a scrum collapsed and I sustained my injury. I remain very positive and I have great support from my family and friends at Leicester Tigers RFC.

I now wish to focus my attention on spinal cord injury research and have begun making inquiries on setting up a registered charity for this cause with the help of my Leicester RFC directorship. I believe the olfactory stem cell procedure is the way forward and would like to offer you my support in any

478

way I can. I have a great respect for your 'dogged' determination and dedication to this very worthy cause, I know how frustrating and time consuming it can be to get the support and backing required to move forward (it took me six months to get a wheelchair).

I am looking forward to being discharged from Stoke Mandeville Hospital on 1st August. It has been extremely disappointing to be in the 'National Spinal Injury Unit' to discover there is little in the way of research being developed. The ethos is not positive or full of hope; it is a miserable environment under resourced with the aim to discharge people as quickly as possible. I hope and pray that your wonderful work will further develop and I would like to be at the front of the queue when your research moves forward. Having written an article recently in the Sunday Times the support has been overwhelming from the Rugby World. I would be delighted to help the cause if you so wish.

Yours sincerely,

Matthew Hampson

FADE TO

Scene 36: INTERIOR — LIVING ROOM — DAY

Roy Jackson is reading a special edition of Sporting Green published with the Leicester Mercury.

WE'VE PROMISED TO HELP MATT FOR LIFE
By Lee Marlow

Leicester Tigers and the *Leicester Mercury* are joining forces to aid injured prop Matt Hampson. The 21-year-old broke his neck in a scrum during an international training session with England Under-21s last year. He was paralysed from the neck down as a result of what is believed to be the worst injury suffered by a Tigers player in the club's long history.

At a time when Tigers, England and most top-flight teams are looking for quality prop forwards, one of the top prospects in the English game will spend the rest of his life in a wheelchair. Well, that's what the doctors say. It's not what Matt says. Matt reckons, one day, he will walk again. The Matt Hampson Trust was set up to help Matt — and he also wants it to help other people with spinal injuries.

For the time being though, his friends and family are trying to convince Matt that he should put his needs first. The *Leicester Mercury* has teamed up with organisers to donate the profit from sales of this special edition of the *Sporting Green*, together with bucket collections at Tigers' Premiership play-off against London Irish, to the Trust.

Leicester Tigers president Roy Jackson is involved in the Matt Hampson Trust campaign and in an interview with the *Mercury* last month, he made this emotional pledge: 'I don't know how much it will cost to look after Matt, it might be £4 million, it might be £8 million. But we, the Tigers, are committed to him. We're here for Matt forever and that's a promise.'

It is a noble and ambitious vow.

'But it's true,' says Roy. 'The Leicester board of directors have promised to help Matt for life. This campaign will go on.'

It is possibly the biggest fundraising drive ever undertaken in Leicestershire. There is no time limit. There is no neat and final financial target to aim at. Instead, the Trust hopes to raise as much money as possible to aid Matt — and to also raise awareness of the injury which confined one of English rugby's young hopefuls to a wheelchair.

At the moment, Matt requires round-the-clock, seven days a week care. He breathes with the help of a ventilator. And even that, explains Roy, is not without its perils. 'We were driving back from a charity function a few weeks ago and we heard this high-pitched beeping,' he explains. 'It was Matt's ventilator. It had stopped working. So his dad, Phil, had to physically hand pump air into Matt's lungs. I don't mind admitting we were a little worried by this.'

But not Matt. 'He said, 'I don't know why you two are flapping about — it's me that's going to die if you don't get that air in my lungs,' ' says Roy. 'And that's him. He refuses to let this injury drag him down. He has all these grand ambitions of raising awareness for other people in the same situation. He wants to help them.'

Jackson believes eventually, Matt will become a fine ambassador for people with spinal injuries. 'But I have to keep telling him 'not yet'. I have to rein him in constantly, tell him that these plans are fine but, first things first, let's get things sorted out for you first. I love him for that. I wish that everyone reading this could meet him and see him for the lad he is. But I want him to get his priorities right. I have to keep reminding him that we have to put him first. He is a remarkable, inspiring and decent young man.'

FADE TO

Scene 37: INTERIOR — STUDY — DAY

Susan Polley, a housewife and mother from New-market in Suffolk, has just composed a letter.

Dear Matt,

I have just read your story of your tragic accident. That is why I decided to write to you. I used to help look after a man in my village who was paralysed from the neck down so I do understand some of the huge problems that you and your family have to cope with.

Sadly this has now happened to a dear young friend of my sons. Chris Clements is

30 and a father to three wonderful young sons. He has also broken his spinal cord through a party accident at my son's 30th birthday on July 29 2006.

We will never forget him dressed in the Sumo Wrestling outfit having fun, laughing and enjoying himself when he was struck by his opponent Darren who is now his brother in law. He went down on his back and horrifically never got up again, his spinal cord broken.

The horror in front of us will live with us forever. We have known Chris from birth. Sadly his sister Cheryl and Darren went on to marry five days later. Only a church service was celebrated, everything else cancelled. But they have said we will all celebrate their wedding when Chris comes home.

Chris is like you, a very fit young man who loved cycling, 'kung fu' — which his sons did with him — and motorcycling. You know how he must be feeling. I just wondered if you would find the time to write to him to give him encouragement. He is a fighter and is doing well. He can breathe unaided and is paralysed from the chest down with no use of his hands. He has recently had to have yet another operation to hold his neck so he can go without a collar.

He is in the Royal Orthopaedic Hospital Stanmore (Alan Brey Unit). He has huge support from family and friends and when he comes home we are going to raise money for a good wheelchair. He is a lovely young man, cheerful, clever and a doting father. It would be lovely if you could cheer him on.

Yours sincerely with good wishes to you.
Susan Polley

FADE TO

Scene 38: INTERIOR — BEDROOM — DAY

Matt Hampson is having breakfast at home in Cold Overton, reading a letter he has received in the mail.

Dear Matt,

I have just heard from my son that you have visited Chris. May I say a huge thank you from the bottom of my heart. I never expected you to make the journey to London. What a true sportsman you are. I do hope you got on well with Chris, he is quite a joker. I am sure it has given him a huge boost. I never told anyone that I had wrote to you so everyone was a bit gob-smacked as I did not even know if the letter would find you. Thank the postman as well!

I hear that you are teaching that is won-derful. We hope that Chris will also find employment when he is well enough. Once again thank you very much for your support.

I have felt so helpless as I felt I could do nothing for Chris. My best wishes to you and your very supportive family.

From

Susan Polley

12

What's special about Matt Hampson? Nothing.
I can't make speeches like Winston Churchill;
I can't do compassion like Mother Teresa; I
am never going to be Nelson Mandela,
Muhammad Ali or Bono. And I don't want to
be. The only thing that sets me apart is my
wheelchair and the pipe coming out of my
neck, but I would like, and have tried, to
make a difference.

In the summer of 2007, almost a year had
passed since my discharge from Stoke Mandeville, when I returned to visit Dan James, a
22-year-old former England schoolboy international who had been paralysed the previous
March playing for Nuneaton. We met in Jimmy's,
the hospital café. He was wearing a wool ski
hat, had lost quite a bit of weight and was
using his arms to propel his chair. The first
thing that struck me was that he had come
down from the ward on his own — he didn't
have a Natalie or an Alison or a Daryl
supporting him. The second thing was how
reluctant he was to engage. I encouraged him
to focus on the possibilities, not the problems,
and spoke of some of the things I had enjoyed
since leaving hospital. The sun kissing my face
on a warm summer's day. The smell of fillet
steak grilling on the barbecue. The laughter of
friends sipping beer in the garden. The Six

Nations Championships and autumn internationals at Twickenham. The pleasure of watching Tigers beat Wasps. The Christmas tasting menu at Gordon Ramsay's in Chelsea:

- Pumpkin soup, tortellini mushroom
- Pressed foie gras, carrot purée, almond foam
- Pan-fried foie gras, pickled veg brioche
- Pig's trotter, confit pork terrine, pastry cheese, quail egg
- Confit shoulder, breast of lamb, stuffed pepper
- Mango, lychee and passion fruit soup, coconut cream
- Prune Armagnac crème brûlée, apple crisp, apple juice
- Chocolate and ginger mousse and blackcurrant sauce, chocolate truffles, strawberry ice cream, white chocolate mince pies, raspberry sorbet

'But make sure you bring your wheelchair,' I joked, 'because you won't be able to walk out of there.'

But it just seemed to wash over him. He wasn't interested in talking about the future. He just wanted me to go.

I thought of him several times in the weeks and months that followed. Phil Boulton, the tight-head at Nuneaton, shared a house with my friend Dave Young (the same house I was supposed to move into before my accident), and kept me posted on Dan's progress. Physically, he seemed to be doing okay; mentally, he was struggling. A year later, in October 2008, I was having dinner with my parents when the news of his death was announced. He had travelled to Dignitas, the Swiss clinic that offers assisted suicide.

13

One night, about a year after my accident, my father came into my room at Stoke Mandeville with a new DVD. 'This is supposed to be good,' he said, brandishing a copy of *Million Dollar Baby*. My sister had warned me off it shortly before. 'Whatever you do, do not watch that film,' she said, almost freaking. I let him down gently. 'Maybe this is not the place, Dad.'

It wasn't as if suicide hadn't crossed my mind — Daryl used to joke about it regularly at Stoke Mandeville. He called it Plan B: 'If they don't find a cure for spinal cord injury through stem cell research, I'm going to book myself a sky dive and unclip the parachute,' he would joke.

The death of Dan James was no laughing matter and forced me to ask questions of myself I had never previously considered. Was there something wrong with me? Was my life really so bad? Did I truly cherish life or was I too scared to die? Tougher still was the frenzied response of the media. Dan and I were suddenly opposite sides of a coin. Heads or tails? Pick a side. Who had more courage? The prop boy who chose to live or the boy who chose to die? It made me very uncomfortable.

14

During the last sixteen months of his life as a ventilator-dependent tetraplegic, there was little that made Stuart Mangan uncomfortable.

He had a view on the choice Dan had made: 'Everybody has been saying to me, 'You're so brave and he wasn't as brave' but I say that's not true. If you look at it this way, some people are too scared to die, and others are too scared to live. He may have been too scared to live and took the easy option to die. Or he may have been too scared to die, but said, 'You know what, I'll do it anyway, because it'll be easier on my parents, and just make life easier for everybody.' So he may have done the brave thing.'

He had a view on the choice facing him: 'Sometimes I do think it gets too tough and you say, really, 'What's the point in battling or forcing yourself to live every day.' You do start thinking about life and death and what's out there after death. If you're going to die anyway, whether you die now or whether you die later shouldn't make a difference. So sometimes I think if things got too tough or I felt I wasn't getting the full enjoyment out of life, then I wouldn't feel bad about saying, 'I could end my life.' But it wouldn't be easy because I couldn't do it myself.'

Stuart was braver, brighter and better travelled than me. He had an international law degree, a masters in business and was fluent in five languages. The youngest of four boys born to his parents, Brian and Una, he was a native of Fermoy in County Cork and had lived and worked in Paris and Madrid before moving to London in July 2007. Eight months later, on Saturday 5 April 2008, he was paralysed.

He had his hair cut that morning, his shoes repaired and a new tube fitted to his mountain bike before racing off to play a match at Hammersmith and Fulham rugby club. He was too clever, rounded and sane to be a proper rugby player. He would never have drank his own piss or fought for the back seat of the bus. No, Stuart was an amateur, a true Corinthian. He broke his neck — C2 complete — in a crunching tackle, trying to clear a ruck.

He had been in Stanmore for a couple of months when I first heard of him. Ed Clark, a friend of my friend Tom Armstrong, was a team-mate of Stuart's at Hammersmith and asked if I would pay him a visit. It was a boiling hot afternoon. He had picked up a pressure sore and was lying on his side, facing the window. There was a framed picture of his girlfriend beside the bed. He smiled and said something and I didn't catch a word — as much to do with his thick Cork accent as the perils of learning to speak on a ventilator — but we connected immediately.

I showed him my laptop and explained the workings of my head-mouse. I told him about my van, my care team and the changes he would need to make at home. I told him about my sports memorabilia business, my journalism and plans to raise awareness and help others with spinal injury. We spoke about my recent trip to Paris — a city he adored — and my ambition to visit New York. He absorbed every word like a sponge.

Stuart had plans, big plans of his own: a microphone that would allow him to project and control the volume of his speech in a nightclub, a seat to prevent pressure sores, a brace so he could ski and sail and ride a horse again. He could not wait to get started, and left Stanmore before Christmas — just eight months after his accident. It was too much, too soon, but some birds aren't meant to be caged.

We shared some good times together in the months that followed, but I was really still getting to know him when he died suddenly from pneumonia on 7 August 2009. I'd like to think some of his brain would have sharpened me. I'd like to think some of my brawn would have toughened him up. I'd like to think we were kindred spirits. I'd like to think I will get to tell him, some day, how much I admired him.

15

Dare we hope? We dare.

Can we hope? We can.

Should we hope? We must.

We must, because to do otherwise is to waste the most precious of gifts, given so freely by God to all of us. So when we do die, it will be with hope and it will be easy and our hearts will not be broken.

— Andy Ripley OBE

16

Remember Red, hope is a good thing, maybe the best of things, and no good thing ever dies.

— Andy Dufresne,
The Shawshank Redemption

17

Rosamond Hutt, a reporter with the Press Association, is perusing an article she has just written for the Newswire.

PARALYSED RUGBY STAR OFFERS HOPE TO DISABLED

A former England and Leicester rugby player who was left paralysed from the neck down following an accident whilst training is backing a new charity dedicated to helping disabled people live life to the full.

Matt Hampson was seriously injured in a rugby scrum during a training session with the England Under-21 team in 2005.

Immediately afterwards, he was unable to speak and could only move his eyes, but thanks to specialist software he was still able to use a computer.

Almost three years on, the 23-year-old is running his own business selling sportswear and, in his new role as patron of the SpecialEffect charity, wants to help others in his position and make the most of cutting-edge technologies.

Matt said: 'Even if you can't have all the technology available immediately, it's when

495

you're there in hospital that you need to know that this technology is out there and this project will help people in exactly this way.'

Matt's mother, Anne, added: 'If you're in hospital for a long time — which, in a spinal injuries hospital is often the case — you need that stimulation desperately.'

SpecialEffect is the brainchild of Dr Mick Donegan, who specialises in using technology to assist disabled people and who has worked closely with Matt over two years.

Dr Donegan said he was delighted that Matt had agreed to be patron of the charity, which will lend specially adapted technology, such as gaze-controlled computer software and electronic games, to disabled people.

'We can't think of anyone who could be a more genuinely inspiring example to the many young people that we support,' he said.

The charity was officially launched by Matt with the support of the Leicester Tigers at the rugby club's headquarters on Wednesday.

Dr Donegan said: 'Matt has already been a huge help with providing contacts and advice and he is very keen to become even more actively involved in the charity in the future.'

18

Scene 40: INTERIOR — COURTROOM — DAY

Anne Hampson has been recalled by the tribunal.
She is the final witness.

BARRISTER
Mrs Hampson, I'm so sorry for dragging you back
to London but there are a couple of issues arising
from your correspondence with the RFU that
require clarification.

ANNE HAMPSON
How can I help?

BARRISTER
(Raises a newspaper) This is an interview your
son gave to the Sunday Times on 18 March 2007.
The journalist spent a day with Matthew and you
travelled together to Twickenham for the England-
France Six Nations game.

ANNE HAMPSON
Yes, I remember. It was the second anniversary of
Matthew's accident and his second interview with
the paper.

BARRISTER
This is a passage from the interview: 'The journey
to Twickenham takes two hours. We are greeted

by Dave Phillips, a friendly Rugby Football Union official, who facilitates our arrival at the ground.' Is that correct?

ANNE HAMPSON
Yes.

BARRISTER
'Lunch is served in the Spirit of Rugby suite. Matt's sister Amy and her boyfriend Adam have joined him at the table and Rob Andrew and a host of RFU officials drop by to say hello. Twenty minutes before kick-off, Matt steers his chair along the ramp to his usual position behind the Royal Box.' Is that an accurate representation?

ANNE HAMPSON
(Smiles) Yes.

BARRISTER
Did Martyn Thomas, Chairman of the RFU's Board of Management, 'drop by to say hello'?

ANNE HAMPSON
Yes, I believe he did.

BARRISTER
So it would be fair to state, would it not, that the attitude of the RFU towards you and your family had changed considerably since the turbulence of the previous winter? You are welcomed at the gate, treated to lunch and seated just behind the Royal Box for the biggest game of the Six Nations?

ANNE HAMPSON
(Smiles) It might also have had something to do with the presence of a journalist from the Sunday Times.

BARRISTER
Mr Thomas sent you an email — Exhibit Z — the previous November. I quote: 'Although Matt is and must be the focus of all our thoughts, I would take the opportunity to say how much I admired the quiet dignity and fortitude shown by you and Phil.' Are you suggesting Mrs Hampson that he was being insincere?

ANNE HAMPSON
Not at all, I'm just disappointed his 'focus' or commitment to Matt was so short-lived. It was not Martyn Thomas's decision, and I don't mean to personalize this, but two years after they had treated him to lunch and swarmed all over him at Twickenham, Matt couldn't even get a car-park pass from the RFU.

BARRISTER
I'm sorry, Mrs Hampson, I don't understand.

ANNE HAMPSON
(Raises a sheet of paper) This is the copy of an email Matt received from the RFU during the Six Nations last year on 8 March 2009.

The email is copied and passed around.

Hi Matt,

Hope you are well and not too disappointed with the England performances of late. I think we gave a great defensive display against the Irish and were unlucky with the ref in Wales.

Re the next 2 internationals at Twicken-ham. I believe that it has been explained to you that the RFU President elect will be bringing his wife to the games and all the games next season. Joan is a wheelchair user and due to health and safety require-ments, it means we will be unable to sit you at the rear of the Royal box as normal. However, I have secured you a place for both games on the wheelchair terrace in the West stand, which is situated next to the Council members' lounge. You may recall being there last August for the Middlesex 7s tournament.

This also means that you will be restricted to 3 tickets for the France & Scotland game and there will be no lunch provided for you. I will still try and get you a car park pass for the West as usual and include it in your ticket pack when it gets sent out, however I can't promise this.

If you have any issues you need to discuss, please get back to me and I will see if I can sort them out. I will be at both games so we can catch up then and discuss next season's tickets etc.

Cheers

Dave

ANNE HAMPSON
And this is a copy of my response to Martyn Thomas.

The letter is copied and passed around.

Dear Martyn,

I was extremely upset and disappointed to receive the insensitive email from Dave Phillips this week. Once again the RFU has shown its lack of care and long-term commitment to Matthew. His condition has not improved after four years and unfortunately for your organisation he has disappeared into the abyss of disabled people enabling the RFU to shake their hands of the whole matter. That is how your insensitive response feels to myself, my family and people who are providing support.

Following four difficult years, we are still living with false promises and these feelings are very much echoed by the PRA and Leicester Tigers. I am an extremely positive person and believe our life is on hold until medical advancements will cure Matt of his paralysis. I also believed you Martyn, when you said you would offer us long-term support so why has the RFU not honoured the many promises you have made?

It may be useful for other members of the RFU to visit us and really understand how real people feel who are in our situation. We would particularly welcome Francis Baron, who has not yet found time to speak to Matthew! Maybe he is from a higher order exempt from understanding the issues of the real world i.e. the human side of life?

The RFU need to realise they own Matt's accident: he was on England duty and his life has been devastated as a result of his accident! That responsibility will not go away. I am sure that the general public would agree that it is not too much for the RFU to invite Matt as a guest particularly during the SIX Nations Tournament. The RFU's handling of the whole situation has made our life more difficult in many ways and last year I truly believed you were beginning to show commitment. It has been interesting to reflect on the stresses and strains of life since Matt's accident, as we prepare to write the final chapter of Matt's book.

The promises made to our family to give Matt an ambassadorial role have fallen long by the wayside. A new charity has been developed following Matt's accident, but he has not been included when the RFU had a perfect opportunity to positively use his status and spirit to help others. He has already raised thousands of pounds for other charities in particular Spinal Research and SpecialEffects.

The timing of your email was impeccable! During a week when we receive a full medical expert report following an investigation into Matt's accident, which conclusively shows that if he had been treated correctly and the pressure on his spinal cord relieved within 4 hours he would not be on a ventilator (A medical paper has been published outlining these facts concerning slow velocity injuries). A stark reminder of the extremely poor support we received from yourselves immediately after the accident! How different things would be for our family if Matt could only breathe independently

The date of Matt's <u>exclusion</u> from the Spirit of Rugby at Twickenham, the 15th March, just happens to be the anniversary of his accident during the Six Nations 2005. It certainly has not been a psychological boost for my son during recent difficult days. I feel my intelligence has been insulted! On more than one occasion Matt has sat on the Royal stand balcony with other people in wheelchairs. At one particular match he believes it was the President's wife herself who sat beside him. The Health and Safety reason seems a rather tenuous excuse to remove Matt's presence from the Spirit of Rugby. The final blow for us all was the final sentence in the email 'and by the way Matt we won't be giving you a car park pass'. It just proves the lack of awareness of the severity of

Matt's injury if his ventilator should break down.

Please, please Martyn think about what you are creating by taking these actions. I am losing patience with the constant lack of sensitivity which is upsetting us all and I hope you will reconsider some of the decisions which have been made. I wait to hear from you in due course.

Yours in sport
Anne Hampson

BARRISTER
And did you hear from Mr Thomas, Mrs Hampson?

ANNE HAMPSON
He sent me a letter. It was the same old story: 'We continue to firmly believe that we have supported Matt and his family fully since his original accident and that we continue to be as flexible and supportive as we can be. It is time though that we brought this in line with the support we offer to all our catastrophically injured players, all of whom are deserving of the investment and resource we can give them.' He just wants to get rid of us. They just want us to go away. The last meeting we had was in January . . .

BARRISTER
With Mr Thomas?

ANNE HAMPSON

Yes. I said to him, 'It's not about the money; it's about caring and showing you understand. I just need to know that you care about my son; I need you to understand that he broke his neck playing for you guys and that you value him and will always look after him.' He said, 'We have lots of injured people and Matt gets his allocation of tickets (for Twickenham) in the wheelchair stand.' I said, 'The wheelchair stand is open. Matt can't control his temperature.' He says, 'Well, our other wheelchair users have to do the same. Why can't Matt do the same?' I said, 'Okay, Martyn, share with me: how many other former England players or Premiership players have you got who cannot breathe?' Dave Phillips was also there. I said, 'How many have you got?'

BARRISTER

What was his reply?

ANNE HAMPSON

He said, 'None.' Matt is the only one. But even if he wasn't the only one they could do more. Matt came up with this great idea of having a box. 'It would be really nice if injured players had a box where they could watch a game in comfort.' They went for it. 'That's a really good idea, Matt,' they said. Then we thought that maybe they would make Matt an ambassador — he is doing such great work for charity now — and we thought it would be a great role for him to go into the box and meet people.' And they said, 'Oh no, he'll have to wait his turn like everybody else.' I said,

'What about making him a patron?' They said, 'No, we've asked Prince Harry. He's going to be the patron.' And I just found myself getting really angry. All I ever asked of them was to give him a role that would enable him to feel valued. And now he doesn't want any part of it.

BARRISTER
What do you mean, Mrs Hampson?

ANNE HAMPSON
He has not watched England at Twickenham since they sent him that email.

BARRISTER
You say it was never about the money, Mrs Hampson?

ANNE HAMPSON
No, it was never about the money. You just want things to be fair. There has got to be a moral purpose and it has got to be fair. I felt the RFU weren't fair. I felt that they lacked emotional intelligence. Matthew's introduction to the game was mini rugby at Oakham and we always had the impression that the RFU was this big family of a rugby organization — that it was all about families and embracing people. But when you unpicked it, you realized that wasn't what it was about at all. They have no ability to understand how people feel whatsoever.

BARRISTER
Your son has moved into a new house, I believe?

ANNE HAMPSON
Yes, Phil built it for him last year, a half-mile from where we live in Cold Overton.

BARRISTER
Tell me about the plaque on the kitchen wall: Omnia Causa Fiunt.

ANNE HAMPSON
Everything happens for a reason.

BARRISTER
Do you believe that, Mrs Hampson?

ANNE HAMPSON
I've always been quite fatalistic, I suppose, but it is quite a hard thing to take in. I suppose he feels his purpose in this world is to help other people. And if he had not been injured, he would not have had that opportunity because he would have been too full of his own selfish existence.

BARRISTER
(Raising a sheet of paper) My final question concerns this document, Mrs Hampson.

The clerk hands the sheet of paper to Mrs Hampson.

BARRISTER
You've seen it before?

ANNE HAMPSON
Yes, it's a release notice Matthew had to sign for the underwriters in order to claim his insurance.

BARRISTER
But that's your signature on the document?

ANNE HAMPSON
Yes, well, obviously I had to sign it for him.

BARRISTER
That must have been difficult for him?

ANNE HAMPSON
It wasn't at all difficult. Matt has never seen it.

BARRISTER
You didn't show it to him?

ANNE HAMPSON
He had been in hospital for six months. The game was his life. Would you have shown it to your son?

BARRISTER
Would you mind reading it for us please?

ANNE HAMPSON
'Having considered and accepted the medical advice which Leicester Tigers Rugby Club and I received from Dr Simon Kemp, following the injury I sustained on the 15th March 2005 whilst training, I agree with the concluding prognosis that as a result of the injury I am now permanently and totally unable to follow in my occupation as a professional rugby player.'

19

Sometimes, when the road is long and the gentle rocking of the van induces one of those deep and almost comatose sleeps, I will open my eyes to my reflection in the window with no memory of how I got here. Why am I in a wheelchair? How the fuck did this happen to me? Then the penny will drop and I'll start to feel really sorry for myself . . .

Why me?

Why me?

Why me?

A favourite scene from *Shawshank* always helps me to refocus. It's the one where Andy has come out of a long spell in solitary and is telling Red about Zihuatanejo, a warm place on the Pacific Ocean in Mexico.

'You know what the Mexicans say about the Pacific?' Andy asks.

'No.'

'They say it has no memory. That's where I want to live the rest of my life — a warm place with no memory . . . Open up a little hotel right on the beach . . . Buy some worthless old boat, fix it up as new and take my guests out charter fishing.'

Red smiles. 'Z-i-h-u-a-t-a-n-e-j-o.'

'In a place like that I could use a man who knows how to get things,' Andy says.

But Red isn't sure. 'I don't think I could make

it on the outside, Andy. I've been in here most of my life, I'm an institutional man now, just like Brookes was.'

'Well, I think you underestimate yourself,' Andy says.

'I don't think so. In here I'm the guy who can get things for you, sure, but outside all you need is the Yellow Pages. Hell, I wouldn't even know where to begin . . . The Pacific Ocean? Shit! That would scare me to death, something that big.'

'Not me,' Andy says. 'I didn't shoot my wife and I didn't shoot her lover. Whatever mistakes I've made, I've paid for them and then some . . . That hotel, that boat, I don't think that's too much to ask.'

'I don't think you ought to be doing this to yourself, Andy. This is a shitty pipe dream. I mean Mexico is way the hell down there and you're in here and that's the way it his.'

'Yeah, right, that's the way it is,' Andy snorts, suddenly pissed. 'It's down there and I'm in here.' And then he says it, the greatest line in the history of cinema, and my creed: 'I guess it comes down to a simple choice really — get busy living or get busy dying.'

20

I've been ribbing Paul for months about the book.

'For fuck's sake when are you finishing? Is there any chance I might see it before I die? This is only Part 1. I don't want it to be my epitaph.'

This morning, at last, he arrived with the completed manuscript.

'What's the final scene?' I ask. 'Do I escape? Have you found a way to get me to Zihuatanejo?'

'I'm afraid not,' he replies, 'I was thinking of something like this . . . '

Scene 41: INTERIOR — LIVING ROOM — DAY

Matt Hampson is watching TV in the living room of his new home in Cold Overton when a new Adidas commercial featuring Jonah Lomu is aired. The commercial starts with Lomu picking up a marker and sketching on a screen.

JONAH LOMU
My name is Jonah Lomu and this is my story.

FADE TO

The sketch: Lomu has drawn a huge man lying in a hospital bed and wired to a machine.

JONAH LOMU
When I sat down with one of the top kidney specialists and he turned and said to me, 'You are
facing life in a wheelchair', that was tough to
accept.

FADE TO

The drawing: The man has abandoned the bed for a
wheelchair but is still wired to the machine.

JONAH LOMU
If anything I didn't accept it.

FADE TO
The drawing: The man is working his arms on a
set of parallel bars and using walking sticks.

JONAH LOMU
For a guy who used to run around the world playing rugby, being chained to a machine for eight
hours six nights a week I had to look deep down
inside me. And I found the power within me.

FADE TO

The drawing: The man casts off the wires from the
machine, and the sticks, and starts walking . . . and
running . . . and playing rugby again.

JONAH LOMU
I've got out there and played rugby when I
shouldn't have. I had to fight for every step to get
there.

512

FADE TO

Lomu writing the punchline: 'Impossible Is Nothing.'

FADE TO

. . . a tear running down the cheek of Matt's face.

I swallow hard and look away.
'What do you think?' he asks.
'Yeah, I've always loved that ad, but I'm not sure it works as a final scene. You're over-egging the pudding. You've got the old violin out again.'
'Okay, well, I'm open to suggestions,' he says, shifting uneasily in his chair.
'What about this?' I propose.

Scene 41: EXTERIOR — VILLAGE — NIGHT

A terrible storm is shaking the Leicestershire village of Cold Overton.

FADE TO

A crash of thunder, a darkened bedroom, a man shaken from his sleep by a terrible premonition . . .

PHIL HAMPSON
Matthew!

FADE TO

Phil Hampson reaching for a dressing gown and

513

sprinting up the street to his son's red-brick bungalow . . .

PHIL HAMPSON
Matthew!

He bursts through the front door and races to his
son's bedroom. He's worried something terrible has
happened, but when he opens the door his son is
not only sleeping peacefully but there's a smile on
his face.

'What's the smile?' Paul interrupts. 'No, let me
guess . . . He's dreaming his favourite dream.
He's back at Twickenham making his debut for
England. He has made it down the tunnel and
joined Haskell in the dressing room.'
'Yeah, maybe he is,' I reply. 'Or maybe he's
just dreaming about tomorrow.'

EPILOGUE

BEING MATT HAMPSON

Twenty-six years ago, on a warm Sunday afternoon in September 1985, I was racing my bicycle down a narrow, gravel-lined descent in northern France when I misjudged a corner and was thrown over the handlebars. I was 23-years-old and on the cusp of achieving my dream of becoming a professional cyclist. Two weeks earlier, I'd finished sixth at the World Amateur Championships in Italy and had just opened discussions with Jean de Gribaldy — the Bill Shankly of cycling managers — about joining his team. But who knows what the next corner brings?

I don't remember much of what happened next, just an acute pain in my back and a desperate struggle to breathe as I was stretchered to an ambulance. I looked like I'd gone twelve rounds with Mike Tyson; I had shattered my left wrist, fractured a T4 vertebra and would spend the next five days cursing my misfortune at a hospital in Béthune. My season was over. It would be five months before I raced my bike again.

I had only a vague idea back then about the workings of the spinal column and it would take another twenty years, and a lecture from Dr Ali Jamous . . .

Sometimes the damage to the (spinal) cord is far less in a high-velocity accident where the bone has burst open than a low-velocity accident where there is no break in the bone.

. . . before I was reminded of the crash and how fortunate I was. But I've thought of it a lot since. It was as close as I have come to being Matt Hampson.

* * *

The first time Matt and I met was at Stoke Mandeville hospital, a year after his accident in March 2006. Jennie was gone and Matt was just coming to terms with the reality of his condition. I had never interviewed a 21-year-old ventilator-dependent-quadriplegic before and was not looking forward to the experience. I mean, where did you begin? How could I ask this kid to look forward? How could I ask him to look back?

He was sitting up in bed and wearing a grey Nike T-shirt when I tiptoed into St George ward and the first thing that struck me was his sense of humour. 'I've never been interviewed by the *Sunday Times* before,' he smiled. But my abiding memory that morning was a contribution from his father, Phil, who had joined us as the interview was winding to a close: 'One thing Matthew said to me early in his injury which I couldn't believe was 'I'll be a better person for this in the long run, Dad'.

It seemed an extraordinary thing for a twenty-year-old to say. I don't think I could have said that.'

. . . Or me. The notion seemed preposterous.

The interview was well received and a year later, during the 2007 Six Nations Championship, I spent a night with him at his home in Cold Overton after we had travelled up and down from Twickenham for the England/France game. The following morning, a Monday, I followed Michelle Metcalf, one of his carers, into his bedroom and she started ribbing him about talking in his sleep.

'What did he say?' I asked.

'Trade secret,' she replied.

'A lot of swear words apparently,' Matt smiled.

'Normally it's about his brother,' she explained. ' 'Fucking hell, Tom!' And you run in and he's asleep.'

Michelle left us and I asked him about his dreams. 'It's funny,' he said, 'but in my dreams I'm always walking, I am never in a wheelchair. I dream that I've been playing. I dream all sorts of things but I'm able-bodied . . . it's quite strange. Or maybe that's not strange. Maybe eventually I'll get used to it and dream that I'm in a wheelchair, but I'm not sure I will. In the back of my mind is this thought that I will walk again; I think you've always got to have that slight . . . '

'Hope?' I suggested.

'Yes, hope, it's always good to have hope — even if it's completely unrealistic at times,

519

you've got to believe that you are going to get better.'

I sat for a moment trying to absorb his words, the silence peppered by the constant whoosh of his ventilator. Then he said: 'I've been thinking about writing a book. Would you do it for me?'

'Yes, Matt,' I replied.

. . . but to be honest, I almost threw up.

Confession: I used to think cycling was the hardest profession in the world. In 1985, I was so tired after racing the Bordeaux-Paris — at 585 km, the longest single-day bike race in the world — that I (literally) crawled to bed on my hands and knees. In 1989, during a blizzard at the Tour of Italy, my hands were so cold one day that I urinated on them. In 1986, I watched the leader of the Tour de France ride by one day with diarrhoea pouring down his legs. But it didn't compare with the pain of writing; none of it hurt like writing a book, and I swore after my last that I would never suffer again. But Matt had made me an offer I could not refuse.

There was one condition: 'It has to be honest,' I insisted. 'I'm going to point my torch in some very dark places and it's really going to hurt.'

'Okay,' he replied.

We started six months later, in September 2007, but there were problems I hadn't envisaged. The nature of Matt's disability and the target we had set — a true and vivid portrait of his life — meant that every interview had to be conducted face-to-face, but I can get to the Algarve more quickly than I can to Cold

Overton. And if we were going to be left alone, I would have to learn how to 'bag' him if his ventilator failed.

There was also the generation gap — Matt wasn't two years old when I rode my first Tour de France — and the only thing we had in common was a love of sport and a favourite film: *The Shawshank Redemption*. Some of the early sessions were hopeless; I was pushing all of his buttons but there was nothing coming back. And then, one morning, on the third or fourth trawl of his childhood, his eyes welled up with tears as he recounted the tragic story of his boyhood friend, Will Trower. And in that moment everything changed.

I kept pushing. I asked questions no 21-year-old should have to answer and at times pushed too hard. In November, after three months of interviews, Matt took ill and was hospitalised with a potentially fatal chest infection. A week before, he had launched a new website, conducted a training session at Oakham and attended three functions. The doctors warned him he was doing too much and needed to slow down.

On 11 November, a week after he was released from hospital, he showed me an email he had received requesting 'advice and guidance' from a friend of Aaron Williams, a young amateur rugby player who had been paralysed playing for Basildon. The following morning we left for Stoke Mandeville. It was my first visit to the hospital and, after an hour spent chatting with Williams, Matt offered me a guided tour.

'I hate this place,' he said. 'The smell of it, the look of it; there is no sense of community, everyone is by themselves. There are so many ways it could be better. They've got a projector screen and a big room they never use but why not let people watch films together? Or play games at night? But there's nothing. It's like a mortuary. I don't know how anyone can be fucking positive in this place. It's horrible.'

We took the lift upstairs to a room on St Andrew ward. 'There's someone I want you to meet,' he said. I followed him into the room. A young woman, Megumi Wilson, was lying in a bed. 'Hi, Megumi. How are you?' he announced. Megumi stared at the ceiling and didn't reply. There was a notice on the wall.

MEGUMI COMMUNICATES BY BLINKING:
ONE BLINK = YES
TWO BLINKS = NO.

Megumi has locked-in syndrome. Two years before, she had been the victim of a hit-and-run near her home in Wales. 'Now you know why I feel I'm one of the lucky ones,' Matt observed when we left the room.

In April 2008, I took a break from my job at the *Sunday Times* and sat down to start work on the manuscript. Three weeks later, I had plucked all my eyebrows and written 3000 words. It was depressing; I can chisel more quickly than that,

522

but for a year that's how it was. The easy option was your standard meat-and-two veg sports autobiography:

CHAPTER 1

My name is Matt Hampson. I'm a 21-year-old ventilator-dependent quadriplegic. That probably sounds like French to you but let me tell you what it means . . .

(Actually, to be fair, that doesn't read too badly but that wasn't going to work for Matt. He was not Martin Johnson. He'd never chinned Lawrence Dallaglio or won the World Cup. But he did have one hell of a story to tell . . . but how to tell it?)

Five months later, in September 2008, I showed him the first draft of 'The Prisoner of Franklin's Gardens' and tried to explain what I was thinking. 'When you hit the ground that morning, it wasn't just your life that changed. The screenplay gives me the latitude and the licence to explore that.'

'No, it's good,' he concurred.

But when I read him Scene 5 . . .

She pulls at the buckle of his belt and unzips his fly. He enters her right then and there, impaling her against the wall. She grinds against him, her body shuddering with pleasure.

. . . he almost choked.

(Confession: like Matt, I've never had sex that good. I can't even write it that good and am indebted, once again, to the brilliance of Frank Darabount.)

*   *   *

Two summers (and deadlines) passed. Phil Hampson built his son a magnificent new home in the village, with splendid views, but Matt still didn't have a book. He never complained: 'It will be done when it's done,' he'd say. 'Just get it right.' Getting it right wasn't easy; he's a perfectionist, I dot my i's and cross my t's, and it made for some interesting text messages . . .

> Me: You're writing about your 'member'. How do you refer to it? (Don't say 'huge'.) Willy? Johnson? Mickey?
> Him: Old boy.
> Me: You said old boy was how the girl in Chinawhite described it. Would a girl use that term?
> Him: No.
> Me: What term would she have used?
> Him: Cock.
> Me: Are you happy with that or do you want to bounce it off some of your girlfriends?
> Him: I think I'm happy with that.

By the autumn of 2010 we had reached the finishing straight and I spent six weeks writing the final chapters at his home in Cold Overton. It was a special time, not because we had finally

524

reached the end, but because it enabled me truly to appreciate the guts and courage and spirit that make him special. It takes three hours of washing and wiping and winching and suctioning to get him out of bed every day. But stand outside his bedroom door any morning and you'll hear his carers laughing and his music blaring and his little Jack Russell, Alfie, licking his face. This is the gospel according to Hambo . . .

'Get busy living or get busy dying.'

. . . Or maybe it was Johno who described him best: 'Whenever you see him, he always makes you feel better rather than the other way round.'

Thank you, Hambo: I'm a better person for having known you.

★ ★ ★

I've got some other people to thank. That first meeting with Matt, in March 2006, was also my first meeting with his parents, Anne and Phil. We have much in common — age, three children and a mutual appreciation of a nice glass of wine, but they have reset the bar on what it takes to be a parent and my admiration for them knows no bounds. My thanks also to Matt's sister, Amy, his brother, Tom, and to the remarkable Adam Wheatly.

I am indebted to all of Matt's care team for the kindness extended to me during my time at Cold Overton and in particular to Dean Clarke (a great story waiting to be told), Ruby Kullar Rai and the lovely Jacqui Pochin. My thanks also to Tommy Cawston, Matt's PA.

Confession: before meeting Matt, I had always hated Leicester Tigers . . .

Bastards, bastards, bastards: hateful, spiteful place . . .

. . . but to know them is to love them. And if you're unfortunate enough to have a catastrophic accident playing rugby, this is the place. Better or more loyal team-mates there are none. My thanks to Tigers past and present: James Buckland, Richard Cockerill, Matt Cornwell, Alex Dodge, Darren Garforth, Roy Jackson, Graham Rowntree, Tom Ryder and Dave Young. My thanks also to Michael Cusack and James Haskell who know what it's like to play at Welford Road. And to the inimitable Tony Spreadbury.

Matt Grimes understands better than anyone what it's like to be Matt Hampson and made a huge contribution to the book. I am also enormously indebted to Alison Brown, Dr Ali Jamous, Natalie Mackay, Pauline Pratt, Indeep Sidhu and Paul Taiano.

There is no such person as Jennifer Marceau but there's someone very like her trying to build a life in Los Angeles. She has my thanks and best wishes.

It is a great regret that I never got to meet Stuart Mangan, but having watched the BBC documentary (*Stuart: The Day My Life*

Changed) I felt I'd known him all my life. One night, during my sejour with Matt, we watched it again and laughed and cried. My thanks to Stuart's father, Brian, who was kind enough to send me the DVD, and to his brother, Barry. I would also like to thank Kathy Sheridan for her brilliant interview with Stuart in the *Irish Times*.

We've lost some good people since the project began: Stuart, Jackie Burnham, Joan Davis, Andy and Maureen O'Donnell, Anita Matthews, Lily Moriarty, Pat Nolan, Alan Ruddock and Matt's great friend and mentor, Grandad Fred. We also lost the great Andy Ripley. Five years ago, on the morning after my first interview with Matt, I sent Andy an email joking that I had 'just met someone even more special than him'. I could almost hear him chuckling when he replied: 'Impossible, dear boy.' It wasn't boastful. Andy was the most unique and gifted person I've ever met. He died last year after a heroic battle with prostate cancer but I am reminded of him constantly.

I've two reasons to thank Alex Butler, my sports editor at the *Sunday Times*: (1) for sending me to interview Matt in March 2007 and running his story across two pages. (2) For his support when that interview became *Engage*. I would also like to thank my colleague Rob Maul — the hardest working journalist I know — for his brilliant work on the transcripts.

I am grateful to my agent, David Welch, for securing a terrific contract with Simon &

Schuster and even more grateful to Ian Chapman for not enforcing it when I missed my deadlines. I've known Ian for almost ten years now and our business is always a pleasure. Thanks also to Mike Jones and Rory Scarfe for their diligence and patience.

Emma Hanratty was the first person to read 'The Prisoner of Franklin's Gardens' and gave me some very helpful feedback about how to pretend to be a barrister . . .

> The main rule for barristers is they cannot ask leading questions about the evidence but they must put the evidence to the witness.

. . . She will probably be horrified when she reads what I've made of her advice ('Stick to the day job, Paul') but she has my sincere thanks.

I've been a poor friend and a retired golfer for almost four years now but intend to right those wrongs soon. FORE! My apologies to Micheal and Brid O'Braonain, David and Mary Walsh, Gary and Sorcha O'Toole, Tony Cascarino, John and Canice Leonard, Ray and Annette Leonard, Paul Nolan, Donal Nolan, Adhamhnan O'Sullivan, Alan English, Tom English, Aidan Harrison, Fanny Sunesson, Iain Forsyth, Tom Humphries (Mozart), Gwen Knapp, Billy Stickland, Evelyn Bracken, Dermot Gilleece, Richard Stanton and Lionel Birnie. Incredibly, I also made two new friends — Andrew and Joanna Croker — during a long bike ride from

528

Rome to Edinburgh.

I was tempted to nominate Anne and Phil as the world's best parents but that title has been held for some time now by Christy and Angela Kimmage. With every day that passes, I love and cherish them more. I am also fortunate to have three great brothers and three great sisters-in-law. Cheers to Raphael, Deborah, Kevin, Aileen, Christopher and Eilish.

There's a place I know on the Algarve that's a lot like Zihuatanejo; a warm place with good memories; a place I want to live the rest of my life. As I type these words, my wife, Ann, is getting ready to head out there for the Easter weekend with our kids, Evelyn, Eoin and Luke. I'll be joining them soon. We'll find a warm terrace and a chilled bottle of wine and raise our glasses ('How bad we are') as the sun sets on the ocean.

Now that, my friends, is paradise.

Paul Kimmage, April 2011

BIBLIOGRAPHY

Jean-Dominique Bauby, *The Diving Bell and the Butterfly*, HarperCollins

Richard Cockerill with Michael Tanner, *In Your Face: A Rugby Odyssey*, Mainstream Publishing

Lawrence Dallaglio, *It's in the Blood: My Life*, Headline

Frank Darabont, *The Shawshank Redemption: Screenplay & Notes* (shooting script), Nick Hern Books

Will Greenwood, *Will: The Autobiography of Will Greenwood*, Century

Austin Healey, *Me and My Mouth*, Monday Books

Victor Hugo, *The Hunchback of Notre-Dame*, Penguin

Martin Johnson, *The Autobiography*, Headline

Stephen King, *Misery*, Hodder

Jason Leonard with Alison Kervin, *Jason Leonard: The Autobiography*, Willow

Lewis Moody with Paul Morgan, *Year of the Tiger: Living Dangerously with Leicester, England and the Lions*, Vision Sports Limited

Brian Moore with Stephen Jones, *Brian Moore: The Autobiography*, Corgi

David Peace, *The Damned United*, Faber & Faber

Christopher Reeve, *Still Me: A life*, Century

Andy Ripley, *The Enthralling Story of the British Lion's Most Crucial Battle*, Mainstream Publishing

The Matt Hampson Foundation

The support I have received since my accident from all walks of life has been overwhelming. The Matt Hampson Foundation has given me a platform that has enabled me to give something back and has given me the opportunity to start a new, very important, chapter in my life and find a new focus to concentrate my mind.

The Matt Hampson Foundation aims to inspire and support young people seriously injured through sport. I feel that with the experiences I have gone through I can support people in a similar situation to myself and raise awareness of not just spinal cord injuries but all different types of paralysis. My foundation will also support a number of other organisations through various fundraising events.

If you would like to find out any more information about The Matt Hampson Foundation and help me help others, then please visit us at www.matthampsonfoundation.org

Matt Hampson, April 2011